PREPARING FOR BABY

ALL THE LEGAL, FINANCIAL, TAX, AND INSURANCE INFORMATION NEW AND EXPECTANT PARENTS NEED

NIHARA K. CHOUDHRI

Cover design by Elmarie Jara / ABA Design

Printed in the United States of America.

19 18 17 16 15   5 4 3 2

Library of Congress Cataloging-in-Publication Data

Choudhri, Nihara K., author.
Preparing for baby : all the legal, financial, tax, and insurance information new and expectant parents need / Nihara K. Choudri.
pages cm
Includes bibliographical references and index.
ISBN 978-1-63425-187-7 (alk. paper)
1. Domestic relations--United States. 2. Children--Legal status, laws, etc.--United States. 3. Parent and child (Law)--United States. 4. Pregnant women--Legal status, laws, etc.--United States. 5. Child care--United States I. Title.
KF505.C46 2015
332.0240085'0973--dc23

2015034391

Discounts are available for books ordered in bulk. Special consideration is given to state bars, CLE programs, and other bar-related organizations. Inquire at Book Publishing, ABA Publishing, American Bar Association, 321 N. Clark Street, Chicago, Illinois 60654-7598.

www.ShopABA.org

Contents

Introduction

CONGRATULATIONS! If you are reading this, chances are you have a new baby on the way—or your little one just arrived. Whether this is your first child or your third, you are in for an amazing adventure. So much wonder and enchantment lie ahead, from your baby's first steps and words to your child's first days at kindergarten and beyond. We hope you'll savor every fleeting moment.

Along with the joy of parenthood comes a hefty set of responsibilities. You have so many things to worry about "doing right," starting from the basics (like nutrition and sleep) to the more complex task of overseeing your child's emotional, social, and educational development. Parenthood is going to keep you busier than you ever imagined.

Between diaper changing and midnight feedings, you probably won't have much time or energy to tackle the legal and financial aspects of being a good parent. We doubt you'll want to spend baby's precious nap time researching the ins and outs of life insurance or the tax breaks you might be eligible for as a new parent.

That's where this book comes in. We created *Preparing for Baby* to help new and expecting parents navigate the many legal, financial, tax, and insurance issues that are part and parcel of the parenting process. No need to lie awake at night wondering how many weeks of leave you can take after your baby arrives, or whether you can claim a tax deduction for your child care expenses. We've done the research for you in this all-in-one resource that tells you what you need to know—and only what you need to know—about everything from setting up a college savings plan to creating a will.

Our approach to writing this book was simple: We wanted to make it as easy as possible for parents like you to understand the important but complicated legal and financial issues that affect new and expecting parents. You won't find any "legalese" or textbook-style explanations here. Instead, we cover each topic step-by-step in plain English, in an accessible question-and-answer format.

If we've done our job right (and we're pretty sure we have), this book will save you hours of time and maybe even a little money. You can spend that time doing far better things—like enjoying the magic of parenthood, or just taking a much-needed nap.

How to Use This Book

Don't get scared by the size of *Preparing for Baby*. It's not meant to be read cover to cover.

We have designed this book so that each chapter stands alone. You don't need to read the first three chapters, for example, if you're interested in learning about the material covered in Chapter 4. Instead, you can just read the chapter or the sections that address the topic that concerns you at any given time. Feel free to jump around as needed. We expect that you'll pick up this book to learn about a particular issue that is on your mind—say, college savings plans, for example—and then you'll set it down until the next issue arises. Think of *Preparing for Baby* as a reference guide rather than a "how to" manual you have to read page by page.

Throughout the book, you'll see a few different icons that break out particular types of information.

Symbol indicates helpful information you might need to know.

Symbol warns you of something you may have to be careful about.

Symbol suggests an idea you might want to consider.

Symbol lists additional resources where you can learn more about a particular topic.

Symbol tells you a fact or statistic you might find interesting.

Symbol thanks an expert for reviewing the information in the chapter.

Frequently Asked Questions

Can I use this book instead of hiring a lawyer or a financial expert?
No. You should use *Preparing for Baby* only as a starting point when considering particular legal or financial issues, like choosing a guardian for your child or weighing your disability insurance options. This book is in no way a substitute for the advice of a lawyer or financial expert. Only a lawyer can provide you with guidance on how the law applies in your particular situation. Similarly, only a financial expert can advise you on whether a specific financial product is the right choice for your family, or whether you are eligible for a particular tax break.

Is all of the legal and financial information in* Preparing for Baby *accurate and up to date?
We have done our very best to ensure that all of the material in *Preparing for Baby* is accurate and up to date, both through independent research and by consulting experts. Having said that, it's important to remember that laws change constantly, particularly at the state level. Similarly, the rules governing tax breaks, and the details of financial products, also change frequently. Be careful to check the latest laws and rules before making any important decisions.

Where can I get up-to-date information on the latest laws and financial information?

Throughout this book, we list additional resources where you may be able to find the latest laws and the most up-to-date financial information. (Webpages are much easier to update than books!) The safest course of action, however, is to check with a lawyer or a financial professional in your state before making any decisions based on the information in *Preparing for Baby*.

CHAPTER 1

Your Workplace Rights before and after Baby Arrives

FEW life events can make work more complicated than the arrival of a new baby. If you are pregnant, you may worry that your employer might treat you differently because you are expecting. You may also need to take time off from work during your pregnancy, or request modifications to your job, because of a pregnancy-related medical condition.

After your baby arrives, you will almost certainly want to take several weeks off from work to care for and bond with your little one. At the same time, you have to make sure that you will still have a job waiting for you when you are ready to return to work.

This chapter covers many of the most pressing workplace challenges and concerns you might face as a new or expecting parent, including:

- Pregnancy-related workplace issues. We discuss pregnancy discrimination, your right to pregnancy-related job modifications, and your right to take time off from work during your pregnancy.
- Maternity and paternity leave. We cover your rights under the federal Family and Medical Leave Act (FMLA). We also touch on your right to take leave under state law.

- Breastfeeding-related issues. We address your right to take reasonable breaks during the workday to pump for your little one.

Many thanks to the National Partnership for Women & Families for providing an expert review of this chapter. The National Partnership for Women & Families is a nonprofit organization dedicated to promoting fairness in the workplace and helping both women and men meet the dual demands of work and family, among other issues. The organization's website (nationalpartnership.org) provides a wealth of information on the legal rights of new and expecting parents. Special thanks to the following individuals from the National Partnership's Workplace Programs team for helping to make sure that the material in this chapter is accurate and up to date: Vasu Reddy, policy counsel, Sarah E. Towne, researcher and writer, and Amaryllis Rodriguez, program assistant.

This chapter only covers federal laws addressing the workplace rights of new and expecting parents. However, many states have laws in place that provide broader benefits than those provided under federal law. You can find helpful summaries of these state laws in *Expecting Better: A State-by-State Analysis of Laws That Help New Parents*, published by the National Partnership for Women & Families and available online at nationalpartnership.org. (Use the "search" feature to find the latest edition of the report.)

Many employers provide new and expecting parents with far greater benefits than the law requires. Depending on who you work for, you may be entitled to much more than the minimum legal requirements when it comes to issues like time off from work or workplace accommodations. For example, plenty of companies provide new parents with at least a few weeks of paid leave, even though there is no federal law that makes paid leave mandatory. Check with your employer's human resources department to see what you are eligible for under your company's policies.

Pregnancy-Related Workplace Issues

Being pregnant raises unique challenges in the workplace. On the one hand, you deserve to be treated the same as your colleagues when it comes to issues like compensation and promotion. On the other hand, you may require special accommodations in the event that your pregnancy interferes with your ability to do certain aspects of your job. You may even need to take time off from work during your pregnancy if you suffer from pregnancy-related complications.

Here we'll help you understand your rights under the federal Pregnancy Discrimination Act and the Americans with Disabilities Act. We'll also tell you what you need to know about pregnancy leave.

Your Right to Fair Treatment at Work during Your Pregnancy

Do I have to tell my employer as soon as I find out I am pregnant?
No. In fact, it is perfectly legal for you to keep your pregnancy under wraps until you feel comfortable sharing the news with your employer.

> A B C *You will have to provide your employer with at least thirty days' notice if you plan on taking leave under the Family and Medical Leave Act (see pages 29 through 34 below).* You may also have longer notice requirements under your state's family leave laws. As a practical matter, however, your pregnancy will probably announce itself long before these notice requirements take effect.

I am concerned that my employer might start treating me differently based on my pregnancy. Are there any laws that protect me from pregnancy-based discrimination?
Yes. The federal Pregnancy Discrimination Act prohibits employers from discriminating against pregnant women in any aspect of their

employment, including:

- hiring and firing;
- compensation;
- work assignments;
- promotions;
- training; and
- fringe benefits, such as leave and health insurance.

The Pregnancy Discrimination Act only applies to employers with fifteen or more employees. If you work for a small employer, then you are not entitled to the protections of the federal Pregnancy Discrimination Act. However, you may have rights under a state pregnancy discrimination law. You can find helpful details on state pregnancy discrimination laws in *Expecting Better: A State-by-State Analysis of Laws That Help New Parents*, published by the National Partnership for Women & Families and available online at nationalpartnership.org. (Use the "search" feature to find the latest edition of the report.)

Can my employer take me off a promotion track or give me less demanding assignments because of my pregnancy?

No. Under the Pregnancy Discrimination Act, employers may not treat pregnant women differently when it comes to promotions and work assignments.

It is illegal for your employer to modify your job or your career track based on your pregnancy, even if your employer has good intentions. For example, let's suppose that you work at a major consulting firm, and your job requires regular trips to Japan. Let's further suppose that when your supervisor learns of your pregnancy, he reassigns you to work with a local client because he is worried that international travel might be too difficult and stressful for you. Your supervisor's actions would violate the Pregnancy Discrimination Act, even though your supervisor was acting out of kindness and concern rather than malice or ill will.

Reassure your boss that you are still capable of meeting all of your usual job responsibilities even though you are pregnant. If you are enjoying a healthy pregnancy, then head off potential problems by letting your supervisor know that you can still handle all of your normal work assignments while you are pregnant.

Can my employer fire me because of my pregnancy?

No. The Pregnancy Discrimination Act prohibits your employer from firing you because of your pregnancy. However, your employer can let you go while you are pregnant for other reasons, like poor performance or company-wide layoffs.

My morning sickness has made it very hard for me to get to work on time and to complete my assignments. Can my employer terminate my employment for poor attendance and performance?

Yes. The Pregnancy Discrimination Act does not prohibit employers from firing pregnant employees for attendance or performance-related reasons. If your pregnancy has interfered with your ability to attend work or complete your assignments, then it is perfectly legal for your employer to terminate your employment. (The Pregnancy Discrimination Act does not provide *special* treatment for pregnant employees, just *equal* treatment.)

Consider taking unpaid leave during your pregnancy. If your pregnancy symptoms are making it hard for you to do your job, then it may be best for you to take some time off from work. See pages 15 through 16 below for details on your right to take pregnancy leave.

As part of a restructuring, my company is laying off my entire department. Can my employer terminate my employment even though I am pregnant?

Yes. As long as your employer is terminating your employment for reasons unrelated to your pregnancy, it is perfectly legal for your employer to let you go as part of a company-wide restructuring. Remember that the Pregnancy Discrimination Act does not provide pregnant women with the right to *special* treatment, only to *equal* treatment.

Your Right to Pregnancy-Related Job Modifications

I am having trouble doing certain aspects of my job (like lifting heavy boxes) because of my pregnancy. Do I have any legal right to a job modification during my pregnancy?

It depends. If you are suffering from a serious pregnancy-related health condition, like sciatica or hypertension, then you are probably entitled to the protections of the Americans with Disabilities Act. The Americans with Disabilities Act requires employers to make "reasonable" job-related modifications for women with temporary pregnancy-related disabilities. (See pages 6 through 9 below for more information on the Americans with Disabilities Act.)

If you are experiencing normal pregnancy-related health issues, however, then the Pregnancy Discrimination Act is the only federal law that governs your right to pregnancy-related job modifications. The Pregnancy Discrimination Act does not entitle all women to pregnancy-based job modifications. Rather, the Pregnancy Discrimination Act only requires that employers treat pregnant women the same as other temporarily disabled workers who are "similar in their ability or inability to work." If your employer has made accommodations for temporarily disabled employees in the past, then your employer may have to make similar accommodations for pregnant employees. (For more information on your right to job modifications under the Pregnancy Discrimination Act, see pages 10 through 14 below.)

Both the Americans with Disabilities Act and the Pregnancy Discrimination Act only apply to employers with fifteen or more employees. If you work for a small employer, then you are not entitled to the protections of either law.

You may be entitled to additional rights under your state's laws. You can find helpful details on state pregnancy-related laws in *Expecting Better: A State-by-State*

Analysis of Laws That Help New Parents, and *Reasonable Accommodations for Pregnant Workers: State and Local Laws*, both published by the National Partnership for Women & Families and available online at nationalpartnership.org. (Use the "search" feature to find the latest edition of both reports.)

Now that I am pregnant, I am finding it very challenging to work full time. Do I have any legal right to cut down to a part-time schedule during my pregnancy?

Possibly. Under the federal Family and Medical Leave Act (FMLA), eligible employees suffering from a "serious health condition"—including pregnancy—can take up to twelve weeks of *unpaid* leave per year. Eligible employees can take leave under the Family and Medical Leave Act in the form of reduced hours for a period of time. For more information on your right to cut down to a part-time schedule during your pregnancy under the Family and Medical Leave Act, see page 19 below.

A B C *The Family and Medical Leave Act applies to women with a broader range of "serious health conditions" than the Americans with Disabilities Act.* The Americans with Disabilities Act only applies to pregnant women suffering from serious pregnancy-related health conditions, like sciatica. Pregnancy itself is not a temporary disability for the purposes of the Americans with Disabilities Act. Under the Family and Medical Leave Act, on the other hand, pregnancy counts as a serious health condition.

Pregnancy-Related Job Modifications under the Americans with Disabilities Act

How does the Americans with Disabilities Act (ADA) apply to pregnant women?

The Americans with Disabilities Act provides workplace protections for employees who suffer from a "physical or mental impairment that substantially limits one or more major life activities." Many temporary but significant pregnancy-related health conditions—such as preeclampsia, sciatica, and gestational diabetes—count as disabilities for purposes of the Americans with Disabilities Act.

> *The ADA Amendments Act of 2008 makes it much easier to show that a medical condition is a covered disability under the Americans with Disabilities Act.* You can learn more about the ADA Amendments Act of 2008 at eeoc.gov/laws/regulations/adaaa_fact_sheet.cfm.

Does the Americans with Disabilities Act protect all pregnant women?

No. While certain pregnancy-related conditions are considered disabilities under the Americans with Disabilities Act, pregnancy itself is not a disability for purposes of the Americans with Disabilities Act. Put simply, the Americans with Disabilities Act only applies to pregnant women who suffer from a significant pregnancy-related health condition.

Does the Americans with Disabilities Act require employers to provide job modifications to women suffering from pregnancy-related disabilities?

Yes. Under the Americans with Disabilities Act, an employer must provide "reasonable" workplace "accommodations" to women with pregnancy-related disabilities. Reasonable workplace accommodations include:

- *Offering a flextime work schedule.* For example, an employer might permit a pregnant woman suffering from severe morning sickness to arrive later than usual and leave later than usual.
- *Modifying a pregnant woman's job responsibilities.* An employer might exempt a pregnant woman with a serious back problem from the physically demanding aspects of her job, like lifting heavy boxes.
- *Permitting an employee to telecommute.* An employer could allow a pregnant woman who has been placed on bed rest to work from home if possible.

- *Temporarily reassigning an employee to a light-duty position.* For example, an employer might reassign a pregnant construction worker to a desk job for the duration of her pregnancy.

An employer does not have to provide a "reasonable accommodation" if it would be an "undue hardship." A reasonable accommodation might pose an undue hardship if it would involve "significant difficulty or expense" in light of the employer's size, financial resources, and the nature of its operations. However, if one type of job modification would pose an undue hardship while a second type would not, then the employer must provide the employee with the second type of job modification.

What do I have to do to obtain a job modification under the Americans with Disabilities Act?

Just ask! Your employer does not have to provide you with reasonable workplace accommodations under the Americans with Disabilities Act unless you request a job modification based on your pregnancy-related disability.

Have a plan before you request a reasonable accommodation. Before talking to your employer about modifying your job, come up with a proposal for how your employer could adjust your responsibilities or your work schedule in a way that would not be difficult or disruptive for your employer. Taking your employer's needs into account will help ensure that your relationship with your employer remains positive both during and beyond your pregnancy.

You can learn more about the Americans with Disabilities Act as it applies to pregnant women in the Equal Employment Opportunity Commission's Enforcement Guidance on Pregnancy Discrimination, available at eeoc.gov/laws/guidance/pregnancy_guidance.cfm.

Pregnancy-Related Job Modifications under the Pregnancy Discrimination Act

Does the Pregnancy Discrimination Act require employers to provide job modifications to pregnant employees?

No. The Pregnancy Discrimination Act only requires employers to treat pregnant employees "in the same manner" as other "employees who are similar in their ability or inability to work." If your employer has previously made job modifications for employees with health issues, then your employer may have to make similar modifications for you during your pregnancy.

For example, let's suppose that Sarah's job involves lifting heavy boxes on to a conveyor belt. Sarah's doctor has advised her that lifting heavy boxes could risk her baby's health. Sarah asks her employer to put her on "light duty" for the remainder of her pregnancy. Let's further suppose that last year one of Sarah's coworkers threw out his back while shoveling snow. Because Sarah's coworker could not lift heavy boxes, Sarah's boss assigned him to light-duty desk work until he recovered from his back injury. Since Sarah's boss has previously made job modifications for an employee similar to Sarah in his inability to work, Sarah's boss may have to make similar job modifications for Sarah under the Pregnancy Discrimination Act.

A B C *The United States Supreme Court recently addressed the question of when an employer must make job modifications for pregnant employees under the Pregnancy Discrimination Act.* The court's decision in *Young v. United Parcel Service* may make it more difficult for employers to refuse to provide job modifications to pregnant employees if those employers have previously provided job modifications for nonpregnant employees who are "similar in their ability or inability to work." You can read the decision on the Supreme Court's website, supremecourt.gov/opinions/14pdf/12-1226_k5fl.pdf.

It seems unfair that women are not entitled to pregnancy-based job modifications under the Pregnancy Discrimination Act. Is it possible that the laws might change at some point?
Yes. A big movement is underway to enact the Pregnant Workers Fairness Act, which would require employers to provide pregnant employees with reasonable workplace accommodations regardless of whether or not employers have previously provided job modifications to nonpregnant employees who are "similar in their ability or inability to work." You can learn more about the Pregnant Workers Fairness Act at the National Partnership for Women & Families website, nationalpartnership.org/issues/fairness/pregnant-workers-fairness-act.html.

Are there any state laws that require employers to provide pregnant women with job modifications where necessary?
Yes. Several states have laws in place requiring employers to provide pregnant women with reasonable workplace accommodations. You can find helpful details on state pregnancy-related laws in *Expecting Better: A State-by-State Analysis of Laws That Help New Parents*, published by the National Partnership for Women & Families and available online at nationalpartnership.org. (Use the "search" feature to find the latest edition of the report.)

Filing a Claim under the Pregnancy Discrimination Act or the Americans with Disabilities Act

If you believe that you have been the victim of pregnancy discrimination or discrimination based on a pregnancy-related disability, then you may want to consider taking formal legal action against your employer.

Pregnancy discrimination is more common than you might think. In 2014, the Equal Employment Opportunity Commission received 3,400 charges of pregnancy discrimination. That same year, the Equal Employment Opportunity Commission resolved more than three thousand pregnancy discrimination cases and collected over $14 million from employers in connection with Pregnancy Discrimination Act violations.

I think my employer may have violated the Pregnancy Discrimination Act or the Americans with Disabilities Act. How can I determine whether I have a valid claim?

The rules governing pregnancy discrimination and discrimination based on a pregnancy-related disability are confusing! Fortunately, the Equal Employment Opportunity Commission has an online assessment tool that can help you evaluate whether or not you have been the victim of illegal discrimination. You can access the online assessment tool at egov.eeoc.gov/eas/.

Keep careful records of what happened. Memories fade, and documents and e-mails can get lost. If you think your employer might have violated the Pregnancy Discrimination Act or the Americans with Disabilities Act, then start to gather e-mails, communications, and other materials that might help you prove your case. You should also write down exactly what happened, with as much detail as possible. In addition, you should also see whether any of your coworkers would be willing to corroborate your story.

What are my legal options if my employer has discriminated against me because of my pregnancy or my pregnancy-related disability?

If you work for an employer with a human resources department, you may wish to file a complaint internally before taking formal legal action.

If your company does not have a human resources department, or if you would prefer not to report the discrimination internally first, then you will need to file a formal charge with the Equal Employment Opportunity Commission, the federal government agency in charge of employment discrimination claims. You may also wish to file a complaint with your state's department of labor, if your state has a pregnancy discrimination or disability discrimination law that may apply to your situation.

Give serious thought to contacting an employment lawyer before taking action. An experienced employment attorney can help you understand your options and ensure that you don't miss any important filing deadlines. If you're not sure who to call, you can find a directory of employment lawyers at the National Employment Lawyers Association website (nela.org). Click on the link marked "Find a Lawyer Directory" in the left-hand menu bar. Select your state and check the boxes for lawyers experienced in "Gender Discrimination" and "EEOC Practice." Another option is to contact your local bar association's lawyer referral service. You can find links to legal referral organizations in your area at the American Bar Association's website, apps.americanbar.org/legalservices/findlegalhelp/home.cfm. Click on your state on the interactive map and then click on the link for "Lawyer Referral" under "Find a Lawyer."

How do I file a charge of pregnancy discrimination (or discrimination based on a pregnancy-related disability) with the Equal Employment Opportunity Commission?

You can file a complaint in person at one of the Equal Employment Opportunity Commission's field offices, or by mail. You can learn more about filing a charge at eeoc.gov/employees/howtofile.cfm.

Don't wait too long to file a charge of discrimination. Strict time limits apply to discrimination claims under the federal Pregnancy Discrimination Act and the Americans with Disabilities Act.

Special rules apply to federal government employees. You can learn more about the complaint process for federal government employees at eeoc.gov/federal/fed_employees/complaint_overview.cfm.

I am afraid that my employer will fire me if I file formal discrimination charges. Does the law provide me with any protections?
Yes. It is illegal for your employer to fire, demote, or in any way "retaliate" against you in the workplace for:

- filing a charge of pregnancy discrimination (or discrimination based on a pregnancy-related disability) with the Equal Employment Opportunity Commission;
- reporting pregnancy discrimination (or discrimination based on a pregnancy-related disability) to your employer; or
- participating in legal proceedings involving claims of pregnancy discrimination (or discrimination based on a pregnancy-related disability), such as an Equal Employment Opportunity Commission investigation or a lawsuit.

Taking Time Off from Work during Your Pregnancy

If your pregnancy turns out to be more difficult than you had anticipated, you may need to consider taking time off from work during your pregnancy. You may be able to take unpaid job-protected leave under the federal Family and Medical Leave Act (FMLA). In addition, you may be eligible for additional leave under your state's laws or your employer or union policies.

What is the Family and Medical Leave Act?
The Family and Medical Leave Act (FMLA) is a federal law that provides eligible working parents with the right to take up to twelve weeks of *unpaid* leave per year to care for a new baby or bond with a newly adopted child. The FMLA also entitles women to take time off from work for pregnancy-related reasons. For example, if your pregnancy is high risk, you can take FMLA leave to attend frequent appointments with your neonatologist.

The FMLA provides *job-protected* leave. When you return from FMLA leave, your employer must give you back the same job you had before or place you in a comparable position with equivalent seniority, compensation, benefits, and working conditions.

> *If you are one of the company's "key employees," then you may not be entitled to the same position or an equivalent position when you return from leave.* An exception to the FMLA's job-protection rule applies if you are one of the company's highest-paid employees in your region. See pages 33–34 below for more details.

Are there any state laws that provide women with the right to take pregnancy leave?

Yes. A number of states have family and medical leave laws that allow women to take time off for pregnancy-related reasons. Some state laws provide more job-protected time off than the FMLA, and apply to a broader range of employees. You can find helpful details on state family and medical leave laws in *Expecting Better: A State-by-State Analysis of Laws That Help New Parents*, published by the National Partnership for Women & Families and available online at nationalpartnership.org. (Use the "search" feature to find the latest edition of the report.)

> *Any time you take off under your state family and medical leave law counts against your FMLA leave.* You cannot take the full amount of leave allowed under your state family and medical leave law and then also take twelve weeks of FMLA leave. Rather, your state law-based leave runs concurrently with your leave under the FMLA. If you take fourteen weeks of leave under your state law, for example, then you cannot take any additional FMLA leave because twelve of your fourteen weeks of state law leave count as FMLA leave.

Am I eligible for unpaid pregnancy leave under the FMLA?

To qualify for pregnancy leave under the FMLA, you must work for one of the following categories of *covered employers*:

- A private employer who employs fifty or more employees for at least twenty workweeks a year.
- A federal, state, or local government employer.

- A public elementary or secondary school.

You must also meet *all* of the following eligibility requirements:
- You must have worked for your employer for a total of at least twelve months.
- You must have worked for your employer for at least 1,250 hours during the twelve-month period preceding your leave. (You will meet this requirement if you have worked at least twenty-four hours per week over the past year.)
- You must work at a location where your employer has fifty or more employees within a seventy-five-mile radius.

A B C *Special hours-worked rules apply to airline flight attendants and flight crew members.* (See page 26 below for more details.)

You may still be eligible for FMLA leave even if you did not work for your employer for twelve consecutive months. As a general rule, you can add up all of the time you have worked for your employer over the past seven years for purposes of meeting the twelve-month requirement. However, you must separately meet the hours-worked requirement to qualify for FMLA leave.

Will I get paid during my FMLA pregnancy leave?

No. FMLA leave is *unpaid* leave.

However, you may be entitled to short-term disability benefits during some or all of your pregnancy leave. Employees in five states (California, Hawaii, New Jersey, New York, and Rhode Island) are generally entitled to short-term disability coverage. Many employers in other states voluntarily provide short-term disability coverage as part of their standard employee benefits package. If you are eligible for short-term disability benefits, then you will receive some portion of your usual paycheck (but not the whole amount) while you are on pregnancy leave. Check with your employer's human resources department for details on whether you qualify for short-term disability benefits, as well as your coverage amount.

Will I continue to have health insurance coverage during my FMLA pregnancy leave?

Yes. While you are on FMLA leave, your employer must continue to provide you with health insurance coverage under the same terms that applied before you took leave. However, if you normally contribute toward your health insurance premiums through payroll deductions, then you must continue to make those contributions during your FMLA leave.

> *You may have to write a check to your employer to cover your premium contributions.* Depending on your employer's rules, you may have to pay your contributions to your health insurance premiums out of pocket during your FMLA pregnancy leave.

Will I need a doctor's note to take pregnancy leave under the FMLA?

Yes. You will need to provide your employer with a "medical certification" stating why you need to take FMLA leave and how long you expect to be on leave. If you are requesting FMLA leave in the form of a part-time schedule (see page 19 below), then your medical certification should also explain why you can only work part time rather than full time.

If I take pregnancy leave under the FMLA, can I still take FMLA leave after my baby is born?

It depends on how many weeks of pregnancy leave you take. Under the FMLA, you cannot take more than a *total* of twelve weeks of unpaid job-protected leave per twelve-month period. Any unpaid FMLA leave you take during your pregnancy will limit the number of weeks of unpaid FMLA leave you can take after your baby is born. For example, let's suppose you take three weeks of unpaid FMLA leave during your pregnancy because you are suffering from severe morning sickness. You will then only be entitled to take nine weeks of unpaid FMLA leave after your baby arrives.

Can I choose to remain on pregnancy leave until my baby is born?

Yes. Bear in mind, however, that your *total* leave under the FMLA cannot exceed twelve weeks. In other words, any time off you take during your pregnancy limits the number of weeks of unpaid leave you can take after your baby is born.

Can my employer require me to remain on leave until my baby is born?

No. You are legally entitled to return to work as soon as you are physically able to do so. Your employer may not require you to remain on leave until you deliver.

Does my employer have to give me back my job once I return from FMLA leave?

Yes. Once you return from FMLA leave, your employer must restore you to the same job you had before you went on leave, or an equivalent job. You are entitled to a position at the same location with the same salary, benefits, and seniority level as the position you had before you took leave. Moreover, the position must involve the same types of job responsibilities and the same general work schedule as the job you had before you took leave.

> *Your employer does not have to give you your job back if your job was eliminated during company-wide layoffs.* If your company terminated your position while you were on leave, then your employer does not have to give you back your job—or offer you an equivalent job—after your leave.

> *Special rules apply to "key employees."* If you are one of the company's highest-paid employees in the region, then your employer does not have to give you back your old job—or an equivalent job—when you return from leave.

> *If you are a teacher, your school can extend your leave until the end of the school term.* Depending on when your leave ends, your school might determine that it would be disruptive to have you return to the classroom—espe-

cially if there are only a few weeks left in the school year. In that case, your school can keep you on leave until the end of the term. The school must continue your health insurance coverage while you remain on leave, and give you back your position when you return.

I am suffering from a fairly serious pregnancy-related health condition. Can I use my FMLA leave to cut down to a part-time schedule during my pregnancy?

Yes. Under the FMLA, you can take leave on an intermittent basis, rather than as a continuous block of time off from work, when it is medically necessary because of a serious health condition. For example, if you are having a high-risk pregnancy that requires frequent monitoring, you may be able to use FMLA leave to cut down to a part-time schedule during your pregnancy.

Your employer could require you to transfer to a different position during this time. Depending on the type of job you have, it may be difficult for your employer to permit you to work a part-time schedule in your current job. Your employer could require you to work in a different position (but with equivalent pay and benefits) while you are taking FMLA leave in the form of a part-time schedule.

Job Hunting While Pregnant

I am interviewing for a new job. Do I have to tell my prospective employer that I am pregnant?

No. You have no obligation to tell prospective employers that you are expecting.

Hiding your pregnancy might get your new employment relationship off to a rough start. As a practical matter, it may be wise to let your prospective employer know that you are expecting before you commit to the job (unless you will deliver your baby before your scheduled start date). Otherwise, your employer could incur undue hardship by your maternity leave—and that could damage your long-term relationship with your new employer.

I am worried that I won't get the job if I tell prospective employers that I am pregnant. Can employers refuse to hire me because of my pregnancy?

No. Under the federal Pregnancy Discrimination Act, employers cannot take pregnancy into account when making hiring decisions *unless* the job involves work that is too strenuous or hazardous for a pregnant woman to perform (like heavy-duty construction work).

However, it is perfectly legal for an employer to pass you over for another candidate who is more qualified, more personable, or just a better fit for the company. Because of the many different factors that go into hiring decisions, it can be hard to prove that a prospective employer decided not to hire you for illegal pregnancy-related reasons.

Is it legal for prospective employers to ask whether I am pregnant during a job interview?

Technically, yes. The Equal Employment Opportunity Commission—the federal government agency in charge of enforcing employment discrimination laws—has explained that the Pregnancy Discrimination Act "does not prohibit employers" from asking candidates whether they are pregnant. However, the agency has advised that "such questions are generally discouraged" because employers may not legally take pregnancy into account when making hiring decisions. The Equal Employment Opportunity Commission has further stated that if an employer asks a job applicant whether she is pregnant, the agency will take that question into account "when evaluating a charge alleging pregnancy discrimination."

Health Insurance Issues If You Quit or Lose Your Job during Your Pregnancy

I am pregnant, and I just lost my job because of company-wide lay-offs. What are my health insurance options?

Your best option may be to continue your company-sponsored health insurance coverage through the Consolidated Omnibus Budget Reconciliation Act of 1986 (COBRA). The COBRA coverage is expensive—you will have to pay the *full* cost of your premiums out of pocket, plus a 2 percent administrative cost. Though pricey, COBRA coverage may be the only way to ensure that you have adequate health insurance coverage during your pregnancy.

If you are married, another option is to enroll in health insurance coverage through your spouse's employer. (An employee whose spouse loses employer-sponsored health insurance generally qualifies for a special enrollment period to make benefits changes without having to wait for the annual enrollment period.)

A third option is to purchase your own health insurance policy through your state's health insurance marketplace. You can find links to your state's marketplace at healthcare.gov.

You can learn more about COBRA coverage in "An Employee's Guide to Health Benefits under COBRA," available at the Department of Labor's website dol.gov/ebsa/pdf/cobraemployee.pdf. If you work for the federal government, then you are eligible for continued health insurance coverage through the Temporary Continuation of Coverage (TCC) program rather than COBRA. You can learn more about TCC coverage at the U.S. Office of Personnel Management's website, opm.gov/healthcare-insurance/healthcare/temporary-continuation-of-coverage/#url=Pamphlet. Finally, if you work for an employer with less than twenty employees you are not eligible for COBRA coverage, but you may qualify for continued coverage if your state has enacted a "mini-COBRA" law.

A waiting period may apply for new health insurance coverage. If you enroll in new health insurance, either through your spouse's employer-sponsored plan or through the health insurance marketplace, you may be subject to a waiting period of up to ninety days before your coverage takes effect. During this time, you will have no health insurance coverage. With COBRA coverage, on the other hand, your coverage takes effect immediately and applies continuously provided you make the premium payments in full and on time.

I am switching jobs midway through my pregnancy. Will my new employer's health insurance plan cover my pregnancy-related health care costs?

Perhaps. Your new employer's health insurance plan almost certainly covers pregnancy-related health care costs. (The federal Pregnancy Discrimination Act requires plans sponsored by employers with fifteen or more employees to cover pregnancy-related expenses the same way that the plan covers expenses for other medical conditions.)

However, your new employer's health insurance plan may impose a waiting period of several months before you can obtain coverage. To avoid a coverage gap, you may want to opt for continued COBRA coverage under your previous employer's plan.

Do your health insurance homework carefully before switching jobs when you are expecting a baby. Otherwise, you could be left without health insurance coverage at the time you need it most.

Can my new health insurance plan exclude coverage for my pregnancy based on the exclusion for preexisting conditions?

No. Thanks to the federal Patient Protection and Affordable Care Act, a health insurance plan cannot deny benefits for pregnancy based on a preexisting condition exclusion. In other words, your new health insurance plan must provide you with coverage for your pregnancy-related health care costs from the first day you become eligible for coverage.

Maternity and Paternity Leave

In the weeks after your baby arrives, you will likely need to take some time off from work to recover from childbirth or just bond with your new baby. Here we'll discuss your right to maternity and paternity leave under the federal Family and Medical Leave Act (FMLA). We'll also touch on your right to take parental leave under state law.

You may be entitled to additional leave, or paid leave, under your employer's policies. Your employer may choose to provide more leave or greater benefits than the law requires. In fact, many companies do! Check with your employer's human resources department or your employee benefits manual to see what you are eligible for under your company's policies.

If you belong to a union, you may have additional rights to paid or unpaid leave. Check with your local union representative for more details.

If you still want more information on the Family and Medical Leave Act after reading this chapter, a useful resource is the National Partnership for Women & Families' "Guide to the Family and Medical Leave Act," available at nationalpartnership.org/research-library/work-family/fmla/guide-to-fmla.pdf.

What is the Family and Medical Leave Act (FMLA)?

The Family and Medical Leave Act (FMLA) is a federal law that provides eligible working parents with the right to take up to twelve weeks of *unpaid* leave per year to care for a new baby or bond with a newly adopted child. The FMLA also entitles pregnant women to take time off from work for pregnancy-related health conditions, such as severe morning sickness or medically required bed rest.

The FMLA provides *job-protected* leave. When you return from

FMLA leave, your employer must give you back the same job you had before *or* place you in a comparable position with equivalent seniority, compensation, benefits, and working conditions.

You may not be entitled to the same position, or an equivalent position, if you are one of the company's key employees. An exception to the FMLA's job-protection rule applies if you are one of the company's highest-paid employees in your region. See pages 33–34 below for more details.

The FMLA is not just for new parents. The FMLA provides eligible employees with the right to take time off from work for a broad range of health and family-related reasons. You can learn more about the full scope of the FMLA in "The Employee's Guide to the Family and Medical Leave Act," published by the U.S. Department of Labor and available at dol.gov/whd/fmla/employeeguide.pdf.

Are there any state parental leave laws?

Yes. A number of states have family and medical leave laws that allow parents to take time off from work after the birth of a new baby or the adoption of a child. Some state laws provide more job-protected time off than the FMLA, and apply to a broader range of employees. You can find helpful details on state family and medical leave laws in *Expecting Better: A State-by-State Analysis of Laws That Help New Parents*, published by the National Partnership for Women & Families and available online at nationalpartnership.org. (Use the "search" feature to find the latest edition of the report.)

Any time you take off under your state family and medical leave law counts against your FMLA leave. You cannot take the full amount of leave allowed under your state family and medical leave law and then also take twelve weeks of FMLA leave. Rather, your state law-based leave runs concurrently with your leave under the FMLA.

Does the FMLA provide fathers with the right to take paternity leave?
Yes. Under the FMLA, eligible fathers may take up to twelve weeks of unpaid job-protected leave to care for or bond with a new baby or a newly adopted child.

Does the FMLA provide adoptive parents with the right to take parental leave?
Yes. Under the FMLA, eligible parents may take up to twelve weeks of job-protected leave to care for and bond with a newly adopted child. You may also be able to take FMLA leave to complete adoption-related requirements, such as a home study or a trip abroad to bring your child back to the United States.

Does the FMLA provide same-sex partners with the right to take unpaid leave to care for a new baby?
Yes. If you are in a same-sex relationship and your partner has a baby, then you may take FMLA leave to bond with and care for the baby even if you are not the baby's biological or legal parent.

FMLA Eligibility Requirements

Unfortunately, not everyone is eligible for FMLA leave. The FMLA only applies to about 60 percent of the American workforce. You will only qualify for FMLA leave if you work for a *covered employer* and meet certain strict eligibility criteria.

Do all businesses and employers have to comply with the FMLA?
No. The FMLA only applies to the following *covered employers*:

- Private employers who employ fifty or more employees for at least twenty workweeks a year.
- Federal, state, and local government employers.
- Public elementary and secondary schools.

Small businesses do not have to provide employees with FMLA leave. If you work for a business with less than fifty employees, you won't qualify for FMLA leave but you may still be eligible for unpaid leave under your state's laws.

Are all employees eligible for unpaid job-protected leave under the FMLA?

No. To qualify for unpaid leave under the FMLA, you must meet *all* of the following eligibility requirements:

(1) You must work for a *covered employer* (see the question above).
(2) You must have worked for your employer for a total of at least twelve months.
(3) You must have worked for your employer for at least 1,250 hours during the twelve-month period preceding your leave. (You will meet this requirement if you have worked at least twenty-four hours per week over the past year.)
(4) You must work at a location where your employer has fifty or more employees in a seventy-five-mile radius.

Special hours-worked rules apply to airline flight attendants and flight crew members. If you are an airline flight attendant or a flight crew member, you can meet the hours-worked requirement provided that in the twelve months preceding your leave, you (1) worked or were paid for at least 60 percent of your applicable monthly guarantee; and (2) worked or were paid for at least 504 hours, not including personal commute time, vacation time, or medical or sick leave.

You may still be eligible for FMLA leave even if you did not work for your employer for twelve consecutive months. As a general rule, you can add up all of the time you have worked for your employer over the past seven years for purposes of meeting the FMLA's twelve-month requirement. However, you must separately meet the hours-worked requirement to qualify for FMLA leave.

I work for a small local office of a national company. Do I qualify for FMLA leave?

It depends on the number of company employees that work in your area. The FMLA only applies if your employer has at least fifty employees within a seventy-five-mile radius of your office location. If you work in a branch office with only twenty employees and there is no other office location within seventy-five miles, then you do not qualify for FMLA leave. However, you may still qualify for unpaid leave under your state's laws.

Salary and Benefits during FMLA Leave

Will I get paid during my FMLA leave?

No. FMLA leave is *unpaid* leave.

The United States is one of only three countries worldwide without a paid maternity leave law! The other two countries with that notable distinction are Papua New Guinea and Oman. A movement is well underway to enact paid family leave legislation in the United States. To learn more, go the National Partnership for Women & Families website at paidleave.org.

Is paid parental leave available under my state's law?

Only three states—California, New Jersey, and Rhode Island—provide paid parental leave to eligible employees. (Washington also passed a paid family leave law, but the law was never implemented.)

You can learn more about state paid family leave programs in "State Paid Family Leave Laws," published by the National Partnership for Women & Families and available online at nationalpartnership.org. (Use the "search" feature to find the latest edition of the report.)

Will I receive short-term disability benefits during my FMLA leave?

If you are an expecting mother, you may be eligible for short-term disability benefits for the first several weeks after you deliver. Employees in five states (California, Hawaii, New Jersey, New York, and Rhode Island) are generally entitled to short-term disability coverage. Many employers in other states voluntarily provide short-term disability coverage as part of their standard employee benefits package.

Short-term disability insurance usually provides six weeks of benefits for a normal delivery, and eight weeks of coverage for a C-section. Typically, you will only receive a percentage of your usual paycheck (not the whole amount) in short-term disability benefits. To find out whether you qualify and your coverage amount, check with your employer's human resources department or your state's department of labor.

Can I apply my accrued vacation days toward my FMLA leave?

Yes. In fact, many people begin saving up their days off as soon as they learn that they are expecting. By using your vacation days, you can turn unpaid FMLA leave into paid time off.

As a general rule, your vacation days will count as part of your FMLA leave, unless your employer provides otherwise. For example, let's suppose that you have four weeks of accrued vacation. You would not be entitled to take sixteen weeks of job-protected leave (twelve weeks of FMLA leave plus four weeks of vacation). However, you would be paid for the first four weeks of your FMLA leave because of your accrued vacation leave.

Can I apply my accrued sick days toward my FMLA leave?

It depends on your employer's sick leave policy. If your employer only permits you to use sick days when you yourself are ill or injured, then you may not be able to use sick leave to care for or bond with a new baby.

Will I continue to have health insurance coverage during my FMLA leave?

Yes. While you are on FMLA leave, your employer must continue to provide you and your family with health insurance coverage under the same terms that applied before you took leave. However, if you normally contribute toward your health insurance premiums through payroll deductions, then you must continue to make those contributions during your FMLA leave.

You may have to write a check to your employer to cover your premium contributions. Depending on your employer's rules, you may have to pay your contributions to your health insurance premiums out of pocket during your FMLA leave.

Will I accrue seniority or vacation time during my FMLA leave?
Probably not. While you are on FMLA leave, your employer can "stop the clock" on the accrual of benefits or privileges—including seniority and vacation time.

The Nuts and Bolts of Taking Parental Leave under the FMLA

Do I provide my employer with any notice before taking FMLA leave?
Yes. As a general rule, you must provide your employer with at least thirty days of advance notice before taking FMLA leave.

Don't wait until the last minute to tell your employer that you plan to take FMLA leave. Give your employer as much advance notice as possible, and do everything you can to ensure that there will be a smooth transition while you are on leave. Going the extra mile will ensure good relations with your employer both during and after your leave.

Do I have to take FMLA leave immediately after my baby is born or adopted?
No. You may take FMLA leave anytime within a year of your baby's birth or adoption.

Consider beginning your FMLA leave after your child's other parent's leave has ended. Instead of taking FMLA leave at the same time as your spouse or partner takes leave, you may want to think about starting your leave after his or her leave has ended. You'll save on child care costs, and you'll each get the opportunity for high-quality one-on-one bonding time with your new arrival.

Do I have to take my twelve weeks of FMLA leave all at once after my baby arrives?

As a general rule, you must take your twelve weeks of FMLA leave in one continuous block of time after the birth or adoption of a baby. However, your employer may permit you to break up your twelve weeks of leave, or to take the equivalent of twelve weeks of leave in the form of a temporary part-time work schedule.

Special rules apply if your child has a serious health condition. In the event that your child has significant health needs, you can take your twelve weeks of FMLA leave intermittently, on an as-needed basis. You are also exempt from the rule that you must take your twelve weeks of FMLA leave within a year after your baby's birth or adoption.

My state provides for longer parental leave than the FMLA. Can I take the full amount of leave allowed under my state's family leave law?

Yes. As long as you are eligible for coverage under your state's family leave law, then you may take the maximum amount of leave allowed in your state. However, any time you take off under your state family and medical leave law counts against your FMLA leave. You cannot take the full amount of leave allowed under your state family and medical leave law and then also take twelve weeks of FMLA leave. Rather, your state law-based leave runs concurrently with your leave under the FMLA.

I have two weeks of paid vacation saved up. Can I take paid vacation in addition to my FMLA leave after my baby arrives?

Probably not. Unless your employer provides otherwise, your vacation days will count as part of your FMLA leave. For example, let's suppose that you have four weeks of accrued vacation. You would not be entitled to take sixteen weeks of job-protected leave (twelve weeks of FMLA leave plus four weeks of vacation). However, you would be paid for the first four weeks of your FMLA leave because of your accrued vacation time.

My spouse and I work for different companies, and each of us is eligible for FMLA leave. Can we both take FMLA leave after our baby arrives?
Yes. You are each entitled to take the full twelve weeks of FMLA leave after your baby arrives.

> *You and your spouse don't have to take FMLA leave at the same time.* The FMLA does not require you to take FMLA leave right after your baby arrives. Rather, you have one full year after your baby is born or adopted to take FMLA leave. You and your child's other parent can take advantage of this flexibility to stagger your FMLA leaves, so that one parent is on unpaid leave while the other parent is back at work collecting a paycheck. This could save you a few weeks' worth of child care expenses, and help with cash flow in the challenging weeks after your baby arrives.

My spouse and I both work for the same company. Can we both take FMLA leave after our baby is born?
Yes, but your employer may limit your *total* FMLA leave to twelve weeks. For example, if your spouse takes eight weeks of FMLA after your baby is born, then your employer may legally allow you to take only four weeks of FMLA leave.

I had a baby last year and I took twelve weeks of unpaid FMLA leave. I am expecting another baby. Can I take FMLA leave again?
Yes. You are entitled to twelve weeks of FMLA leave per twelve-month period, as long as you meet the eligibility requirements and you have a qualifying reason for taking FMLA leave (like having another baby).

I am expecting twins. Can I take double the usual FMLA leave?
No. Even if you are carrying twins or triplets, you may still only take

a maximum of twelve weeks of unpaid leave under the FMLA.

Can I use my FMLA leave to cut down to a part-time schedule after my baby arrives?
Employees who take time off from work to care for a new child must generally take leave in one continuous block, rather than using the leave to cut down to a part-time schedule. However, your employer may permit you to take the equivalent of twelve weeks of FMLA leave in the form of a temporary part-time work schedule.

> *Your employer could require you to transfer to a different position if you take FMLA leave in the form of a part-time schedule.* Depending on the type of job you have, it may be difficult for your employer to permit you to work a part-time schedule in your current job. Your employer could require you to work in a different position (but with equivalent pay and benefits) while you are taking FMLA leave in the form of a part-time schedule.

What happens if stay on leave for longer than twelve weeks?
In that case, you will no longer qualify for the FMLA's protections. Your employer will not have to hold your job open for you. Moreover, your employer will be under no obligation to restore you to the same position—with the same salary and benefits—if your employer permits you to return to work. Significantly, your employer will no longer have to subsidize your health insurance coverage.

What happens if I don't return to work after my FMLA leave?
If you decide not to return to work after your FMLA leave, then your employer could ask you to reimburse the company for any health insurance premiums your employer paid on your behalf while you were on leave.

Special FMLA Rules for "Key Employees"

Am I a "key employee" for FMLA purposes?
You may be a key employee under the FMLA if:

- You are among the highest paid 10 percent of your company's employees within a seventy-five-mile radius of where you work.
- You are a salaried employee.
- You would otherwise be eligible for FMLA leave.

Can I take FMLA leave if I am a key employee?
Yes. However, your employer may not have to give you back your job—or an equivalent job—once you return from FMLA leave.

If I am a key employee, does this mean that I will not get my job back after I return from FMLA leave?
Not necessarily. Your employer may only refuse to give you back your job if doing so would cause "substantial and grievous economic injury" to the company. There are no hard and fast rules for determining when this standard is met. However, one factor your employer may consider is whether the company can temporarily replace you or leave your position unfilled while you are on leave.

Does my employer have to tell me if there is a possibility I might not get my job back after my leave?
Yes. If you are a key employee and your employer believes that it may not be able to give you back your job after you return from FMLA leave, then your employer *must* inform you in writing of the possibility that you might lose your position. Your employer has to provide you with this written notice at the time you inform your employer of your plans to take FMLA leave.

If my employer decides that it cannot give me back my job after my FMLA leave, does my employer have to let me know?
Yes. As soon as your employer has made a good faith determination that giving you back your job after your FMLA leave would cause

"substantial and grievous economic injury" to the company's operations, your employer must inform you of its decision in writing. Your employer must explain the reason for its decision, and provide you with a reasonable amount of time to end your FMLA leave and return to your position. If you cut your FMLA leave short and go back to work, then your employer must give you back your old job.

Will I have to pay back the cost of my employer's contributions to my health insurance coverage if I don't return to work?
If you are a key employee and your company informs you that it will not reinstate you to your position after your FMLA leave, then you will *not* have to pay back the amount of any health insurance premiums your employer paid on your behalf during your FMLA leave.

Filing a Complaint for FMLA Violations

After I returned from FMLA leave, my employer refused to give me back my old job or an equivalent job. How do I file a complaint under the FMLA?
You should start by contacting the U.S. Department of Labor's Wage and Hour Division (WHD), the government agency responsible for enforcing the FMLA. You can reach the WHD by phone at 1-866-487-9243. Or you can visit your local WHD office and file a complaint in person. You can find a list of WHD offices at the Department of Labor's website, dol.gov/whd/america2.htm.

A B C *To find out more about the process of filing a complaint for FMLA violations, go to the Department of Labor's website at* dol.gov/wecanhelp/howtofilecomplaint.htm.

I am afraid that my employer will fire me if I file a formal complaint. Does the law provide me with any protections?
Yes. It is illegal for your employer to fire, demote, or in any way "retaliate" against you in the workplace for seeking to enforce your rights under the FMLA.

Breastfeeding and the Working Mother

If you are a nursing mother, you may need special accommodations at your workplace—such as a couple of uninterrupted breaks during the workday, as well as a private place in which to pump. Here we discuss your rights under the federal Fair Labor Standards Act, which provides special workplace protections for nursing mothers.

What workplace protections does the Fair Labor Standards Act provide for nursing mothers?
Under the Fair Labor Standards Act, employers must provide eligible nursing mothers with a reasonable amount of break time to pump, as well as a private space in which to do so. The private space cannot be a bathroom.

Employers with less than fifty employees do not have to accommodate nursing mothers if doing so would pose an "undue hardship" on the employer.

Are all nursing mothers eligible for workplace accommodations under the Fair Labor Standards Act?
Unfortunately not. The Fair Labor Standards Act's protections for nursing mothers only apply to women who are entitled to overtime pay.

The following categories of employees are *not* eligible for overtime pay and are therefore *not* entitled to the Fair Labor Standard Act's protections for nursing mothers:

- executive employees;
- administrative employees;
- professional employees, including teachers and academic administrative personnel in elementary and secondary schools;
- outside sales employees; and
- certain skilled computer professionals.

For a full list of employees exempt from the Fair Labor Standards Act's overtime pay requirements, consult the

U.S. Department of Labor's website at dol.gov/compliance/guide/minwage.htm.

Do employers have to provide* paid *break time to nursing mothers?
No, as long as the nursing mother is completely relieved from all job-related responsibilities during her break times. However, if an employer provides paid break time to other employees, and a nursing mother uses that break time to pump, then the break time must be paid time.

For how long must employers provide accommodations to nursing mothers under the Fair Labor Standards Act?
Employers must provide nursing mothers with workplace accommodations for up to one year after the birth of the employee's child.

Are there are any state laws that protect nursing mothers in the workplace?
Yes. A number of states have laws in place requiring employers to provide workplace accommodations for nursing mothers. These laws often apply to a broader range of employees than the Fair Labor Standards Act.

CHAPTER 2

Establishing a Legal Identity for Your Child

WITH the arrival of a baby comes a big pile of paperwork. You'll have to fill out plenty of forms, and jump through a few hoops, to establish a legal identity for your child. In the pages that follow, we'll give you the information you will need to:

- choose a name for your child,
- obtain a birth certificate for your child,
- determine whether your child is a United States citizen,
- obtain a Social Security number for your child, and
- apply for a United States passport for your child.

We'll also tell you how and when to add your baby to your health insurance plan.

Naming Your Child

If you are like most new parents, you have probably spent months wrestling with the decision of what to name your child. Here we'll fill you in on the legal rules governing baby names.

Select your baby's name before you deliver. You will need to provide your baby's name when you apply for a birth certificate and a Social Security number for your child.

Can I give my child any first or middle name I wish?

As a general rule, you can give your child any name your heart desires. There is no federal law that governs naming. However, a few states do have nitpicky laws that place technical restrictions on what you can name your child. In California, for example, your child's legal name cannot include an accent.

Do I have to give my child his or her father's last name?

No. In most states, you can give your child any last name you choose. You might opt for the mother's last name, the father's last name, or a hyphenated combination of both names. You can even give your baby a completely new last name that belongs to neither parent.

Can I name my baby after a celebrity or other famous person?

Yes. You can give your child just about any name you wish—from Beyoncé to Barack.

If I am unhappy with the name I choose, can I change my child's name down the line?

Yes, but the process may be complicated. Some states allow you to change your baby's name, or add a new first name, simply with both parents' written consent. In most states, however, you will need to file a formal petition for a name change in state court and obtain a judicial name change order. You will then need to make sure that this name change is reflected on all of your child's legal documents, including your child's Social Security number and passport.

Save yourself the trouble by choosing your child's name carefully and thoughtfully before you apply for your child's birth certificate.

Applying for a Birth Certificate

A birth certificate is your baby's most important identification document. You will need a birth certificate to do everything from applying for your child's passport to registering your child for kindergarten.

How do I apply for a birth certificate?

If you deliver in a hospital, then you simply have to fill out the birth certificate application form that you will usually receive during your stay. You will need to provide your baby's name, as well as the names of both parents, on the application form. The hospital will generally take care of submitting the application form for you. You should receive an official birth certificate in the mail a few weeks later.

If you don't deliver in a hospital, then check with your county's department of health for instructions on how to obtain a birth certificate for your child.

What happens if I can't decide on a name for my baby while I am still in the hospital?

In that case, the hospital may send you home with the birth certificate application form. It will then be your responsibility to make sure that your child's birth certificate application form is completed and submitted on time to the appropriate government agency.

Don't take a chance with your baby's birth certificate! Life with a new baby can be chaotic, and administrative details (like applying for a birth certificate) can get lost in the shuffle. Check one thing off your to-do list by completing the birth certificate application form while you are still in the hospital.

I am not married to my baby's father. Can I name him as the father on the application for my baby's birth certificate?

If you are not married, then you can only list the baby's father on the birth certificate application if the father signs an *acknowledgment of paternity* form. (The hospital should be able to provide you with a copy of this form.)

Signing an acknowledgment of paternity ensures that your child's father is considered your child's legal parent. Without an acknowledgment of paternity or a court order establishing paternity, your child's father will not have the legal rights and responsibilities (including the obligation to pay child support) that come with parenthood.

We are adopting a child born in the United States. Can we apply for a birth certificate that replaces the birth parents' names with our names?

Yes. Once your adoption is finalized, your state's department of health will issue an amended birth certificate that replaces the birth parents' names with the adoptive parents' names. The amended birth certificate will reflect the name you have given your adopted child, rather than the name your child was given at birth.

We are adopting a child born in the United States. Will our adopted child's original birth certificate be sealed?

In many states, an adopted child's original birth certificate is permanently sealed. However, several states—including Alabama, Alaska, Colorado, Kansas, Maine, New Hampshire, and Oregon—provide adoptees with access to their original birth certificates once they are adults. A number of other states allow adult adoptees to obtain copies of their original birth certificates when certain requirements are met.

To learn the access laws that apply in your state, check the American Adoption Congress's website at americanadoptioncongress.org. The American Adoption Congress lobbies for adoption reform, including state legislation that provides adult adoptees with unfettered access to their original birth certificates.

We are adopting a child from overseas. Can we obtain a United States birth certificate for our child?

Yes. In order to obtain a United States birth certificate for a child adopted from overseas, you will need to readopt your child in a court in your home state. Following readoption in the United States, you can apply for a state birth certificate for your adopted child.

Your adopted child's United States-issued birth certificate will reflect the name you have given your adopted child, and will list you and your child's other adoptive parent as your child's parents. However, your adopted child's United States-issued birth certificate will list your child's actual country of birth—and not the United States—as your child's birthplace.

> *A United States-issued birth certificate is not proof of citizenship for a foreign-born adopted child.* A birth certificate only serves as proof of citizenship for a child who is born in the United States. For an adopted child born overseas, you will need to obtain a Certificate of Citizenship or a U.S. passport to establish proof of citizenship. (See pages 42 through 45 below for more details.)

I am afraid I might lose my child's original birth certificate. Can I order an extra official copy of my child's birth certificate?

You should be able to obtain an extra official copy of your child's birth certificate through your state's department of health. You will have to pay a small fee for every copy you order.

> *One option is to use VitalChek to order an official birth certificate.* If you don't mind paying a few extra dollars, you can obtain an extra copy of your child's birth certificate with just a few clicks at vitalchek.com.

Determining Whether Your Child Is a United States Citizen

If you are not a United States citizen, or if your child is born outside of the United States, you may have questions regarding your child's citizenship status. Here we'll give you the answers to questions you may have on citizenship issues.

My baby was born in the United States. Is my baby a United States citizen?

Yes. Almost any child born in the United States or in certain United States' territories is a United States citizen. An exception applies for children of foreign diplomats.

> *It does not matter whether the child's parents are citizens, or even legal residents of the United States.* All children born in the United States (except for children of foreign diplomats) are entitled to United States citizenship, regardless of who their parents are or whether their parents are citizens or legal residents.

> *Some Americans oppose birthright citizenship.* Conservative legislators are pushing for changes to the citizenship law that would restrict United States citizenship to children whose parents are American citizens or lawful residents.

Do I have to file any papers to obtain proof of United States citizenship for a child born in the United States?

No. You simply need a birth certificate establishing that your child was born in the United States.

I am a United States citizen, but my child was born while I was abroad. Is my child a United States citizen?

Probably. The citizenship rules governing children born abroad are somewhat complex, and depend on both the citizenship and marital status of the child's parents.

If you and your child's other parent are married to each other, then your foreign-born child is a United States citizen provided that:

- you and your child's other parent are both United States citizens

and one parent lived in the United States or its territories at any time prior to the child's birth; *or*
- one parent is a United States citizen *and* the United States citizen parent lived in the United States or its territories for *at least five years* prior to the child's birth.

If you and your child's other parent are not married to each other, then your foreign-born child is a United States citizen provided that:

- the child's mother is a United States citizen *and* the mother lived in the United States or its territories for a continuous period of at least one year prior to the child's birth; *or*
- the child's father is a United States citizen *and* the father lived in the United States or its territories for a continuous period of *at least five years* prior to the child's birth.

For more details on the citizenship rules governing foreign-born children, go to the U.S. Citizenship and Immigration Services website at uscis.gov/us-citizenship/citizenship-through-parents.

Do I have to obtain legal proof of citizenship for my foreign-born child?
Yes. You must apply for proof of citizenship for your foreign-born child as soon as possible after your child's birth.

You should apply for a Consular Report of Birth Abroad of a Citizen of the United States of America (CRBA), also known as Form FS-240, at the nearest U.S. embassy or consulate. A CRBA documents that your foreign-born child is a United States citizen. You can use a CRBA to apply for a United States passport for your child and register your child for school in the United States.

For more information on applying for a CRBA, consult the U.S. Department of State's website at travel.state.gov/content/passports/english/abroad/events-and-records/birth.html. You can find contact information for the nearest U.S. embassy or consulate at usembassy.gov.

You should also apply for a U.S. passport for your foreign-born child. Like a CRBA, a valid U.S. passport is considered proof of citizenship. As a general rule, parents of foreign-born children should apply for *both* a CBRA and a United States passport for their children.

> *Make sure you apply for a CRBA or a U.S. passport for your child as soon as practically possible.* Failing to obtain appropriate documentation could lead to problems with establishing your child's United States citizenship and your child's right to enter the United States.

Can I obtain a formal certificate of citizenship for my foreign-born child?

Yes. You can apply for a Certificate of Citizenship using Form N-600, available at the U.S. Citizenship and Immigration Services website at uscis.gov/n-600.

> *You can only apply for a Certificate of Citizenship for your child once you have legal proof of your child's citizenship status.* To obtain a Certificate of Citizenship, you will need to provide either a valid U.S. passport or a CRBA (also known as Form FS-240) for your child.

I am adopting a child from overseas. Will my child be a United States citizen?

Yes. Under the Child Citizenship Act of 2000, your adopted child will generally be entitled to United States citizenship if:

- you or your child's other parent is a United States citizen, and
- your adopted child will reside permanently in the United States in the legal and physical custody of the United States citizen parent.

If your child's adoption is finalized abroad, then your child will be issued an IR-3 visa and will acquire U.S. citizenship on the day your child enters the United States. If your child's adoption is not finalized before your child enters the United States, then your child will be issued an IR-4 visa. Your child will become a United States citizen only after you have readopted your child in the United States and your child's adoption is finalized.

You can learn more about the Child Citizenship Act of 2000 at the U.S. Department of State's website at travel.state.gov/content/travel/english/legal-considerations/us-citizenship-laws-policies/child-citizenship-act.html.

Do I have to obtain legal proof of citizenship for my foreign-born child?

Your foreign-born adopted child will automatically be entitled to United States citizenship provided your child meets the requirements of the Child Citizenship Act of 2000 (see above). However, it is a smart idea to obtain proof of United States citizenship for your foreign-born child in the form of a Certificate of Citizenship.

If your child's adoption is finalized before your child enters the United States, and your child has an IR-3 visa, then U.S. Citizenship and Immigration Services will mail you a Certificate of Citizenship after your child arrives in the United States.

If your child's adoption is not finalized before your child enters the United States, then you will need to apply for a Certificate of Citizenship for your child once you have readopted your child in the United States and the readoption is finalized.

You can apply for a Certificate of Citizenship using Form N-600, available at the U.S. Citizenship and Immigration Services website at uscis.gov/n-600.

Obtaining a Social Security Number for Your Child

One of your child's most important pieces of identification is his or her Social Security number. You will need a Social Security number for your child in order to claim child-related tax breaks. In the years to come, your child will use his or her Social Security number to do everything from opening a bank account to applying for a driver's license.

How do I apply for a Social Security number for my child?
The easiest way to apply for a Social Security number for your child is to request a Social Security number at the same time that you apply for your baby's birth certificate. Typically, you simply have to check a box on the birth registration form requesting a Social Security number for your child. The Social Security Administration will then mail you a Social Security card for your child.

How much will it cost for me to obtain a Social Security number for my child?
There is no charge for obtaining a Social Security number for your child.

I did not apply for a Social Security number for my child at the hospital. How do I obtain a Social Security number for my child?
You can apply for a Social Security number for your child at your local Social Security office. You will need to complete Form SS-5, available at ssa.gov/forms/ss-5.pdf. You will also have to present a certified copy of your child's birth certificate, along with one other form of identification for your child (such as your child's passport, or a copy of your child's hospital record). In addition, you will need to provide proof of your own identity, such as a driver's license or a U.S. passport. Once the Social Security Administration has reviewed your child's application and verified your child's documents, the Social Security Administration will mail you your child's Social Security card.

You can find out more about applying for a Social Security number for your child at the Social Security Administration's website ssa.gov/ssnumber/. Another useful resource is "Social Security Numbers for Children," a helpful brochure published by the Social Security Administration (available at ssa.gov/pubs/EN-05-10023.pdf). To find your local Social Security office, you can call 1-800-772-1213 or go to secure.ssa.gov/ICON/main.jsp.

My child was born overseas. How do I obtain a Social Security number for my child?

The process for applying for a Social Security number for a U.S.-born adopted child is essentially the same as the process for U.S.-born children (see above). However, you will need to provide evidence of your child's U.S. citizenship. Acceptable documents include a Consular Record of Birth Abroad (a CRBA, or Form FS-240), a Certificate of Citizenship, or a U.S. passport.

How do I obtain a Social Security number for my U.S.-born adopted child?

The process for applying for a Social Security number for a U.S.-born adopted child is essentially the same as the process for natural-born children (see page __ above). However, you will need to provide your child's amended birth certificate that reflects your child's new name.

> *If your child already has a Social Security number, you can change your child's name on his or her Social Security card and records using Form SS-5, available at* ssa.gov/forms/ss-5.pdf. You may also be able to apply for a new Social Security number for your adopted child.

How do I obtain a Social Security number for my foreign-born adopted child?

The process for applying for a Social Security number for an adopted child is essentially the same as the process for natural-born children (see above). However, you will need to provide evidence of your child's U.S. citizenship.

You can prove your child's citizenship status by presenting your child's Certificate of Citizenship (see page __ below) or your child's United States passport. If you do not yet have a Certificate of Citizenship or a United States passport for your child, you may be able to apply for a Social Security number for your child using the documents issued to your child by the U.S. Department of Homeland Security when your child arrived in the United States. For more information, go to the Social Security Administration's website at ssa.gov/people/immigrants/children.html.

Can I obtain a Social Security number for my child if the adoption is not yet final?

You cannot obtain a Social Security number for your child if your adoption is not yet final, but you may be eligible to obtain an Adoption Taxpayer Identification Number (ATIN) for your child. An ATIN allows you to claim valuable child-related tax breaks before your *domestic* adoption is finalized. You cannot obtain an ATIN if you are adopting a child internationally.

You can learn more about obtaining an ATIN—including eligibility requirements—at the Internal Revenue Service's website, irs.gov/Individuals/Adoption-Taxpayer-Identification-Number. To obtain an ATIN, you will need to complete IRS Form W-7A, available at irs.gov.

Applying for a Passport for Your Child

Even if your child is just an infant, you will need a valid United States passport for your child in order to travel overseas with your child.

How do I obtain a United States passport for my child?

The process of applying for a passport for your child is fairly complicated. Unfortunately, you can't just check a box on your birth certificate application to get a passport for your child.

In order to obtain a passport for your child, you must apply in person *with your child* at your local passport acceptance facility. You must complete Form DS-11, available at state.gov/documents/organization/212239.pdf, and provide a passport photo of your child. You must also provide:

- Evidence of your child's United States citizenship—such as a U.S. birth certificate, a Consular Report of Birth Abroad (a CRBA, or Form FS-240), or a Certificate of Citizenship.
- Evidence of your parental status—such as a U.S. or foreign birth certificate listing you as your child's parent, or an adoption decree.
- Photo identification for you (the parent)—such as your driver's license or United States passport.

For a complete list of application requirements, consult the U.S. Department of State's website at travel.state.gov/content/passports/english/passports/under-16.html.

Do both parents need to be present for a child's passport application appointment?

No. However, if only one parent can attend the child's passport application appointment, then the other parent must provide his or her written consent in the form of a completed and *notarized* Form DS-3053, available at state.gov/documents/organization/212243.pdf.

How much does it cost to obtain a United States passport for a child?

A little over $100, not including expedited service or delivery fees. You can find a list of current passport application and execution fees at travel.state.gov/content/passports/english/passports/information/fees.html#minor_passport.

How long does it take to obtain a United States passport for a child?

It typically takes four to six weeks to receive a passport. If you pay for expedited service you may be able to receive your child's passport within three weeks. There are also services available that you can use to obtain a passport sooner, if necessary.

Will I need an appointment to apply for a passport for my child?

Typically, yes. You can find a list of local passport acceptance facilities at iafdb.travel.state.gov/. Call ahead of time to book an appointment and verify all of the application requirements.

My child was born overseas. How do I obtain a United States passport for my child?

The process of applying for a United States passport for a child born overseas is essentially the same as that for children born in the United States (see above). Instead of applying at a local passport acceptance facility, however, you will need to apply at your local United States embassy or consulate. Call ahead to confirm the application requirements, and make sure you have all the necessary paperwork before your appointment.

How do I obtain a United States passport for my U.S.-born adopted child?

The process for applying for a United States passport for a U.S.-born adopted child is essentially the same as that for children born in the United States (see above). However, you will need to provide certified copies of your child's amended birth certificate and the adoption decree.

How do I obtain a United States passport for my foreign-born adopted child?

The process for applying for a United States passport for a foreign-born adopted child is essentially the same as that for children born in the United States (see above). However, you will need to provide a certified copy of the final adoption decree (as well as a translation, if the decree is not in English). You must also present either the child's foreign passport showing an I-551 stamp or the child's permanent resident card.

> *Obtaining a United States passport is no easy task.* Double check the application requirements at travel.state.gov/content/passports/english/passports/under-16.html.

Adding Your Child to Your Health Insurance Plan

As soon as your baby is born, you should contact your health insurance company to add your baby to your plan. If you wait too long, you risk losing benefits for your child.

Will my new baby be automatically added to my health insurance plan?

No. Even though your health insurance company may be covering the cost of your obstetrician appointments and your delivery fees, your health insurance company will not automatically learn of your baby's arrival and add your baby to your plan. *It is your responsibility to reach out to your health insurance company to add your baby to your plan.*

If you don't contact your health insurance company to add your baby to your plan, you could forfeit full health insurance coverage for your baby until the next open enrollment period. Reaching out to your health insurance company should be very high on your post-baby-to-do list (right up there with calling the grandparents to share the good news).

How long do I have to enroll my baby in my health insurance plan?
As a general rule, you must contact your health insurance company within thirty days of your child's birth to add your baby to your health insurance plan.

We are adopting a child. How long do we have to enroll our adopted child in our health insurance plan?
You must usually contact your health insurance company within thirty days of your child's adoption or placement for adoption.

Do I have to wait until open enrollment to obtain health insurance coverage for my baby or adopted child?
No. The birth or adoption of a child entitles you to a "special enrollment" period, which means that you can add your child to your health insurance plan without waiting for the open enrollment period.

Does coverage begin on the date I enroll my child in my health insurance plan?
No. As long as you enroll your child within the thirty-day period, coverage is retroactive to the date of your child's birth, adoption, or placement for adoption. For example, let's suppose your baby was born on March 1, 2015, but you did not enroll your baby in your health insurance plan until March 25, 2015. Your health insurance company would have to pay your child's health care costs beginning on March 1, 2015, the date your child was born.

Will I need my baby's Social Security number in order to add my baby to my health insurance plan?
No. Health insurance companies recognize that it takes several weeks to obtain a Social Security number for a new baby or a newly adopted child. You can add your child to your health insurance plan without a Social Security number. However, you should provide your health insurance plan with your child's Social Security number as soon as you receive it.

My baby was born with a heart condition. Can my health insurance company apply the preexisting condition exclusion to deny benefits to my baby?
No. As long as you add your child to your health insurance plan within thirty days of the child's birth, adoption, or placement for adoption, your health insurance company cannot deny coverage for your child based on the preexisting condition exclusion.

You can learn more about your rights to add your baby to your health insurance plan at the U.S. Department of Labor's website, dol.gov/ebsa/publications/newborns.html. The U.S. Department of Labor's site explains both the Newborns' and Mothers' Health Protection Act and the Health Insurance Portability and Accountability Act as they apply to newborns, adopted children, and new parents.

CHAPTER 3

Hiring a Nanny

FINDING and managing good child care can be a challenge. If you choose to enroll your child in day care, the process is fairly straightforward—at least from a legal point of view. All you really have to worry about is completing some basic paperwork and abiding by the terms of the contract you sign with your day care provider (like paying your bills and picking your child up on time).

If you opt to hire a nanny, on the other hand, you will have to comply with an onerous and administratively burdensome set of legal requirements. You will become a household employer in the eyes of the law, and you will be subject to many of the same rules and regulations that govern small business employers.

In the pages that follow, you'll learn all about hiring and paying your nanny legally. This chapter covers:

- The basics of hiring a nanny. We'll answer questions you may have on topics like working with a nanny placement agency, conducting a nanny background check, using a "nanny cam," and letting your nanny drive your car.
- Setting your nanny's salary. We'll help you understand the taxes

you must pay on your nanny's salary, as well as the taxes your nanny will owe on her wages. You will also learn about minimum wage and overtime laws, workers' compensation insurance, and the other expenses that come with hiring a nanny. (See Appendix A: State Minimum Wage, Overtime, and Workers' Compensation Requirements.)
- Providing your nanny with benefits. In addition to a salary, you may decide to offer your nanny fringe benefits, ranging from small perks like cell phone service to major benefits like contributions toward your nanny's health insurance premiums. We'll help you understand the tax implications and other considerations involved with providing these extras.
- Drafting a nanny employment agreement. We'll explain why you need a contract with your nanny and what you should cover in your agreement.
- Complying with the initial administrative requirements of hiring a nanny, as well as the ongoing payroll and tax obligations of employing a nanny. You'll learn about everything from verifying your nanny's employment eligibility to your tax withholding requirements.

In addition, we'll address the many risks inherent in paying a nanny "off the books."

While the process of legally hiring a nanny may seem overwhelming, it's far from impossible, especially if you get some professional assistance with legal and tax compliance. Doing things right from the start can help pave the way for a successful nanny relationship that could last for years.

Many thanks to HomePay (myhomepay.com) *for providing an expert review of this chapter.* HomePay handles the full range of employment obligations—including payroll management and tax filings—for families who hire nannies, housekeepers, and other domestic workers. Special thanks to Tom Breedlove, HomePay's director, and Erik Johnson, HomePay's marketing communications specialist, for helping to make sure that the material in this chapter is accurate and up to date.

The rules governing hiring and paying a nanny are tremendously complex and vary by state. If you attempt to comply with the many requirements for legally hiring a nanny on your own, you run the risk of inadvertently missing an important rule or regulation. The safest course of action is to hire a comprehensive "nanny tax" agency to handle everything from verifying your nanny's eligibility to work in the United States to managing your tax and payroll obligations. Three agencies to consider are HomePay (homepay.com), HomeWork Solutions (homeworksolutions.com), and GTM Payroll Services (gtm.com).

The Basics of Hiring a Nanny

Hiring a nanny can be overwhelming. Here we'll provide answers to the some of the most frequently asked questions on the process of finding and managing a nanny.

I am considering hiring a nanny. What is the first thing I should do?
You should first consider what your family needs and wants in a caregiver. You'll need to decide:

- Whether you want to hire a live-in nanny or a live-out nanny.
- The hours and days you want your nanny to work.
- What you would like your nanny to do for your family. For example, would you like her to make meals and do light housekeeping in addition to child care?
- Whether your nanny must be able to drive. Will she need her own car?
- Whether you have any other special requirements for a nanny. For example, do you want a nanny who speaks fluent English? Would you like a nanny with a college degree? Do you want a young,

energetic nanny or an older, more experienced nanny?

I have a good sense of the kind of nanny I am looking for and the schedule I would like my nanny to work. What is the next thing I should do?

You should then determine how much you would like to pay your nanny, and whether you will provide any benefits, such as contributing toward your nanny's health insurance premiums. Bear in mind that there are many expenses that come with hiring a nanny, as well as compensation rules you must follow. When setting your nanny's salary, you will need to take into account the taxes you must pay on your nanny's salary, as well as the taxes your nanny will owe on her wages. You will also have to comply with minimum wage and overtime requirements. (See pages 65 through 66 for more details on setting a nanny's salary.)

I am ready to begin my search for the "perfect nanny." Should I look for a nanny on my own or use a nanny placement agency?

It depends on your budget and your personal preferences. If you can afford it, a nanny placement agency can streamline the search process by prescreening candidates for you. A good placement agency will match your family with applicants who are willing to work on your schedule and in your salary range.

Before sending candidates your way, a nanny agency will typically:

- confirm that the candidate is legally authorized to work in the United States,
- conduct a background screening,
- check the candidate's references, and
- interview the candidate in person.

All of this prescreening comes at a significant cost. Agencies usually charge a sizable placement fee of 12–15 percent of the nanny's first year's salary, although some just charge a flat rate.

Because of the high cost of using a nanny placement agency, many families opt to handle the nanny search on their own through word-of-mouth referrals and child care websites (such as Care.com and sittercity.com).

I want to hire a nanny placement agency to select candidates for me. What questions should I ask before choosing a placement agency?

You should definitely do a little homework before deciding on a nanny placement agency. Here are a few questions to ask:

- How long has the agency been in business? How many nanny placements has the agency made?
- Are there any minimum requirements for candidates? For example, must candidates have a certain number of years of work experience or a minimum number of references?
- Does the agency check each candidate's references?
- Does the agency conduct background checks? What is covered in the background check?
- Does the agency conduct in-person interviews of each candidate?
- What is the agency's candidate rejection rate?
- Is there an application fee for families seeking a nanny?
- What is the agency's placement fee?
- Are placements guaranteed? If so, for how long?
- What happens if the agency places a nanny who does not work out for some reason? Will the agency conduct a new search at no cost?
- Will the agency assist you with preparing a nanny employment agreement?
- Does the agency offer emergency back-up services if your nanny has to miss work for any reason? How much does this cost?

I have decided to search for a nanny on my own. Should I ask candidates to complete an application form?

Requiring candidates to complete an application form can save you time by helping you prescreen candidates for qualities you are looking for (like CPR certification). You can find a sample nanny employment application form at the HomeWork Solutions website, 4nannytaxes.com/forms/nanny-app.pdf.

Some perfectly wonderful candidates may be uncomfortable completing a comprehensive nanny application before getting to know you. Unlike traditional employment searches, the hunt for a nanny tends to be a bit less formal and a lot more personal. Nanny candidates may want to sit down with you in person before providing you with contact information for their references and other personal details.

I have found a wonderful nanny, but she is undocumented. Can I legally hire an undocumented nanny?

No. You can only legally hire a nanny who is authorized to work in the United States. You will need to confirm your nanny's employment eligibility by completing Form I-9 (see pages 92–93 below).

I have checked my potential nanny's references and now I want to run a background check. How can I do this?

Under the Fair Credit Reporting Act, you will need your potential nanny's written consent to run a background check on her.

There are a number of companies that will conduct a nanny background check for you at a modest cost (typically less than $100) with a quick turnaround time. In order to run a background check on your nanny, you will need your nanny's legal name, her date of birth, her Social Security number, and her authorization.

When choosing a nanny background check service, make sure you understand exactly what the screening includes. A nanny background check should ideally include:

- Social Security number verification to confirm the candidate's identity and to determine whether she has used any other names, as well as to obtain her former addresses.
- A felony and misdemeanor check in every jurisdiction where the candidate has worked and lived for the last seven years, run on every name used by the candidate in the last seven years.
- A search of the National Sex Offender Registry.
- A driving record check.

You can find helpful information on the nanny background check process at the Association of Premier Nanny Agencies' website, theapna.org/about/standards-of-practice/required-background-checks/. You can also find useful articles on hiring a safe caregiver on Care.com, care .com/safety-resources-p1377.html.

One company to consider is Nanny Background Check, which has been in the nanny screening business for more than fifteen years. You can begin the screening process at nannybackgroundcheck.com.

Once I find the "perfect nanny," will I need an employment agreement with her?

The law does not require that you have an employment agreement with your nanny. However, depending on the state in which you live, you may need to provide your nanny with notice of her hourly rate, her overtime rate, and her pay frequency. (Both California and New York impose this requirement.)

Even though you are under no legal obligation to have a "nanny contract," having an agreement in place can help to make sure that there are no misunderstandings on important issues such as working hours, compensation, vacation days, sick days, bonuses, and raises. (You can learn more about nanny contracts on pages 87 though 90.)

My nanny is starting work next week. What do I need to do to hire and pay my nanny legally?

First, you'll need to comply with a few basic administrative requirements. You will have to verify your nanny's employment eligibility using Form I-9. If this is your first time hiring a nanny, you will need to apply for a federal employer identification number (EIN) and a state EIN to register as a household employer. You will also have to report your new hire to your state's new-hire reporting agency. (See pages 91 through 94 for more information.)

Next, you will need to get payroll set up to pay your nanny legally. If your nanny would like you to withhold income taxes from her salary, you must have your nanny complete a W-4 and a state income tax withholding form (if you live in a state with income taxes). Throughout the year, you will need to make periodic federal and state tax payments. You will also have to provide your nanny with a W-2 at the end of the year. (See pages 62 through 71 for more information on complying with your tax and payroll obligations.)

Finally, you will need to make sure you are adequately insured with workers' compensation, disability insurance, and automobile insurance (if applicable). (See pages 80 through 87 for more information on these insurance issues.)

Hiring and paying a nanny legally seems so complicated and expensive. What happens if I just pay my nanny "off the books" instead?
Many families (probably the vast majority) pay their nannies off the books instead of complying with the multitude of rules and requirements for hiring and paying a nanny legally. However, paying a nanny off the books is a very risky practice from a legal perspective. (See pages 99 through 101 below for information on the potential problems that can arise when you pay a nanny this way.)

Can I claim any tax breaks if I pay my nanny "on the books"?
Yes. You may be eligible to use an employer-sponsored dependent care flexible spending account to pay a portion of your nanny's wages with pretax dollars. You may also be able to claim the child care credit. (See pages 220 through 223 of Chapter 6 for more information on these valuable tax breaks.)

I have found a terrific nanny, but she does not want to be paid on the books. What should I do?
Try explaining to your nanny that there are many benefits to getting paid legally. If you pay your nanny on the books, she may be eligible to receive valuable government benefits—including unemployment benefits if you terminate her employment due to no fault of her own, and Social Security and Medicare benefits when she reaches retire-

ment age. She will also have a record of verifiable income, which she may need to rent an apartment, obtain a credit card, lease a car, or take out a loan.

I am hiring a nanny for a two-week trial period. Do I need to comply with the many requirements for legally hiring and paying a permanent nanny during this trial period?

At a minimum, you will need to confirm your nanny's eligibility to work in the United States (see pages 91 through 93 below). You must also comply with minimum wage and overtime requirements (see pages 71 through 80 below).

Depending on how much your nanny earns during her two-week trial period, you may not have to pay Social Security and Medicare taxes on her wages for that time. You do not have to pay these taxes if you pay a nanny or babysitter less than a certain amount per year. (In 2015, this amount was $1,900.)

Check with a "nanny tax" professional about any applicable requirements for hiring a nanny on a trial basis. You may still owe state taxes on your nanny's salary. In addition, you may need workers' compensation insurance during your trial period.

I want one-on-one in-home care for my child, but I don't want to go through all the trouble of legally hiring and paying a nanny. Are there any other options?

You may want to consider hiring a caregiver through the au pair program, which allows young women and men from abroad to spend a year or two with a host family in the United States. When you hire an au pair, you do so through one of the nationally accredited au pair agencies. You usually won't have to pay Social Security, Medicare, or federal unemployment taxes on your au pair's salary because au pairs are J-1 nonimmigrants. You simply pay a fixed stipend for a set number of child care hours each week.

Compared to hiring a nanny, hiring an au pair is a bargain. However, the au pair program is not for everyone. First, you have to be willing to deal with the unique challenges of having a young person live in your home seven days a week. Second, there are restrictions on an au pair's responsibilities and working hours. You cannot ask your au pair to work more than ten hours a day, or more than forty-five hours a week, even if you pay her extra to do so. You also cannot ask your au pair to do any household chores other than those that directly relate to your child (like your child's laundry). Third, you may not leave an au pair alone with an infant under the age of three months. Finally, and perhaps most importantly, an au pair cannot stay with your family for longer than two years. Most au pairs leave after one year. Depending on your family's needs, it might be disruptive to have to change caregivers so frequently.

For more information about the au pair program, go to j1visa.state.gov/programs/aupair. If you would like more detailed information on program requirements and benefits, a useful resource is aupairinamerica.com.

My nanny will be driving my children. Are there any legal or financial issues I need to worry about?

Yes. First, you should make sure that your nanny's driver's license is up to date and that your nanny has a good driving record. You can do this through a background check. However, if you live in Alaska, New Hampshire, or Pennsylvania, you will have to ask your nanny for a copy of her driving record because Department of Motor Vehicles records are not available through a background check in these states.

If your nanny will be driving your car on a regular basis, you will need to add your nanny as an additional driver on your automobile insurance policy. This could raise your premiums, particularly if your nanny is younger than age twenty-five. Check with your automobile insurance company for coverage information.

If your nanny will be driving her own car while she is working for you, you should make sure that the car is safe enough for your children, and that your nanny has adequate automobile insurance coverage. You may need to purchase nonowned auto coverage, which provides coverage for accidents that occur when an employee is using her own vehicle for work-related reasons. Check with your automobile insurance company for more details.

You should also reimburse your nanny for gas, maintenance, and wear and tear if she regularly uses her own car to drive your children. You can use standard mileage rates published by the IRS to reimburse your nanny for these costs. (In 2015, the rate was 57.5 cents per mile.) Mileage reimbursements are nontaxable, which means that neither you nor your nanny will owe taxes on these costs.

Finally, you should give some thought to what will happen if your nanny has a car accident on the job. If she is driving her own car, will your family cover the deductible? If she is driving your car and she is at fault, will you hold her responsible for some of the costs of repair? You may want to spell out the terms of who will pay for what in your nanny employment agreement (see pages 87 though 90 below).

What happens if my child has a medical emergency during my nanny's shift?

It's a smart idea to provide your nanny with a signed medical authorization form so that your nanny can consent to any necessary medical treatment in your absence. You can find a sample "Consent to Treat Form" at the website of the American College of Emergency Physicians, acep.org/medicalforms/.

You should also provide your nanny with:

- a copy of your child's health insurance card;
- contact information for your child's pediatrician and any of your child's other health-care providers; and
- the name and address of the hospital that you would like your nanny to go to in the event of an emergency.

I am considering sharing a nanny with another family. How does that work from a legal perspective?

If you share a nanny with another family, both you and your nanny's other family will have to comply with the legal requirements for hiring and paying a nanny. You will each owe employment taxes on your share of the nanny's salary, and you will each have to give your nanny a W-2 form at the end of the year.

Because there are two families involved with two separate sets of needs, nanny share arrangements can get complicated quickly. A comprehensive employment agreement between your family, the other family, and the nanny can help head off possible problems (like coordinating vacation days so that the nanny can have a full week off a couple of times a year).

> *Nanny share arrangements can raise unique legal issues.* It's best to work with a "nanny tax" professional to craft a tax-compliant compensation arrangement, and to ensure that both families are following all applicable legal rules for hiring and paying a nanny.

I am worried about leaving my baby in the hands of a stranger. Can I legally install a "nanny cam" in my home so I can keep an eye on my nanny?

Yes. You do not need your nanny's consent to install an audio-free nanny cam in any common area of your home, such as your kitchen or your playroom. However, a number of states have laws in place protecting against audio recordings. If you install a nanny cam that records both video and audio, you should obtain your nanny's written consent beforehand.

If my "perfect nanny" turns out to be a poor fit for my family, can I terminate her employment?

Yes. Unless you provide otherwise in your employment agreement with your nanny, your nanny is considered an "at will" employee. This means that you can generally terminate your nanny's employment at any time and for any reason.

> *Your state may have special laws governing how and when you can fire your nanny.* For example, the Massachusetts Domestic Workers Bill of Rights provides protections for live-in nannies who are terminated without cause. Massachusetts families must provide written notice to a live-

in nanny and do one of the following: (1) allow the nanny to continue living in the family's home for at least thirty days, (2) pay for comparable off-site housing, or (3) give two weeks of severance pay.

Will I have to provide my nanny with severance pay if I terminate her employment?

No. You are not legally obligated to provide your nanny with severance pay. However, you may wish to provide termination provisions in your nanny employment agreement that specify whether or not you must give your nanny advance notice of termination and/or severance pay.

Can my nanny apply for unemployment benefits if I terminate her employment?

Provided you pay your nanny on the books, your nanny may be eligible for unemployment benefits if you let her go. Your nanny will likely qualify for unemployment benefits if you terminate her employment for reasons unrelated to her performance. For example, you might let your nanny go if there is a change in your family's circumstances, or if your nanny is simply not a good fit for your family's needs. However, your nanny will likely be ineligible for benefits if you terminate her employment for performance-related reasons (or "cause"). For example, if your nanny is never on time, or if she does not care for your child appropriately, then she will likely not qualify for unemployment benefits.

Setting Your Nanny's Salary

Before beginning your search for the perfect nanny, you should first decide how much you are willing to pay in salary and benefits.

When you pay your nanny on the books, you will owe Social Security, Medicare, and unemployment taxes on your nanny's salary. You may also have to pay for workers' compensation and disability insurance. You will have to factor in these expenses when calculating the out-of-pocket costs of hiring a nanny.

You will also need to consider what your nanny's take-home pay will be each week. Your nanny will owe Social Security and Medicare taxes, in addition to income taxes, on her salary. She may also owe state taxes, such as disability insurance taxes. As your nanny's employer, you are legally required to withhold Social Security and Medicare taxes from your nanny's salary, but your nanny can choose whether or not to have you withhold federal and state income taxes. You should determine approximately how much your nanny will owe in taxes, so that you can let prospective candidates know what their take-home pay will be each week. Otherwise, your nanny may be unpleasantly surprised to see that her weekly check is a fair bit less than the salary you advertised.

Significantly, you will have to be very careful to comply with federal and state minimum wage and overtime laws when setting your nanny's salary. These laws apply regardless of whether you pay your nanny a fixed weekly salary or on an hourly basis because nannies are considered nonexempt employees for purposes of the minimum wage and overtime laws.

Finally, you may want to consider holiday bonuses and annual raises when setting your nanny's starting salary. The law does not require either, but many nannies expect both. If you set your nanny's base salary too high, you may not have enough of a cushion to pay bonuses and raises each year.

Employment Taxes You Must Pay on Your Nanny's Salary

As a household employer, you will be responsible for paying Social Security, Medicare, and federal and state unemployment taxes on your nanny's salary. This will add approximately 10 percent to your out-of-pocket costs of hiring a nanny. In addition, you may owe modest additional state taxes, such as a state disability insurance tax.

You probably won't have to pay Social Security and Medicare taxes if you hire an occasional babysitter. These taxes only apply if the amount you pay to a babysitter or nanny exceeds a certain amount annually. In 2015, this amount was $1,900.

How much will I have to pay in Social Security and Medicare taxes on my nanny's salary?

In 2015, household employers were required to pay 6.2 percent in Social Security taxes and 1.45 percent in Medicare taxes on their nanny's salaries. For a nanny who earned $500 a week, a household employer would have been required to pay $38.25 in Social Security and Medicare taxes.

The combination of Social Security and Medicare taxes is frequently referred to as "FICA taxes."

Why do I have to pay Social Security and Medicare taxes on my nanny's salary?

Your Social Security and Medicare taxes, or FICA taxes, help to pay for the cost of your nanny's future Social Security and Medicare benefits.

When you pay your nanny on the books, you help to ensure that your nanny will be eligible for Social Security and Medicare benefits years from now. Your nanny will only be able to claim Social Security benefits if she works on the books for at least ten years. The amount of her Social Security benefits will depend on her lifetime on the books earnings. Similarly, your nanny will generally only qualify for Medicare benefits if she (or her spouse) is also eligible for Social Security benefits.

How much will I have to pay in federal and state unemployment taxes on my nanny's salary?

The amount you will owe in federal and state unemployment taxes on your nanny's salary varies depending on the state in which you live.

In 2015, federal unemployment taxes (or FUTA taxes) were 6 percent of the first $7,000 of an employee's salary, or $420. (No FUTA taxes were due on an employee's salary above this amount.) Like the FUTA tax rate, each state has its own unemployment tax rate as well as a cap on how much of your nanny's wages will be subject to that tax rate.

You may be able to claim a credit against your FUTA taxes based on the state unemployment taxes you pay on your nanny's salary.

Taxes That Must Be Withheld from Your Nanny's Salary

Just like any other employee, your nanny will owe taxes on her salary. Your nanny must have Social Security and Medicare taxes withheld from her salary, and may also elect to have federal and state income taxes withheld as well. In some states, you may have to withhold additional taxes—such as a disability insurance tax—from your nanny's salary.

How much do I need to withhold in Social Security and Medicare taxes from my nanny's salary?
In 2015, household employees were required to have 6.2 percent in Social Security taxes and 1.45 percent in Medicare taxes withheld each pay period from their gross wages. A nanny who earned $500 a week in 2015 would have had $38.25 in Social Security and Medicare taxes withheld from her paycheck each week. Her net salary (before accounting for federal and state income taxes) would have been $461.75.

You and your nanny will pay the same amount in Social Security and Medicare taxes. In 2015, the total Social Security and Medicare tax obligation on a household employee's salary was 15.3 percent. The family employing the nanny owed 7.65 percent in taxes, while the nanny had the other 7.65 percent in taxes withheld from her salary.

You could opt to pay your nanny's share of Social Security and Medicare taxes. Some families choose to pick up the full tab of their nanny's Social Security and Medicare tax liability. If you do this, you will have to add the amount of Social Security and Medicare taxes you pay on your nanny's behalf to the taxable wages reported on your nanny's W-2. Your nanny will then owe federal and state income taxes on this higher amount of income.

How much will my nanny have to pay in federal and state income taxes?

It depends on your nanny's salary and the state in which you reside, as well as your nanny's filing status and the number of allowances she can claim. To get an estimate of how much your nanny will owe in federal and state income taxes, use the "nanny tax" calculator at myhomepay.com. Just click on the "Calculators" link on the right-hand side of the menu bar in the middle of the page.

You are not legally obligated to withhold income taxes from your nanny's salary. While you must withhold Social Security and Medicare taxes from your nanny's salary, your nanny can opt to pay her income taxes entirely on her own. Just make sure your nanny understands that she will be responsible for paying estimated tax payments during the year, or else she might face a sizable income tax bill at the end of the year, as well as a possible tax underpayment penalty.

Will my nanny or I have to pay disability insurance taxes?

It depends on the state in which you reside. If you live in New Jersey, both you and your nanny must pay disability insurance taxes. If you live in California, Hawaii, Rhode Island, or Puerto Rico, then only your nanny has to pay disability insurance taxes. The tax rate varies by state.

By paying disability insurance taxes, your nanny may qualify for benefits if she has a non-work-related illness or injury that prevents her from doing her job. The rules on disability benefits vary by state.

My nanny is undocumented, but she would like to pay taxes on her income to establish a record of compliance with U.S. laws for immigration purposes. Is this possible?

Yes. In fact, the IRS requires undocumented workers to pay taxes on their wages. Similarly, the IRS requires employers of undocumented workers to pay employment taxes on those wages.

Establishing a record of paying taxes can help your nanny in the event that she has the opportunity to apply for legal immigrant status. On the flip side, the Department of Homeland Security often denies immigration petitions based on nonpayment of taxes.

If your undocumented nanny opts to pay taxes on her salary, she does not have to worry that doing so could result in deportation proceedings. Federal law prohibits the IRS from sharing information concerning the wages of undocumented workers with U.S. Immigration and Customs Enforcement.

In order to pay taxes, your undocumented nanny will need to obtain an individual taxpayer identification number (ITIN) using IRS Form W-7, available at irs.gov. You can use your nanny's ITIN in lieu of a Social Security number on tax forms. Your nanny may also be able to use her ITIN to open a bank or credit card account, or to take out a mortgage loan. You can learn more about ITINs at the IRS website, irs.gov/Individuals/Individual-Taxpayer-Identification-Number(ITIN).

It is illegal to hire an undocumented nanny. Even if both you and your nanny comply with all applicable tax obligations, it is still against the law for you to hire a nanny who is not legally authorized to work in the United States.

I have a live-in nanny. Does my nanny have to pay taxes on the value of the room and board we provide?

From a federal tax standpoint, if your nanny lives in your home, the value of her lodging is considered nontaxable income provided that: (1) you require her to live at your home for your convenience (for example, to provide you with early morning child care or overnight child care if you travel for work); and (2) your nanny agrees to live with you as a condition of employment. Similarly, your nanny does not have to pay taxes on the value of the meals she eats at your home as long as you provide her with meals for your convenience (for example, because you want her to be home during the day with your children instead of going out to lunch).

> *Depending on the state in which you live, your nanny may owe state income taxes on the value of the room and board you provide.* Your nanny should check with an accountant or tax specialist to determine if she is responsible for reporting the value of room and board as part of her taxable wages when she files her tax return.

I want to give my nanny an estimate of her take-home pay. How can I calculate her net pay?

If you would like to run the numbers yourself, a good place to start is the Employee Paycheck calculator available at myhomepay.com/Resources/Nanny-Tax-Withholdings-Calculator. However, the safest course of action is to have your accountant or a payroll service do the calculations for you. This way, you can rest assured that you have factored in all applicable taxes.

Minimum Wage and Overtime Requirements

Nannies are protected under the federal Fair Labor Standards Act (FLSA), as well as state labor laws. You must pay your nanny at least the minimum wage for every hour that she works. You also have to comply with federal and state overtime requirements.

If I pay my nanny a fixed weekly salary, do I still have to worry about hourly minimum wage requirements?

Yes. Under the federal Fair Labor Standards Act, you may not pay your nanny anything less than the federal minimum wage for every hour that she works. State labor laws impose similar requirements on nanny wages.

In some states, like California, it is illegal to pay your nanny a fixed salary rather than paying her on an hourly basis.

Experts recommend that you pay your nanny on an hourly basis to avoid minimum wage and overtime mistakes. If you are set on offering a fixed salary to your nanny, it's wise to break the salary down to an hourly rate based on the number of hours your nanny will work in a typical week. You can then use this hourly rate to adjust your nanny's pay if she works more than the typical number of hours in any given week.

Don't forget about overtime pay. If your nanny works more than forty hours per week, then you will have to pay her overtime at a rate of time and a half. Overtime pay is calculated based on your nanny's hourly rate, not the applicable minimum wage. (See pages 76 through 77 below to learn more about overtime.)

You don't have to worry about federal minimum wage requirements if you have an occasional babysitter. The Fair Labor Standards Act only applies to nannies or babysitters who either (1) work more than eight hours a week, or (2) earn more than a certain amount ($1,900 in 2015) in a single year.

What is the federal minimum wage?

In 2015, the federal minimum wage was $7.25 per hour.

The federal minimum wage could increase in the near future. Unions and other employee organizations are working hard to raise the federal minimum wage to at least $10.10 per hour.

Do I have to comply with any other minimum wage requirements besides the federal minimum wage?

Yes. You also have to comply with your state's minimum wage laws. Many states have imposed higher minimum wage requirements than the federal minimum wage. In Washington, D.C., for example, the minimum wage is $9.50 per hour. (Check the chart on page 293 to find out the minimum wage that applies in your state.)

Depending on the town or city in which you live, you may also be subject to municipal minimum wage laws. For example, the minimum wage in San Francisco is $11.05 per hour.

You must pay the highest applicable minimum wage. If your state's or city's minimum wage is higher than the federal minimum wage, then you must pay your nanny at your state's or city's minimum wage rate (rather than the federal minimum wage rate) for every hour that she works.

What counts as a "working hour" for minimum wage purposes? For example, do I have to pay my nanny when my child is napping or when my nanny is eating lunch?

You must pay your nanny the minimum wage for every hour that she is on duty. Any time that your nanny is required to be at your home—even if your child is napping, or attending preschool—counts as a working hour. You also need to include your nanny's lunch and rest breaks as working time, unless your nanny is completely relieved from her obligations and is not required to be at your home during that time.

Commuting time does not count. You do not have to pay your nanny for the time she spends getting to and from your home.

Special rules apply for round-the-clock shifts. If your nanny works for twenty-four consecutive hours or more, you can exclude up to eight hours of sleeping time provided that your nanny is given adequate sleeping arrangements and she has at least five consecutive hours of sleep time uninterrupted by work-related duties. For example, let's suppose your nanny spends one night a week at your home, so that you and your spouse can enjoy a "date night." Your nanny is scheduled to be on duty for twenty-four hours, from 8:00 a.m. on Friday morning until 8:00 a.m. on Saturday morning. As long as you provide her with a proper place to sleep and uninterrupted sleeping time, you can pay her for only sixteen of the twenty-four hours and count eight hours as unpaid sleeping time.

I plan on paying my nanny a weekly salary rather than an hourly rate. How can I make sure that my nanny's salary complies with minimum wage requirements?

You first need to calculate the number of hours your nanny will work each week. As long as your nanny will work forty or fewer hours per week, you can simply divide your nanny's weekly salary by the number of hours your nanny will work each week to determine whether her salary complies with minimum wage requirements.

For example, let's suppose you live in Washington, D.C. and you plan on paying your nanny $350 per week for forty hours of work. This works out to $8.75 per hour, which is less than Washington, D.C.'s minimum wage of $9.50 per hour. To comply with the minimum wage that applies in Washington, D.C., you would have to offer a salary of at least $380 per week for forty hours of work.

A B C *You will have to pay your nanny more during weeks when she works longer hours.* There may be weeks when your nanny works more hours than her "set" number of hours. For example, let's suppose you offered your nanny a fixed salary of $300 per week for thirty hours of work (or $10 an hour). If your nanny worked thirty-five hours one week because you had a late meeting to attend, you would have to pay your nanny $350—her usual salary of $300, plus an additional $50 for the extra five hours she worked that week.

If your nanny works more than forty hours per week, you must also make sure that your nanny's salary complies with federal and state overtime laws. In addition, California requires you to pay your nanny daily overtime if she works more than a certain number of hours per day. (See pages 76 through 77 below for more information on overtime laws.)

I am paying for my live-in nanny's room and board. Do I also have to pay her the minimum wage for every hour that she works?

The short answer is yes.

Under the Fair Labor Standards Act, you can take a credit against the minimum wage for the "reasonable cost" of room and board provided to your live-in nanny if (1) the room and board is primarily for your nanny's benefit, and (2) you would not have incurred the costs of providing room and board if you did not have a live-in nanny.

As a practical matter, most families won't be able to meet these two criteria. For example, if you provide your nanny with a spare bedroom in your home that would otherwise go unused, you would not be incurring any additional costs above and beyond what you would normally have to spend on housing. Also, if you require your nanny to live at your home (perhaps because you leave for work early in the morning), then you cannot claim a credit for the value of your nanny's lodging because it is provided primarily for your family's benefit.

You may be able to take a modest credit for the amount you spend on providing food for your nanny as long as you can separate your nanny's food expenses from your own family's food expenses. If your nanny eats the same meals as your family, this will be quite hard to do.

Put simply, the safest (and easiest) course of action is to pay your live-in nanny the minimum wage for every hour she works, even if you provide her with room and board.

If you count the value of your nanny's room and board toward your nanny's minimum wage, the value of the room and board is considered "taxable compensation." This means that both you and your nanny will owe taxes on the value of the room and board you provide.

Do I have to pay my nanny overtime if she works more than forty hours per week?

Yes. Under the Fair Labor Standards Act, your nanny is entitled to one and a half times her *hourly rate* (not the federal minimum wage) for every hour that she works beyond forty hours per week.

For example, let's suppose that you agree to pay your live-out nanny $10 per hour. Let's further suppose that your nanny is usually scheduled to work forty hours per week. However, during busy weeks at work, your nanny stays late and works fifty hours per week. Your nanny's regular pay rate during forty-hour weeks would be $400 per week before taxes. However, during weeks when your nanny works fifty hours per week, your nanny would earn $550 per week before taxes—$400 for the first forty hours ($10/hour × 40 hours) and $150 for ten hours of overtime ($10/hour × 1.5 overtime rate × 10 hours).

Federal overtime requirements do not apply to live-in nannies. If you have a live-in nanny, you don't have to pay your nanny overtime under the Fair Labor Standards Act. However, you may have to pay overtime to your live-in nanny under your state's labor laws. (Check the chart on page 293 below to learn your state's requirements.)

If your nanny will be entitled to overtime, be careful not to set your nanny's hourly rate too high. Otherwise, your nanny's total weekly salary might turn out to be much higher than you had expected because of the time-and-a-half overtime rate.

Do I have to comply with any other overtime requirements besides the federal overtime rules?

Yes. You also have to comply with your state's overtime rules. Some states require families to pay overtime to live-in nannies. If you live in California, you may have to pay daily overtime if your nanny works more than a specific number of hours in a day. (Check the chart on page 293 to find out the overtime requirements that apply in your state.)

Rather than paying my nanny overtime, can I give her compensatory time off instead?

No. You must pay her overtime for every hour that she works in excess of forty hours. You cannot compensate her for the overtime hours by "making up" the time with reduced hours the following week.

Do I have to pay my nanny overtime if she works on a holiday or a weekend?

No. Under the Fair Labor Standards Act, you only have to pay overtime for any hours worked in excess of forty hours per week. You do not have to pay your nanny overtime for hours worked on the weekend or on holidays if she works less than a total of forty hours during the week.

A week is defined as a seven-day period for purposes of the Fair Labor Standards Act.

Do I have to pay my nanny if she takes a sick day or a holiday?

Under the Fair Labor Standards Act, you do not have to pay your nanny for any time that she does not work.

However, you may have to provide your nanny with sick days or vacation days under your state or city laws. For example, if you live in New York and your nanny has been with you for at least a year, you must provide your nanny with three paid days off per year.

My live-in nanny regularly works more than forty hours per week. Do we have to pay her overtime under the Fair Labor Standards Act?

No. Under federal law, you don't have to pay a live-in nanny overtime.

Several states have specific overtime laws for live-in employees. These states include California, Hawaii, Maine, Maryland, Massachusetts, Minnesota, and New York.

A nanny who occasionally stays the night is not a live-in nanny for purposes of the overtime exemption. You can only claim the overtime exemption if your nanny stays at your home either permanently, or for five consecutive nights each week. For more information, check "Fact Sheet #79B: Live-in Domestic Service Workers Under the Fair Labor Standards Act (FSLA)," available at the Department of Labor's website, dol.gov/whd/regs/compliance/whdfs79b.htm.

My nanny will be working more than forty hours per week. How do I structure my nanny's weekly salary so that it complies with both minimum wage and overtime laws?

A terrific place to start is the online Hourly Pay Rate Calculator available at the HomeWork Solutions website at 4nannytaxes.com/calculator/hourly.cfm. (You will need to complete a free registration to use the calculator.) The Hourly Pay Rate Calculator will help you break down your proposed weekly nanny salary into a base rate and an overtime rate.

For example, let's suppose you live in New Jersey and you plan to pay your nanny $500 before taxes to work fifty hours per week. You cannot simply offer your nanny an hourly rate of $10 per hour, because you would then have to pay your nanny $550 per week (40 hours × $10/hour plus 10 hours × overtime rate of $15/hour).

Instead, you should offer your nanny an hourly rate of $9.09, with an overtime rate of $13.64. This hourly rate works out to $500 per week for a fifty-hour workweek. This rate also complies with New Jersey's minimum wage of $8.38 per hour.

Do I have to provide my nanny with a salary breakdown, so that she understands her hourly rate and her overtime rate?

Depending on the state in which you live, you may be legally required to inform your nanny of her hourly rate, her overtime rate, and her pay frequency.

Check to see whether your state has any special notice requirements with respect to paying a nanny. In both

New York and California, for example, you must provide you nanny with written notice of her hourly rate and her overtime rate. You can find California and New York wage notice forms at the HomePay website, myhomepay.com/Resources/Forms. You can also find state-by-state requirements for hiring and paying a nanny at HomePay's website, myhomepay.com/Answers/RequirementsByState.

It's a smart idea to inform your nanny of her hourly rate and her overtime rate regardless of where you live. Being clear with your nanny from the start about exactly how much she will be paid and how her salary will be calculated can help avoid salary-related misunderstandings down the line.

My nanny may occasionally come on vacation with us. If I pay for my nanny's airfare and her meals, do I still have to pay her both the minimum wage and overtime for the hours she is on duty?

Yes, assuming you are taking your nanny with you to help care for your children while on vacation (and not so that your nanny can go sightseeing). If your nanny is traveling with you for your family's benefit, the value of the airfare, lodging, and meals you provide for your nanny all count as nontaxable income (or "fringe benefits"). You will still have to pay your nanny no less than the applicable minimum wage for every hour that she is on duty while on vacation with your family, as well as every hour that she spends traveling with you. You will also have to pay your nanny overtime if she works more than forty hours a week while on vacation.

Make sure your nanny has a clear understanding of vacation compensation and working hours before you finalize your plans. Being away from home can make it hard to distinguish between when your nanny is working and when she's off the clock. A good rule of thumb is that if your nanny is free to be on her own away from you and your children, then she's not working and you don't have to pay her for her time. But if she is with your children—even if she is just relaxing by the pool watching your kids play—you should pay her for her time. To avoid misunderstandings, it may be best to have a separate vacation employment agreement that covers the details of hours and pay while you are away together.

Workers' Compensation

Workers' compensation insurance covers your nanny's medical expenses and lost wages in the event that she is injured on the job. Depending on the state in which you live, you may be legally required to purchase workers' compensation insurance.

Which states require families to purchase workers' compensation insurance for their nannies?
Check the Appendix A on page 293 to see whether your state requires you to purchase workers' compensation for your nanny.

You could face fines for noncompliance with state workers' compensation requirements. Failing to purchase required workers' compensation insurance could subject your family to sizable state penalties.

My state does not require families hiring nannies to purchase workers' compensation insurance. Should I purchase workers' compensation insurance anyway?
Workers' compensation is a smart idea because it can cover your nanny's medical expenses and lost wages if she gets hurt while working for your family. For example, your nanny could trip on your child's toy, fall down the stairs, and throw out her back for weeks.

As a general rule, a nanny who accepts workers' compensation benefits cannot sue her employers for on-the-job injuries, even if her employers were at fault in some way (for example, by not shoveling an icy sidewalk). Without workers' compensation insurance, you could face thousands of dollars in liability for your nanny's lost wages, medical expenses, and pain and suffering in the event that your nanny is injured on the job.

If you need help purchasing workers' compensation insurance, a "nanny tax" service can help. Among other companies, both HomePay (myhomepay.com) and GTM Payroll Services (gtm.com) can help you to purchase workers' compensation insurance.

Will my homeowners' insurance policy cover my nanny's on-the-job injuries?

Your homeowners' insurance policy will probably *not* cover your nanny's on-the-job injuries. Your homeowners' insurance policy will not cover your nanny's on-the-job injuries if your state requires workers' compensation insurance (see the chart on page 293). Moreover, your homeowners' insurance policy will not cover injuries that occur outside your home while your nanny is working for you (for example, if your nanny twists her ankle while chasing after your rambunctious toddler at a playground). Check with your homeowners' insurance company to understand the terms of your coverage.

Disability Insurance

Disability insurance covers a percentage of your nanny's lost wages for a period of time in the event that she cannot work because of a non-work-related medical condition or injury. Depending on the state in which you live, you may have to pay disability insurance taxes and/or withhold disability insurance taxes from your nanny's salary to guarantee coverage for your nanny.

Which states require families to purchase disability insurance for their nannies?

New York and Hawaii require families to purchase disability insurance coverage for their nannies.

California, New Jersey, Rhode Island, and Puerto Rico provide disability benefits to employees funded through mandatory payroll taxes.

My state does not require or provide disability insurance. Should my nanny purchase disability insurance anyway?
It's worth considering, especially if there is a possibility that your nanny may become pregnant while working for you.

Let's suppose, for example, that your nanny has a minor medical procedure that keeps her out of work for three weeks. During that time, your family would likely have to hire replacement child care. Would your family continue paying your nanny while she is out sick? Or would you not pay her wages for three weeks, even if your nanny depended on her income to cover her basic living expenses? If your nanny has a disability insurance coverage in place, you won't face these difficult choices because disability benefits would cover all or most of your nanny's wages during the time she is unable to work.

Bonuses and Raises

While there is no law requiring holiday bonuses or annual raises, nannies often expect a little extra compensation at holiday time, as well as a modest increase in compensation each year.

Consider spelling out your raise and bonus policies in your nanny contract. To avoid unpleasant surprises and disappointment, you may want to tell your nanny exactly what she can expect in the way of bonuses and raises in your nanny employment agreement (see pages __ through __).

Do I have to pay my nanny a holiday bonus?
No. You are under no obligation to provide your nanny with a holiday bonus. However, many families give their nannies a holiday bonus each year.

Does my nanny's holiday bonus count as a nontaxable gift?
No. Bonuses, as well as any other "gifts" to your nanny, are considered taxable income. This means that your nanny will owe taxes on her bonus. In addition, you will owe employment taxes on her bonus.

Do I have to raise my nanny's salary every year?
No. However, most families provide their nannies with at least a small raise each year, as long as the nanny worked hard and fulfilled her responsibilities during the year. Families also typically raise their nanny's salary substantially with the arrival of a new baby.

> *Raising your nanny's hourly rate will impact her overtime rate.* If you increase your nanny's base hourly rate, you will have to factor in this increase for overtime purposes. For example, if you raise your nanny's hourly rate from $10 per hour to $12 per hour, your nanny's overtime rate will increase from $15 per hour to $18 per hour—a sizable jump.

Providing Your Nanny with Benefits

In addition to a salary, you may choose to provide your nanny with additional benefits—including paid time off. These "extras" can sometimes make all the difference in attracting and retaining the "perfect" nanny.

Do I have to provide my nanny with paid sick days or vacation days?
Under the federal Fair Labor Standards Act, you do not have to provide your nanny with paid sick days or vacation days. However, you may have to provide your nanny with paid sick days or vacation days under state or city laws. For example, if you live in New York and your nanny has been with you for at least a year, you must provide your nanny with two paid sick days a year.

As a practical matter, your nanny will likely expect at least a couple of paid sick days a year, as well as a week or two of paid vacation. You should clearly specify your vacation and sick day policies in your nanny employment agreement (see pages 87 through 90).

Do I have to provide my nanny with maternity leave or family medical leave?

You have no obligation to provide your nanny with maternity leave or family leave under federal law because the federal Family and Medical Leave Act only applies to employers with fifty or more employees.

However, you may be obligated to provide your nanny with *unpaid* maternity leave under your state's law. For example, under the new Massachusetts Domestic Workers Bill of Rights, a nanny who has worked full time for at least three months is entitled to up to eight weeks of *unpaid* maternity leave and the nanny's family must hold the nanny's job while she is on leave.

> *If it is possible that your nanny may start a family during her time working for you, she should consider purchasing a disability insurance policy.* Disability insurance can provide your nanny with a percentage of her salary if she has to take time off from work for maternity leave or some other non-work-related injury or illness. Families in New York and Hawaii are legally required to purchase disability insurance. Three other states (California, New Jersey, and Rhode Island), as well as Puerto Rico, provide disability benefits to employees that are funded through mandatory payroll taxes.

Do I have to pay for my nanny's cell phone service?

No. While the law does not require you to pay for your nanny's cell phone service, it can make sense to do so. First, neither you nor your nanny will pay taxes on the value of cell phone service you provide. The IRS has ruled that an employer-provided cell phone is considered a nontaxable benefit when the employer has "substantial reasons relating to the employer's business" for providing the employee with a cell phone. If you pay for your nanny's cell phone so that you can stay in touch with your nanny throughout the day and in the event of emergencies, the IRS will consider the cell phone service to be a nontaxable benefit.

Second, your nanny will be much more likely to take your phone calls and answer your text messages if you are the one responsible for her cell phone bill.

Do I have to provide my nanny with health insurance coverage?
No. You are under no obligation to provide your nanny with health insurance coverage.

However, there are tax advantages for paying part of your nanny's compensation in the form of contributions to her health insurance premiums. If your nanny is the only household employee you have, any amount you pay toward her health insurance premiums from a state-licensed provider is considered nontaxable compensation. This means that you will not have to pay employment taxes on your contributions toward your nanny's health insurance premiums. Moreover, your nanny will not have to pay income taxes or any other taxes on your contributions toward her health insurance premiums.

> *If you have any additional household employees besides your nanny, your contributions toward your nanny's health insurance premiums will only be nontaxable if you purchase a policy for your nanny through the Small Business Health Options Program (SHOP).* (Go to HealthCare.gov for more details.)

If your nanny's salary does not exceed $50,000 per year, you may also be eligible to receive a federal tax credit of up to 50 percent of the amount of your contribution toward your nanny's health insurance premiums under the Small Business Health Care Tax Credit. In order to qualify for the credit, you must purchase a health insurance policy through the Small Business Health Options Program (SHOP). Talk to your accountant for more information. You can also learn more about the credit at irs.gov/uac/Small-Business-Health-Care-Tax-Credit-Questions-and-Answers:-Who-Gets-the-Tax-Credit:Questions-and-Answers.

Even if you do not contribute toward your nanny's health insurance premiums, you must provide your nanny with a notice about the federal Health Insurance Marketplace. Under new federal laws every employer—including household employers—must provide employees with information about the Health Insurance Marketplace. You can find a model notice at dol.gov/ebsa/pdf/FLSAwithout-plans.pdf.

Do I have to provide my nanny with any retirement benefits?
No. You should know that by paying your nanny on the books, you are effectively contributing toward her future retirement benefits by paying Social Security taxes on her salary.

If you would like to help your nanny build a retirement fund, an easy way to do so is to have your nanny establish an individual retirement account (IRA) at any financial institution and to make contributions to your nanny's IRA each year. You can learn more about contributing to your nanny's IRA at HomePay's website, myhomepay.com/Answers/Nanny-Retirement.

I want to help pay for my nanny's education. Is there any tax advantage for doing so?
Yes. You can provide your nanny with a certain amount in tax-free educational assistance each year to cover the costs of tuition, books, fees, and supplies. (In 2015, this amount was $5,250 per year.)

As long as you have a written agreement in place that addresses this educational assistance, neither you nor your nanny will owe taxes on the amount you contribute toward your nanny's education (up to the annual limit). For more information on this valuable fringe benefit, turn to IRS Publication 15-B, entitled "Employer's Tax Guide to Fringe Benefits," available at irs.gov.

I want to help pay for my nanny's commuting and parking costs. Is there any tax advantage for doing so?
Yes. You can provide your nanny with a certain amount in tax-free assistance each year to cover your nanny's commuting costs on public transportation or in a ride share. (In 2015, this amount was $130 per month.) You can also provide your nanny with a certain amount in tax-free assistance to cover the costs of parking near your home. (In 2015, this amount was $250 per month.) Neither you nor your nanny will owe taxes on qualifying parking and commuting assistance.

For more information on commuting and parking assistance, turn to IRS Publication 15-B entitled "Employer's Tax Guide to Fringe Benefits," available at irs.gov.

Drafting a Nanny Employment Agreement

Once you have found the "perfect" nanny and negotiated a work schedule and compensation arrangement that works for both of you, you should get it all in writing in a nanny employment agreement. You are not legally required to have a nanny contract. However, having a nanny employment agreement in place can go a long way toward avoiding misunderstandings that could challenge your working relationship with your nanny.

Do I need a lawyer to draft a nanny employment agreement?
Not necessarily. You may be able to use a contract available online. You can find a template for an employment agreement with a live-out nanny at cdn-care.com/media/cms/pdf/nanny-contract-caredotcom.pdf. However, it is best to work with a professional to ensure that your nanny employment agreement complies with all applicable laws. Consider consulting with a nanny tax agency or an employment lawyer before finalizing your agreement.

What should I cover in my employment agreement with my nanny?
A nanny employment agreement can be as simple or as comprehensive as you would like it to be. Here are a few topics you should be sure to address:

- *Your nanny's work schedule.* Specify the hours and days that your nanny will be working each week. Will the hours vary each week? What happens if you need your nanny to work late or arrive early?
- *Your nanny's responsibilities.* Be very clear about what it is that you expect your nanny to do. For example, will your nanny have to prepare meals for your children? Will she have to do the dishes and tidy up afterward? Do you expect your nanny to do your children's laundry and put it away? Try to be as specific as possible about your nanny's job responsibilities. (Many families have run into trouble with differing interpretations of what constitutes "light housekeeping," for example.)
- *Your nanny's compensation.* Specify your nanny's hourly rate, as well as her overtime rate. Your employment agreement should also clarify whether you are providing your nanny with a guaranteed minimum weekly salary that you will pay regardless of the number of hours your nanny actually works. Make it very clear that all of your compensation figures are listed on a pretax basis, in *gross* wages rather than *net* wages.
- *Pay frequency.* Specify how often your nanny will be paid (weekly or biweekly) and on what day of the week.
- *Bonuses and raises.* You may wish to state your holiday bonus policy. For example, you could state in your employment agreement that you will pay your nanny a minimum holiday bonus equivalent to one week's salary on the third Friday in December. You may also provide that your nanny will get a salary increase of a certain percentage every year (perhaps on the anniversary of the date you hire her). In addition, you may want to clarify whether she will receive a raise if you have additional children.
- *Tax issues.* Your employment agreement should state that you will withhold from your nanny's salary her share of Social Security and Medicare taxes, as well as any applicable state taxes subject to mandatory withholding. Your employment agreement should also specify whether or not you will be withholding federal and state income taxes from her salary. In addition, your employment agreement should note that you will provide your nanny with Form W-2 for tax purposes by January 31 each year.

- *Paid and unpaid time off.* Specify whether or not you will be providing your nanny with any paid sick days or vacation days. (Depending on your state's requirements, you may be obligated to provide your nanny with a certain minimum number of paid days off a year.) If you are providing your nanny with paid vacation days, clarify whether she must coordinate her days off with your family's vacation schedule, or give you a certain amount of advance notice before she takes a vacation day or week. You may also want to address what happens if your family does not need your nanny on a particular day or week—will she still be paid? (Most nannies expect to be paid even if the family is on vacation.)
- *Holidays.* Your employment agreement should clearly state whether or not you expect your nanny to work on the major holidays, and whether you will provide your nanny with any paid or unpaid holidays. Be sure to address all of the federal government holidays (including Martin Luther King Day and Veterans Day) in your employment agreement.
- *Benefits.* If you will be providing your nanny with any fringe benefits, such as cell phone service or contributions toward her health insurance premiums, specify the terms of those benefits in your employment agreement. Be sure to note whether there are any caps on the amount you will pay for benefits. (For example, you may state that you will pay up to $50 a month toward your nanny's cell phone bill.)
- *Automobile-related issues.* If your nanny will be driving her own car, you may want to provide in the agreement that your nanny must maintain comprehensive auto insurance and keep her vehicle in good working order. You should also specify that you will reimburse your nanny for on-the-job mileage and general wear and tear on her car at the IRS mileage reimbursement rate. Finally, you may want to establish what you will be responsible for in the event your nanny has an accident while driving her car while working for you. Will you pay the insurance deductible, for example?
- *Termination.* You should specify that your nanny is an "at will" employee and that your family can terminate her employment at

any time and for any reason. The termination provisions of your employment agreement should clearly state that you can immediately terminate your nanny's employment for good cause (for example, if she endangers your children, regularly misses work or arrives late, or otherwise fails to adhere to her responsibilities as outlined in your employment agreement).

- *Notice of termination and severance pay.* You may wish to provide that you will give your nanny a certain amount of notice before terminating her employment, unless you terminate her employment for good cause. You may also choose to specify your family's policy on severance pay. Make it clear that your family will not pay severance in the event that your nanny is terminated for good cause. Finally, your employment agreement should also provide that your nanny will give you a certain amount of notice if she chooses to leave your family.

Should I have my nanny sign the employment agreement?
Yes. Both you and your nanny should sign and date the employment agreement.

Does my nanny need to sign a new employment agreement each year?
No, but you should update your employment agreement with your nanny if any important aspects of your arrangement change. You will need to revise your employment agreement if:

- *Your nanny's compensation changes.* If you give your nanny a raise, you will need to update your employment agreement to reflect her new salary. Be sure to adjust the hourly rate and the overtime rate accordingly.
- *Your nanny's regular work schedule or job responsibilities change.* As your family's needs change, you may ask your nanny to work more (or less) hours. Your nanny's job responsibilities may also evolve if you have another baby, or as your children head off to school.

If you update your employment agreement with your nanny, both you and your nanny should sign and date the revised agreement.

Complying with the Initial Administrative Requirements of Hiring a Nanny

When you hire a new nanny, you will need to comply with certain basic administrative requirements. First, you must verify your nanny's employment eligibility using Form I-9. If this is your first time hiring a household employee, you will also have to obtain an Employer Identification Number (EIN) for federal tax purposes. In addition, you will have to set up state EINs for unemployment and state income tax purposes (if you live in a state with income taxes). You must also inform your state's new hire reporting program of your new nanny hire.

Verifying Your Nanny's Employment Eligibility

Before you can legally hire a nanny, you will need to confirm that your nanny is legally authorized to work in the United States. You must complete Form I-9 (available at uscis.gov/sites/default/files/files/form/i-9.pdf) within three business days of your nanny's first day of work. In order to complete this form, your nanny will have to provide you with documentation establishing her identity and her legal authorization to work in the United States.

Does my nanny have to be a United States citizen?
No. You can also hire:

- a lawful permanent resident of the United States (also known as a "green card holder"),
- an individual with a valid permit to work in the United States, or
- a noncitizen national of the United States. People born in American Samoa, certain former citizens of the former Trust Territory of the Pacific Islands, and certain children of noncitizen nationals born abroad fall into this category.

You cannot legally hire an undocumented immigrant. Hiring a nanny who is not legally authorized to work in the United States is a violation of federal law. If you choose to hire an undocumented nanny, however, you will still owe employment taxes on your nanny's wages. (See pages 94 through 99 below for more information on nanny employment taxes.)

How can I confirm that my nanny is legally authorized to work in the United States?

You must complete Form I-9 (available at uscis.gov/sites/default/files/files/form/i-9.pdf) within three business days of your nanny's first day of work. Form I-9 asks you to certify that you have reviewed your nanny's documentation confirming her legal authorization to work in the United States.

Your nanny can provide you with any of the following documents to confirm her identity and her legal authorization to work in the United States:

- a U.S. passport or U.S. Passport Card;
- a Permanent Resident Card or Alien Registration Receipt Card (Form I-551) (also known as a "green card"); or
- an Employment Authorization Document with a photograph of your nanny (Form I-766).

Alternatively, your nanny can provide you with her driver's license (which establishes her identity) *and* her Social Security card (which establishes her employment eligibility). Make sure that the Social Security card does not specify any restrictions on your nanny's legal authorization to work in the United States (such as "Not Valid for Employment" or "Valid for Work Only with DHS Authorization").

Check Form I-9 for a complete list of acceptable documentation. If your nanny cannot provide you with any of these documents, check page 9 of Form I-9 for a complete list of acceptable documents.

Be careful to check that your nanny's documentation is up to date and not expired.

Consider using electronic I-9 verification, also known as the Department of Homeland Security's e-Verify program, to confirm your nanny's employment eligibility. The easiest way to use e-Verify is to work with a company, such as HomeWork Solutions (homeworksolutions.com), that offers this service.

Do I have to keep copies of documentation confirming my nanny's identity and employment eligibility?
No. You are not legally required to keep copies of your nanny's passport or green card. However, it is a smart idea to keep photocopies of your nanny's documentation along with the completed Form I-9 for your records.

Do I have to submit Form I-9 to the U.S. Department of Homeland Security or any other government agency?
No. You just need to keep a completed Form I-9 in your records for the duration of your nanny's employment. Once your nanny's employment with your family ends, you must keep her Form I-9 until the later of: (1) three years after the date you hired her, or (2) one year after her employment ends.

Obtaining an Employer Identification Number

In order to submit employment taxes to the IRS and comply with your nanny-related tax reporting obligations, you will need an Employer Identification Number (EIN).

You will also need state tax identification numbers to set up state tax withholding and unemployment insurance accounts. Check with your nanny tax payroll service for more details.

What is an employer identification number?
An employer identification (EIN) is a nine-digit number that the IRS uses to identify employer tax accounts. Just as no two people have the

same Social Security number, no two employers have the same EIN.

Your federal EIN stays the same forever. Although nannies may come and go, you will always keep your EIN.

How can I obtain an employer identification number?
You can apply for an employer identification number online, using the IRS's EIN Assistant (available at sa.www4.irs.gov/modiein/individual/index.jsp). You will be asked to provide basic information about yourself, including your name, address, and Social Security number. The EIN assistant will also ask you what type of business or legal structure you are seeking to establish. Select "sole proprietor," which is the structure used for household employers.

At the end of the process, you can opt to receive your confirmation letter with your EIN online. You will need this number to report your new nanny hire (see below) and to fill out nanny-related tax forms.

New Hire Reporting Requirements

When you hire a nanny, you must let your state's new hire reporting program know. States use these reports for statistical purposes.

What information must I provide to my state's new hire reporting program?
The requirements vary by state. In general, you will have to provide your nanny's name, address, Social Security number, and date of hire. You will also have to provide your name, address, and employer identification number.

Where can I learn more about my state's new hire reporting requirements?
You can find links to each state's new hire reporting center at the U.S. Small Business Administration's website, sba.gov/content/new-hire-reporting-your-state.

Complying with the Payroll and Tax Obligations of Employing a Nanny

As a household employer, you will have year-round tax and payroll obligations. You will need to calculate and remit payroll taxes based on your nanny's salary. In addition, you will have to withhold applicable taxes from your nanny's paycheck and remit those taxes to the government on your nanny's behalf. You will also need to provide your nanny with a W-2 form at the end of the year and submit a copy of your nanny's W-2 to the Social Security Administration.

> *Outsource your nanny-related payroll and tax obligations.* Complying with the tax and payroll requirements of hiring a nanny on the books is onerous and fraught with the possibility for unintentional error. Hiring a company that specializes in household employment, like HomePay (myhomepay.com) or HomeWork Solutions (homeworksolutions.com), can take the burden off your shoulders. Alternatively, if you use an accountant to prepare your annual tax return, you may want to consider hiring that same accountant to handle your nanny tax and payroll obligations.

> *For the nitty-gritty details on your federal tax obligations as a household employer, turn to* IRS Publication 926 entitled "Household Employer's Tax Guide," available at irs.gov. You can also find state-specific tax and payroll requirements at HomePay's website, myhomepay.com/Answers/RequirementsByState.

Do I have to pay my nanny every week?

It depends on the state in which you live. Families in Connecticut, New Hampshire, New York, Rhode Island, and Vermont must pay their nannies every week. If you live in any other state, you can generally pay your nanny every other week.

As a practical matter, however, most nannies prefer to be paid on a weekly basis.

Can I pay my nanny in cash?
Yes, but bear in mind that you will owe employment taxes on your nanny's salary regardless of whether you pay your nanny in cash or via check.

If you pay your nanny in cash, have your nanny sign a receipt of payment. Keep the signed receipts as proof that you paid your nanny in full and on time.

Do I have to give my nanny a pay stub each pay period?
Under federal law, you do not have to provide your nanny with a pay stub each pay period. However, it's a good idea to generate pay stubs for your nanny anyway. A pay stub can help you keep track of your nanny's hours for purposes of complying with federal and state minimum wage and overtime requirements. Moreover, a pay stub can help your nanny understand her pay breakdown and the taxes you are withholding from her salary.

Some states require that you give your nanny a pay stub each period. Check your state's requirements. You can find helpful state-by-state nanny tax requirements at HomePay's website, myhomepay.com/Answers/RequirementsByState.

Do I have to keep time sheets for the hours and days my nanny works?
Under the federal Fair Labor Standards Act, you do have to keep track of the hours your nanny works both each day and each week. If your nanny works regular hours, you can meet this requirement with a nanny employment agreement that specifies the hours your nanny works each day and each week. If your nanny's hours vary, however, you should keep a formal record of your nanny's hours to ensure that you are in compliance with minimum wage and overtime laws.

The U.S. Department of Labor offers a handy (and free) iPhone app that can help you keep track of your nan-

ny's hours. Search the App store for "DOL-Timesheet."

Do I have to withhold federal and state income taxes from my nanny's pay?

No. However, you should encourage your nanny to let you withhold federal and state income taxes from her salary so that she won't face a large tax bill at the end of the year. If your nanny opts to have you withhold federal and state income taxes from her paycheck, ask her to complete IRS Form W-4 (available at irs.gov) as well as the applicable state tax withholding form. You can then withhold income taxes according to your nanny's selection on these forms.

If you don't withhold federal and state income taxes from your nanny's salary, make sure your nanny understands that she is obligated to pay those taxes herself. Otherwise, she might not budget for this expense and may be unpleasantly surprised to discover that she owes a hefty lump sum come tax time. She may also owe tax underpayment penalties if she waits until tax time to pay her entire income tax liability for the year.

Do I have to withhold Social Security and Medicare taxes from my nanny's pay?

Yes, unless you are opting to pay your nanny's share of Social Security and Medicare taxes for her (see below). You will need to remit Social Security and Medicare taxes to the IRS four times per year in April, June, September, and January.

If you cover your nanny's Social Security and Medicare tax bill, remember to add this amount to your nanny's total compensation for the year when preparing your nanny's annual W-2 form. You will also need to factor in the taxes you pay on your nanny's behalf when calculating your nanny's income tax withholdings for the year.

Do I have to withhold disability insurance taxes from my nanny's pay?
If you live in California, New Jersey, Rhode Island, or Puerto Rico, you will need to withhold disability insurance taxes from your nanny's salary and remit those taxes to the appropriate state agency.

Do I have to give my nanny a W-2 form at the end of the year?
Yes. A W-2 provides a record of your nanny's annual earnings and tax withholdings. Your nanny will need her W-2 to file her annual tax return.

> *You will need to submit Copy A of your nanny's Form W-2 to the Social Security Administration, along with Form W-3* (available at irs.gov). Form W-3 is a cover form that lets the Social Security Administration know how many W-2s you have issued to your employees. If your nanny is your only household employee, then the information on your W-3 will essentially mirror the information on your nanny's W-2.

Can I wait until I file my tax return at the end of the year to pay taxes on my nanny's salary?
Because of the risk of tax underpayment penalties, you should not wait until you file your tax return to pay federal taxes on your nanny's salary. Most families with full-time nannies make estimated federal tax payments four times per year using IRS Form 1040-ES (available at irs.gov). Some people opt to ask their employers to increase their tax withholdings to account for the impact of nanny employment taxes.

In addition to federal tax payments, most families will also have to make quarterly state tax payments—although some states have monthly or annual filing deadlines.

Do I have to file a separate federal tax return to report employment taxes on my nanny's salary?
No. You can report your nanny's salary on your personal income tax return using Schedule H (available at irs.gov). Your obligation to pay Social Security and Medicare taxes is added to your family's tax liability for the year.

I own a small business. Can I pay my nanny through my business payroll?
As a general rule, you cannot pay your nanny through your business payroll. There are two exceptions to this rule: (1) if you own a business as a sole proprietor, and (2) if your home is on a farm operated for profit.

> *You cannot claim a business deduction for your nanny's salary and employment taxes.* Even if you own a business as a sole proprietor or your home is on a for-profit farm, you may not deduct your nanny's wages and employment taxes from your business income for tax purposes. You also cannot add your nanny to your business's group health insurance plan.

Paying a Nanny "Off the Books"

Complying with the many obligations for hiring and paying a nanny legally can be challenging and expensive. Many families bypass the process entirely by paying their nannies "off the books." Before you decide to go this route, you should understand the various legal and financial risks that come with paying a nanny off the books.

Is it illegal to pay my nanny off the books?
Yes. Failure to pay employment taxes on your nanny's salary is considered a form of tax evasion.

> *Paying your nanny off the books compromises your personal tax return.* You must report nanny taxes on your personal income tax return. If you pay your nanny off the books, then your personal income tax return is inaccurate and incomplete.

Is there any chance that the government could find out that I have been paying my nanny off the books?

Yes. There are a number of different ways that you might get caught by the IRS. First, if you let your nanny go and she then files for unemployment benefits, your state unemployment agency will quickly discover that she was paid off the books because it will have no record of unemployment taxes paid while she was working for you. The government can also discover your off the books arrangement if your nanny applies for government benefits, such as Social Security.

Second, the IRS may audit your tax return if you claim a tax credit for child care, but your nanny never files her personal income tax return because you failed to provide her with a W-2.

Third, your nanny might report her income to the IRS even if you do not provide her with a W-2. Your nanny can report her income using IRS Form 4852, which serves as a substitute for a W-2. Your nanny can also report her income on IRS Form 8919 if you misclassify her as an independent contractor and provide her with a Form 1099 instead of a W-2 at the end of the year.

What happens if the IRS discovers that I have been paying my nanny off the books?

If the IRS finds out that you have been paying your nanny off the books, the IRS can hold you responsible for back taxes, interest, and penalties. There is no statute of limitations on the IRS's ability to recover unpaid nanny taxes. For example, if the IRS discovers that you have been paying your nanny off the books for the past ten years, the IRS can recover ten full years' worth of back taxes, along with hefty interest and penalties.

The government can also pursue criminal charges. In rare cases, the government has brought criminal charges in connection with nanny tax evasion.

Can my family benefit by paying a nanny "on the books"?

Yes. In addition to the peace of mind that comes with following the law, your family could benefit from valuable child care tax breaks if you pay your nanny on the books. (See pages 215 through 219 of Chapter 6 for information on employer-sponsored dependent care flexible spending accounts and the child care credit.) These tax breaks can offset a significant percentage of the costs associated with hiring and paying your nanny legally.

For More Information

To learn more about legally hiring and paying a nanny, two useful websites are homepay.com and homeworksolutions.com. In addition, two books you might find helpful are:

- *How to Hire Your Nanny: Your Complete Guide to Finding, Hiring, and Retaining Household Help* by Guy Maddalone (Sphinx Publishing, 2012).
- *Nannies & Au Pairs: Hiring In-Home Child Care* by Ilona Bray (Nolo, 2012).

The laws governing hiring and paying a nanny are always changing, particularly at the state level. To stay current on legal changes that could affect your family, you may want to check the HomePay blog (myhomepay.com/Blog) from time to time.

CHAPTER 4

Education Savings Plans

AS college costs continue to climb, it's never too early to think about saving for your child's education. The sooner you begin saving for college, the more your family can benefit from the power of compounding interest and returns over time. Even small investments can add up to impressive savings. For example, if you save just $50 a month from the day your baby is born, you could end up with more than $20,000 in college savings by the time your child turns eighteen (assuming a 7 percent interest rate). That's enough to pay for more than two years of in-state tuition and fees at some public universities.

You could save even more if you invest in an education savings plan. Under some plans, your investment earnings are exempt from federal and state taxes if you use the money to pay for qualifying educational expenses. Other plans let you prepay your child's future tuition costs today.

In the pages that follow, we'll tell you everything you need to know about the most commonly used education savings plans. This chapter covers:

- *529 savings plans*, which allow you to save for college and postsecondary school costs. Investment earnings are tax free if used for eligible educational expenses. The contribution limits are high (often up to $300,000 per child), and there are no income-based eligibility criteria. Depending on where you live, you may even qualify for a state tax break on your 529 savings plan contributions. (See Appendix B: State Tax Benefits for 529 Plan Contributors.)

- *Prepaid tuition plans*, which let you pay for your child's college tuition in advance. Most plans do not have income-based eligibility criteria. However, state residency requirements usually apply. To participate, you or your child must live in the state that offers the prepaid plan. Two notable exceptions are the Private College 529 Plan and the Massachusetts U.Plan Prepaid Tuition Program, both of which let you invest regardless of where you live. (See pages 111 through 124 for more information.)
- *Coverdell education savings accounts*, which allow you to invest a certain amount per child per year ($2,000 in 2015) to pay for your child's educational expenses. You can use the funds in a Coverdell education savings account to pay for elementary, middle, and high school costs in addition to college and graduate school expenses. Investment earnings are tax free if used for qualifying educational expenses. However, only families whose income falls below certain limits are eligible to invest in a Coverdell education savings account. (See pages 133 through 143 for more information.)
- *Roth IRAs*, which effectively let you save for college and retirement at the same time. Investment earnings are tax free if you withdraw the money after you are 59.5 years old. However, you can withdraw your contributions penalty free at any time and for any reason, including to cover college and other educational expenses. Withdrawals are not prorated between contributions and earnings. Instead, all of your withdrawals count as a return of your original contribution until you have taken out the full amount of your contributions. While the Roth IRA is a terrific plan for families that qualify, strict income-based eligibility criteria apply. (See pages 143 through 150 for more information.)
- *Education savings bonds*, which let you invest in government savings bonds without paying taxes on the bond interest provided you use the bond proceeds to pay for eligible college and postsec-

ondary school expenses. Education savings bonds are a terrific choice for the risk averse because the bonds are guaranteed to grow in value over time. Unfortunately, you can only claim the interest exemption for educational expenses if your income falls below certain limits at the time you redeem the bonds. (See pages 150 through 154 for more information.)

- *Custodial accounts*, which allow you to gift money, stocks, bonds, and other assets directly to your child without the cost and administrative burdens of setting up a trust. One of the major advantages of investing in a custodial account under the Uniform Trusts to Minors Act (UTMA) or the Uniform Gifts to Minors Act (UGMA) is flexibility. You can invest and spend the money in a custodial account for your child's benefit any way you please. However, your child will gain complete control over the funds once he or she reaches the age of majority under your state's UGMA or UTMA law. You might also have to contend with a tax penalty. Thanks to the "kiddie tax," your child's investment earnings above a certain amount ($2,100 in 2015) will be taxed at your marginal tax rate. (See Appendix C for more information.)

As you can probably already see, there really is no "one size fits all" education savings plan. The plan that works best for your family might not suit another family. This chapter will give you the information you need to evaluate the various education savings plans and to decide whether any of these plans is the right choice for your family.

Many thanks to college savings expert Joseph F. Hurley for reviewing this chapter. Joseph F. Hurley is the founder of savingforcollege.com, a comprehensive website that provides a wealth of information on 529 savings plans and other education savings plans. Savingforcollege.com offers rankings of the best-performing 529 plans, state-by-state plan details, and plenty of helpful articles on everything from the tax benefits of education savings plans to financial aid.

Education Savings Plans 101

Should I start saving for my child's college expenses as soon as my child is born?

Not necessarily. Financial experts generally agree that you should only begin investing in an education savings plan after making sure that your family is in good financial health overall. Before worrying about college savings, you should:

- *Pay down high-interest debt (anything with an interest rate of more than 10 percent).* If you have racked up bills on your credit cards, tackle those balances first before saving for college.
- *Save enough for an emergency fund to cover six months' worth of living expenses.* You never know what life has in store. Having an emergency fund with enough cash to carry you through six months' worth of living expenses will help your family to weather unexpected storms like a layoff or a medical emergency.
- *Make sure your family is well insured.* Unless you have saved up several years' worth of living expenses, a major health crisis or an untimely death could leave your family financially devastated. Protect your family with comprehensive health insurance coverage and a generous life insurance policy. You may even want to invest in a disability insurance policy before you start setting aside funds for college. (To learn more about life and disability insurance, see Chapter 5.)
- *Contribute the maximum amount to your retirement accounts.* It might seem selfish, but you should maximize contributions to your retirement accounts before you think about saving for college. You may be able to borrow funds from your retirement account to pay for college, but you won't be able to take a loan against your child's college savings plan to pay for your retirement. Maximizing your retirement account contributions will also lower your tax bill because contributions to employer-sponsored retirement accounts and traditional individual retirement accounts (IRAs) are tax deductible.
- *Consider buying your first home.* Depending on your financial

situation and the real estate market in your area, it may make sense to purchase your first home before saving for college. You could lower your family's tax bill with the mortgage interest tax deduction and build valuable home equity. When your child is ready for college, you might opt to take out a home equity loan to finance your child's college education and deduct the interest on that loan on your federal tax return.

How much should I save for college?

It depends on your personal financial situation and the type of college that you would like your child to attend. To get a sense of how much you should be setting aside each month, use the College Board's College Savings Calculator, available at bigfuture.collegeboard.org/pay-for-college/paying-your-share/college-savings-calculator. Another useful option is the College Funding Calculator at savingforcollege.com. (You can find it by clicking on the "Tools & Calculators" link under the "Quick Menu" on the left-hand side of the page.)

Don't let the numbers scare you! You might be surprised to learn that most families don't actually pay the full "sticker price" for college tuition. Even if you can't save the amount it would take to cover your child's full tuition bill, remember that every dollar you save for your child's education is one less dollar you may otherwise have to borrow to cover college expenses. Setting aside even a few dollars each month can add up to a respectable savings fund over time.

Collect "free money" for your child's education along the way. An easy way to boost your child's college savings fund is through education rewards programs. The most well-known program is Upromise (upromise.com), which provides you with cash-back rewards for education when you shop at participating retailers. There are also a number of credit cards, like the Fidelity Investment Rewards American Express Card, that allow you to deposit cash-back rewards directly into a 529 savings plan.

Is there any advantage to using an education savings plan instead of a standard savings or brokerage account?

Yes. One of the biggest advantages of using an education savings plan is the built-in tax breaks that come with many of the plans. When you save for college using a standard savings or brokerage account, you have to pay taxes on your investment earnings. But if you invest in a *529 college savings plan*, for example, investment earnings used for qualifying educational expenses are tax free. Depending on the state in which you live, you may even qualify for a state tax deduction on contributions to a *529 college savings plan*.

Another benefit of investing in an education savings plan is the peace of mind that comes with knowing that you already have funds specifically earmarked for your child's future education. When you save for college in a standard savings or brokerage account, on the other hand, it can be tempting to dip into college savings to pay for the many expenses you'll face in the years ahead.

As with any investment option, there are disadvantages that come with education savings plans. You will lose access to your savings to some extent. For example, you can withdraw your investment in a 529 savings plan at any time, but you will owe taxes and a 10 percent penalty on your investment earnings if you use the money for anything other than college or postsecondary school expenses.

Look before you leap. Before investing in an education savings plan, make sure you understand the terms and conditions. You can find answers to frequently asked questions about the various education savings plans in the pages below.

Will an education savings plan affect my child's chances of receiving financial aid?

The short answer is yes, but probably not as much as you might think. To understand how college savings might impact your child's eligibility for financial aid, it helps to understand the basics of the financial aid process.

The key number for financial aid purposes is your expected family contribution (EFC). Your child will only qualify for need-based financial aid if your EFC is less than the cost of attending a particular college. Because college costs vary, your child may qualify for financial aid at one institution but not another.

Qualifying for need-based financial aid is no guarantee that your child will actually receive financial assistance. If your child does receive financial aid, chances are that the aid will be a mix of grants, loans, and work-study programs.

Just about every college and university uses the Free Application for Federal Student Aid (FAFSA) as a starting point for determining EFC. The FAFSA considers the value of your family's assets and income when evaluating how much your family can contribute toward your child's education. Based on current guidelines, parent assets are counted at a rate of up to 5.64 percent, while student assets are counted at a much higher rate of 20 percent. Parent income is counted at a rate of 22 percent to 47 percent, while student income is assessed at a 50 percent rate (after certain allowances).

The financial aid impact of any given education savings plan depends a great deal on whether the plan is considered a parent asset or a student asset for FAFSA purposes. Savings plans that are considered parent assets (like *529 college savings plans* and Coverdell education savings accounts) will not affect your child's financial aid eligibility nearly as much as plans that are considered student assets (like UGMA or UTMA custodial accounts).

Retirement accounts and home equity do not count under the FAFSA formula. If you want to sock away money without affecting your child's eligibility for financial aid under the federal formula, invest as much as you can in retirement assets and home equity. Consider investing in a Roth IRA (see pages __ through __ below), which effectively allows you to save for retirement and college expenses at the same time. However, you will need to be careful when you withdraw Roth IRA funds to pay for college because the full amount of Roth IRA withdrawals will count as parent income for FAFSA purposes.

To make things even more complicated, a number of colleges use other methodologies in addition to the FAFSA for calculating your EFC. These methodologies treat assets somewhat differently than the FAFSA formula. For example, the College Scholarship Service Profile (CSS) will take your family's home equity into account when determining your EFC, but the FAFSA does not.

Finally, you should know that the rules governing financial aid are not set in stone. The financial aid methodologies could all change a great deal in the many years between now and when your child is ready for college.

What factors should I consider when choosing an education savings plan?

Choosing an education savings plan is a major financial decision with important consequences for your child's future. Here are a few factors you may want to consider before making your choice:

- *Eligibility requirements.* Do you meet the requirements (if any) for investing in the plan?
- *Investment flexibility.* Do you want to be able to choose your own investments? Are you comfortable with the investment options offered by the plan?
- *Contribution limits.* How much do you want to be able to save for college each year? Will the plan let you contribute that amount?
- *Eligible expenses.* Do you want to use the money to pay for college expenses only? Or do you want the flexibility to pay for other expenses as well, like private school tuition?
- *School choice.* Does the plan limit your child's school choices? Are you comfortable with the school choices the plan offers?
- *Refund rules.* Do you want the option to withdraw money from the plan, in case your financial situation changes or you want to use the money for something besides college? Is there any penalty for withdrawing the money early to pay for nonqualifying expenses?

- "*What ifs*." What happens if your child decides not to college? Can you change the beneficiary without penalty?
- *Financial aid impact*. How will investing in the plan impact your child's potential eligibility for financial aid?

Can I open more than one type of education savings plan for my child?
Yes. In fact, opening more than one type of education savings plan can make a lot of sense because the different plans offer unique benefits. For example, some families choose to invest in both a prepaid tuition plan and a 529 savings plan because 529 savings plan funds can be used for room and board, which prepaid tuition plans generally don't cover.

Will I owe federal gift taxes on contributions to an education savings plan for my child?
Unless you happen to be very wealthy, you probably won't have to worry about federal gift tax consequences when contributing to an education savings plan for your child.

Every year you can give your child up to the annual gift tax exclusion amount ($14,000 in 2015) without gift tax consequences. The gift tax exclusion applies per parent and per child. For example, let's suppose you are married with two children. In 2015, you and your spouse could each have given $14,000 to each of your children—for a total of $56,000—without triggering the gift tax.

> *Gifts that exceed the annual limit count against your lifetime gift and estate tax exemption*. The federal government allows you to give away a certain amount of your assets during your lifetime (in the form of gifts) and after your death (as part of your estate) without paying gift or estate taxes. In 2015, the lifetime estate and gift tax exemption was $5.43 million per person. Every dollar in gifts or bequests in excess of this amount is heavily taxed (the top federal estate tax rate was 40 percent in 2015).

529 Savings Plans

The 529 savings plans (529 plans) are state-sponsored investment accounts authorized under Section 529 of the Internal Revenue Code. The 529 plans offer tremendous tax benefits. Investments in 529 plans grow tax deferred, and investment earnings are tax free provided you use the money for qualifying college or postsecondary school expenses. Depending on where you live, you may even be eligible for a state tax deduction or credit for some or all of your 529 plan contributions.

> *A penalty applies if you withdraw money from your 529 plan for anything other than eligible educational expenses.* If you use 529 plan funds for some other purpose, like a down payment on a house, you'll have to pay taxes and a 10 percent penalty on your investment earnings.

The 529 plans operate similarly to 401(k) retirement plans. Most 529 plans allow you to choose from a range of ready-made investment options (typically mutual funds) based on your time horizon and your risk tolerance. If your investments do well, your college savings nest egg will grow substantially over time. But if your investments do poorly, or if your child happens to begin college during a bear market, then you may have less available to pay for college than you had anticipated.

One of the most appealing features of 529 plans is that there are no eligibility restrictions. Anyone can open a 529 plan, regardless of income. Moreover, the contributions limits are high. Many plans allow you to sock away $250,000 or more per account.

529 Plan Basics

Am I eligible to open a 529 plan?

Yes. The 529 plans have no income limits or eligibility restrictions of any kind. Anyone can open a 529 plan. Grandparents, aunts and uncles, and even generous friends can establish a 529 plan for your child.

Who owns the funds in a 529 plan?
The person who establishes a 529 plan owns the funds in the account.

If you were to establish a 529 plan for your child, the funds in the account would legally belong to you, not your child. You would be the 529 plan account owner. Your child would simply be the beneficiary of the account.

> *Even when your child turns eighteen, you will still own and control the funds in a 529 plan.* There is no age at which a child automatically gains access to and control over the funds in a 529 plan.

How much can I contribute to a 529 plan?
Each state plan sets its own contribution limits. Most plans allow you to contribute $250,000 or more per account.

Can I choose the investments in a 529 plan?
Yes, but you are limited to the investment options offered by the particular 529 plan you select. Most plans offer a range of mutual funds at different risk levels.

Is there an age limit for 529 plan beneficiaries?
No. You can contribute to a 529 plan for your child regardless of your child's age. In fact, you can keep making 529 plan contributions even after your child begins college.

If I have more than one child, do I need more than one 529 plan?
Yes. You will need to set up a separate 529 plan for each child.

Can I change the beneficiary of a 529 plan?
Yes. You can change the beneficiary of a 529 plan to a different member of your family at any time. You can even name yourself or your spouse as the beneficiary of your 529 plan.

If I change my mind or need the money, can I withdraw funds from a 529 plan?
Yes. You can withdraw funds from a 529 plan at any time and for any

reason. If you use the funds for anything besides qualifying educational expenses, however, you will have to pay taxes *and* a 10 percent penalty on your investment earnings. You may also have to repay any state tax deduction or credit you received for contributing to your state's 529 plan.

Tax Benefits of 529 Plans

Are 529 plan contributions tax deductible for federal tax purposes?
No. Contributions to a 529 plan are made in after-tax dollars, not pretax dollars.

What are the tax benefits of investing in a 529 plan?
The 529 plans offer a number of built-in tax breaks that can add up to substantial savings over the years:

- *Investments in a 529 plan grow tax deferred.* You do not have to pay federal taxes on 529 plan investment earnings as long as the funds remain in the account. You don't even have to report the earnings on your federal income tax return until you start withdrawing funds from the account. Most states mirror the federal tax treatment of 529 plans and defer state taxes on 529 plan investment earnings.
- *The 529 plan investment earnings are tax free, provided you use the funds to pay for eligible college or postsecondary school expenses.* Withdrawals from a 529 plan are exempt from federal taxes on investment earnings as long as you use the funds to pay for qualifying college or postsecondary school expenses (see pages _ through __ below). The 529 plan withdrawals used for qualifying educational expenses are also exempt from state taxes.
- *Some states offer a tax deduction or credit for 529 plan contributions.* Depending on where you live, you may be eligible to claim an annual state tax deduction or credit for 529 plan contributions.

Most states will only allow you to claim a state break if you invest in a 529 plan sponsored by your home

state. A few states—Arizona, Kansas, Maine, Missouri, Montana, and Pennsylvania—offer a state tax deduction for contributions to any state's 529 plan.

529 Plan-Eligible Educational Expenses

What educational expenses can I pay for using 529 plan funds?
You can use the funds in a 529 plan to pay for tuition and fees at just about any private or public college, university, vocational school, or other postsecondary educational institution in the United States.

> *You can use the funds from one state's 529 plan to pay for your child to attend a private or public college in a different state.* If you invest in a New York 529 plan, for example, you can use funds from that plan to cover your child's tuition expenses at a private college in Rhode Island.

You can also use the funds in a 529 plan to pay for books, supplies, and equipment to the extent that they are "required for enrollment or attendance" at an eligible educational institution.

In addition, you can use the funds in a 529 plan to pay for room and board, as long as your child is enrolled in school at least half time at an eligible educational institution.

If you have a child with special needs, you can use 529 plan funds to pay for special needs services when your child attends college or postsecondary school.

Can I use the funds in a 529 plan to pay for private school tuition?
Elementary, middle, and high school expenses are not qualifying expenses for 529 plan purposes.

> *If you want to save money for private school tuition, consider investing in a Coverdell Education Savings Account.* You can use the funds in a Coverdell Education Savings Account to pay for elementary, middle, and high school costs in addition to college and postsecondary school

expenses. (See pages 133 through 143 for more information.)

Using 529 Plan Funds for Other Purposes

What happens if I spend the money in a 529 plan on something other than eligible educational expenses? For example, what if I need the money for a down payment on a house, or to cover an unexpected medical expense?

If you withdraw money from a 529 plan for anything other than eligible college or postsecondary school-related expenses, you will have to pay taxes *and* a 10 percent penalty on your investment earnings. However, you will not owe any taxes on your 529 plan contributions because 529 plan contributions are made in posttax dollars, not pretax dollars.

> *You cannot withdraw contributions only from a 529 plan.* For tax purposes, every withdrawal from a 529 plan includes a prorated portion of the account's investment earnings. For example, let's suppose you have $100,000 in a 529 plan, of which $25,000 represents investment earnings. If you withdraw $10,000 from the plan, then the IRS will consider $2,500 of that amount to represent your investment earnings.

Aside from the obligation to pay taxes and a 10 percent penalty on investment earnings, there are no other restrictions or limits on accessing the funds in a 529 plan. You can withdraw funds from a 529 plan at any time and for any reason.

Can I take a loan against a 529 plan account?

No. You cannot borrow against the value of your 529 plan investments. If you need to access the funds in a 529 plan, you will have to cash out your investments.

529 Plan "What Ifs"

What if my child receives a scholarship?
If your child is lucky enough to receive a scholarship, you can withdraw the funds in a 529 plan without paying a 10 percent penalty on your investment earnings. (The IRS provides an exemption from the 10 percent penalty for scholarship recipients.)

> *You will still have to pay taxes on your investments earnings, however.* You may also have to repay the amount of any state tax deduction you claimed on your 529 plan contributions.

To avoid paying taxes on your 529 plan investment earnings, you could use the 529 plan funds for a different child or family member by changing the beneficiary of the 529 plan or rolling over the funds to a different 529 plan, or you could save the 529 plan funds to pay for your child's graduate school expenses.

Bear in mind that if your child receives a scholarship you will likely still have to pay for room and board, as well as books and supplies. You can make tax-free withdrawals of 529 plan funds to cover these expenses, which can add up quickly.

What if my child decides to study abroad?
If your child attends a foreign university, you may still be able to use 529 plan funds to pay for your child's education.

Eligibility for 529 plan purposes depends on whether a school participates in the U.S. Department of Education's Federal Student Aid (FSA) program. Many international schools participate, including Oxford University in England and McGill University in Canada. You can find a complete list of participating institutions at the Federal Student Aid website (studentaid.ed.gov) by searching for "international schools that participate in the federal student loan programs." (The Federal Student Aid website maintains a spreadsheet of participating schools that it updates regularly.)

What if my child decides not to go to college?
If your child decides against college, your child may still choose to attend some type of postsecondary school, such as an art institute or a trade school. You can use 529 plan funds to pay for educational expenses at most vocational schools in the United States.

Of course, your child may decide not to pursue any type of postsecondary education. In that case, you can change the beneficiary of the 529 plan fund to another child or family member or roll over the funds to a different family member's 529 plan.

> *You can use 529 plan funds for eligible educational expenses for yourself or your spouse.* If your child does not wish to go to college, you can name yourself or your spouse as the beneficiary of your 529 plan. You could use the money to get that graduate degree you have always wanted or pursue your dreams of attending culinary school.

If all else fails you can simply withdraw the funds from the 529 plan, subject to taxes and a 10 percent penalty on the investment earnings. (There is no exemption from the 10 percent penalty for children who simply decide not to attend postsecondary school.)

What if my 529 plan investments lose value by the time my child is ready for college?
Unfortunately, there is no way to know for sure whether your 529 plan investments will grow over time. If an economic downturn hits shortly before your child is ready to go to college, you may have less money to pay for college than you had hoped.

> *For a "guaranteed" college investment, consider a 529 prepaid tuition plan.* Prepaid tuition plans allow you to purchase college credits or semesters of tuition that you can later redeem to pay for your child's college expenses. With a prepaid tuition plan, you won't have to worry about the impact of market swings because you are buying units of education, rather than investing in the market. (See pages

124 through 132 for more information on prepaid tuition plans.)

Financial Aid Impact of 529 Plans

Will a 529 plan affect my child's eligibility for financial aid?
Yes, to a limited extent. The 529 plans are considered parent assets rather than student assets under the Free Application for Federal Student Aid (FAFSA) formula, which most colleges use as a starting point for determining your Expected Family Contribution (EFC) toward your child's college expenses. Based on current guidelines, the FAFSA formula will take up to 5.64 percent of the value of parent assets into account when calculating your EFC. (Child assets are assessed at a much higher rate of 20 percent.)

Custodial 529 plans owned by a dependent child are also considered parent assets rather than child assets under the FAFSA formula. (See pages 155 through 160 for more information on custodial 529 plans.)

Let's consider an example to see how this works in practice. If you have $100,00 saved in a 529 plan by the time your child is ready for college, the FAFSA formula would assume that you could contribute up to $5,640 toward your child's college expenses for the following year.

The FAFSA formula counts all 529 plans, including those established for your other children, as parent assets for financial aid purposes. Suppose, for example, that you have three 529 plans, one for each of your three children. When your first child is ready for college, the FAFSA formula would factor in the value of all three 529 plans when determining your child's financial aid eligibility.

Grandparent-owned 529 plan funds don't count for federal financial aid purposes. If a grandparent sets up a 529 plan naming your child as a beneficiary, the FAFSA formula will not factor in the value of the plan when calculating your child's financial aid eligibility. However, withdrawals from a grandparent-owned 529 plan count as student income and have a significant impact on financial aid eligibility under the FAFSA formula.

Will my child's financial aid be reduced once I start withdrawing 529 plan funds to pay for tuition and expenses?

Under the FAFSA formula, withdrawals from a parent-owned or student-owned 529 plan do not count as either parent income or student income for purposes of your child's financial aid eligibility for the following year. This means that 529 plan withdrawals should not impact your child's financial aid package for future years. Bear in mind, however, that different schools use different financial aid methodologies.

Unlike withdrawals from parent-owned 529 plans, withdrawals from grandparent-owned 529 plan funds count as student income under the FAFSA formula. The FAFSA formula takes 50 percent of student income into account (after certain allowances) when determining your expected family contribution. Once a grandparent begins withdrawing 529 plan funds to pay for your child's education, your child's financial aid eligibility for the following year could be reduced by 50 percent of the amount of those withdrawals. To limit the financial aid impact of withdrawals from grandparent-owned 529 plans, it may make sense to conserve grandparent savings for the child's last year of college.

Gift Tax Consequences of 529 Plans

Will I owe federal gift taxes on contributions to my child's 529 plan?

Most parents won't have to worry about federal gift tax consequences when contributing to a 529 plan. Every year you can contribute up to the annual gift tax exclusion amount ($14,000 in 2015) to your child's 529 plan without gift tax consequences.

The gift tax exclusion applies per parent and per child. If you are married with two children, you and your spouse could have contributed $28,000 in 2015 gift tax free to each child's 529 plan for a total of $56,000 in 529 plan contributions.

Special gift tax rules apply for extra-large 529 plan contributions. Let's suppose you win the lottery and you'd like to invest a large percentage of your winnings in your child's 529 plan. The federal gift tax rules allow you to make a lump-sum contribution to your child's 529 plan equivalent to five times the gift tax exclusion in a single year. Your lump-sum contribution will be treated as though you had made the gift over a five-year period. As long as you don't make any further contributions to your child's 529 plan during that five-year period, you won't have to worry about gift taxes.

Choosing a 529 Plan

I'm ready to consider investing in a 529 plan. Where do I start?
The first thing you'll need to do is choose a 529 plan. There are dozens of state-sponsored 529 plans to choose from. You'll also have to decide whether to choose a direct-sold 529 plan or an advisor-sold 529 plan.

Do I have to invest in a 529 plan offered by my home state?
No. You can invest in a 529 plan offered by any state in the country, provided the plan does not have a state residency requirement. (A few plans, like Louisiana's START Saving Program, will only allow you to invest if you are a state taxpayer.)

However, if your state offers a tax deduction or tax credit for investing in a 529 plan sponsored by your state, it probably makes the most financial sense for you to invest in your own state's 529 program. The tax benefits of investing in your own state's plan will likely outweigh the higher returns you may earn by choosing another state's plan.

Check the chart on page 301 to see whether your state offers a tax break for investing in your state's plan. Some states only offer tax breaks if your income is below a certain amount. Make sure you meet the eligibility criteria for any applicable tax break.

You should also check to see whether your state offers matching grants or other benefits for contributing to a 529 plan offered by your state.

If I invest in my home state's 529 plan, will my child have to attend college in my home state?
No. The state plan you choose has no impact on where your child can attend college. You can use the funds in any state's 529 plan at any public or private college in the country. For example, if you invest in a New York 529 plan, you can use the money in that account to pay for your child to attend college in California.

What is the difference between a direct-sold 529 plan and an investor-sold 529 plan?
A direct-sold 529 plan allows you to invest your savings directly with a financial services company. If you opt for a direct-sold 529 plan, you will be able to choose from a range of preselected investment options, often based on the age of your child and your risk tolerance. You will make all of your investment decisions on your own.

With an advisor-sold 529 plan, however, you invest in a 529 plan through a financial advisor. The advisor can help you to choose and manage your 529 plan investments and maximize the tax benefits.

Direct-sold 529 plans are usually much less expensive than advisor-sold plans. You typically won't pay a "load," or sales fee, for a direct-sold 529 plan. Moreover, direct-sold 529 plans tend to have lower annual expenses than advisor-sold plans.

On the flip side, advisor-sold 529 plans often offer a broader range of investment options than direct-sold plans. Depending on your level of financial sophistication, you may prefer to have an advisor by your side to guide you through the process of choosing 529 plan investments based on your personal risk tolerance and financial goals.

What factors should I consider when choosing a 529 plan?

As with any other investment, you should do a little homework before selecting a 529 plan. Here are a few questions to consider:

- Which financial services company manages the plan? What is the company's track record and reputation?
- What types of investment options does the plan offer? Does the plan offer risk-adjusted investment options based on the age of your child?
- How have the plan's investments performed in recent years compared to the overall market, as well as compared to similar investments?
- What are the applicable fees and expenses for investing in the plan?
- Is there a minimum initial contribution? Is there a minimum amount for future contributions once you have set up the account?
- What is the maximum cap on contributions to the plan?
- Does the plan let you link directly to any rewards programs such as Upromise (Upromise.com)?
- Can you set up automatic payroll deductions or monthly contributions from your savings or checking account?
- Can family and friends contribute directly to your child's 529 plan?
- How user friendly is the plan? For example, is the plan website easy to navigate?

You can find 529 plan rankings, as well as helpful information on choosing a 529 plan, at savingforcollege.com. If you're having trouble deciding between two or more 529 plans, savingforcollege.com offers a useful plan comparison tool. (Just click on the link marked "Compare 529 plans" under the menu box labeled "Learn About 529 Plans" on the savingforcollege.com home page.) You can find another helpful plan comparison tool on the College Savings Plans Network site (collegesavings.org). (Click on the link marked "Compare 529s by Feature" or "Compare 529s by State" under "529 Resources" in the left-hand menu bar.)

I really like two different 529 plans and I can't decide between them. Can I invest in more than one 529 plan per child?

Yes. There are no limits on the number of 529 plans you can open.

Depending on your personal circumstances, it may make sense to invest in more than one type of 529 plan. You may decide to invest some of your money in a 529 plan sponsored by your own state to capture the benefit of a state tax deduction, and the rest of your money in a different state's 529 plan that may offer higher returns.

Can I switch 529 plans down the road?

Yes. You can shift funds from one 529 plan to another with no penalty, once per calendar year.

> *You may have to repay your state tax deduction if you switch to an out-of-state plan.* If your state offers a state tax break for contributions to a state-sponsored 529 plan, you may have to pay back the amount of that deduction or credit if you transfer funds from your state's 529 plan to a different state's 529 plan.

Setting Up a 529 Plan

I've chosen a 529 plan. How do I set up an account?

Once you've selected a 529 plan, you should be able to set up an account online directly from the plan's website. You'll need to set up your investment allocations at the time you set up your account, so you might want to do a little research beforehand to ensure that you make good choices from the start.

For More Information

Where can I learn more about 529 plans?

You can learn everything you ever wanted to know about 529 plans and more at savingforcollege.com. Another useful resource is the College Savings Plan Network's website (collegesavings.org).

If you want to learn the nitty-gritty tax details governing 529 plans, read IRS Publication 970, entitled "Tax Benefits for Education," available at irs.gov.

Prepaid Tuition Plans

If you worry about the ups and downs of the market and how those changes could affect your child's college savings fund, you may want to consider a prepaid tuition plan. These plans allow you to purchase units or credits of tuition today that you can redeem to pay for your child's college expenses years down the line. In essence, prepaid tuition plans give you the option to "lock in" tomorrow's tuition costs today.

While prepaid tuition plans offer the appeal of investment security, there are a few drawbacks to consider. First, you'll have to sacrifice flexibility in college choice. You will only get the maximum benefit from a prepaid tuition plan if your child attends a plan-affiliated school. Second, you won't necessarily pay today's tuition prices with a prepaid plan. Several plans charge a sizable premium over current tuition prices. Third, there is a small possibility that the plan terms could change between when you invest in the plan and when your child is ready for college. A number of prepaid tuition plans have folded or closed enrollment due to underfunding, and one plan (Alabama's prepaid tuition program) now pays less than the full cost of tuition. Finally, each plan comes with its own unique set of rules and restrictions on refunds, beneficiary changes, and other important issues. You'll need to do your homework carefully to avoid unpleasant surprises down the line.

Prepaid Tuition Plan Basics

Which states offer prepaid tuition plans?

Only eleven states offer prepaid tuition plans that are still open to new enrollment:

- Florida
- Illinois

- Maryland
- Massachusetts
- Michigan
- Mississippi
- Nevada
- Pennsylvania
- Texas
- Virginia
- Washington

There is also one private prepaid tuition plan, the Private College 529 Plan.

Do I have to be a state resident to invest in a state's prepaid tuition plan?
Most states require that either the account owner or the beneficiary of the plan be a state resident. There are two notable exceptions to this general rule: You don't have to be a Massachusetts state resident to invest in the Massachusetts U.Plan Prepaid Tuition Program (mefa.org/products/u-plan/). You can also invest in the Private College 529 Plan (privatecollege529.com) regardless of where you live.

Are there any other eligibility requirements for investing in a prepaid tuition plan?
No. As long as you meet any applicable state residency requirements, you can invest in a prepaid tuition plan no matter how much you earn. You don't have to be a child's parent to set up a prepaid tuition plan for the benefit of that child. Grandparents and other relatives can also establish a prepaid tuition plan on your child's behalf.

How much can I contribute to a prepaid tuition plan?
Each plan sets its own contribution limits. Most plans allow you to contribute up to the full cost of tuition and mandatory fees.

Can I prepay the costs of room and board with a prepaid tuition plan?
No. Most prepaid tuition plans will only allow you to prepay the cost of tuition and mandatory fees.

Consider investing in both a 529 savings plan and a prepaid tuition plan. You can use the funds in a 529 savings plan to pay for room and board, as well as books. (See pages 111 through 124 above for more information on 529 savings plans.)

If I invest in a prepaid tuition plan, will my child have to attend a college or university affiliated with that plan?

To get the maximum benefit from a prepaid tuition plan, your child will need to attend a college or university affiliated with the plan. Many prepaid plans allow you to apply the funds in your plan toward tuition at colleges or universities unaffiliated with the plan, but you may only be entitled to the amount you actually contributed to the plan plus a small interest adjustment. This will almost certainly be insufficient to cover the costs of tuition at a college or university unaffiliated with the plan.

Pay close attention to the list of plan-affiliated schools. Make sure that the plan offers enough school options to meet the needs of whomever your child may grow up to be. Your child could be a star athlete, a budding scientist, or a master violinist. Ask yourself whether your child will be happy to choose one of the plan-affiliated schools years from now.

Does a prepaid tuition plan really allow me to lock in today's tuition rates?

It depends on the terms of the plan. Several plans charge a substantial premium over current tuition prices to account for the fact that tuition will almost certainly increase between now and when your child is ready for college.

Don't assume that a prepaid tuition plan is a smart investment. Run the numbers carefully to make sure that investing in a prepaid tuition plan makes good economic sense for your family. Depending on your risk tolerance, you may come out ahead by investing in a 529 savings plan instead.

Can I choose the investments in a prepaid tuition plan?
No. With a prepaid tuition plan, you purchase units of education (typically credits or semesters). The prepaid tuition plan is responsible for investing the funds in the plan to yield returns that meet or exceed the rising cost of tuition. You don't bear the risk that the investment returns will be insufficient to cover future tuition increases. Rather, that risk falls on the prepaid tuition plan.

Are prepaid tuition plans guaranteed? Is there any risk that the terms of the plan could change between now and when my child is ready for college?
Some prepaid tuition plans are guaranteed by the full faith and credit of the state that offers the plan. Other prepaid tuition plans are guaranteed only to the extent of the plan's assets.

Unfortunately, prepaid tuition plans have a checkered history when it comes to staying afloat. Tuition increases have outpaced the returns on most investments, which has made it very difficult for prepaid tuition plans to keep up with their commitments. A number of prepaid tuition plans have folded in recent years, including Colorado's plan. Several plans are underfunded, which means they have less assets available than their projected tuition payment obligations. Alabama's prepaid tuition plan now pays only partial tuition, even though families purchased full tuition contracts, because it simply does not have the resources to meet its commitments.

Does investing in a prepaid tuition plan guarantee my child's admission to a plan-affiliated school?
No. There is no guarantee that your child will be admitted to a plan-affiliated school. However, most plans offer a range of plan-affiliated schools, so it is likely that your child will gain admission to at least one of those schools.

If I have more than one child, do I need more than one prepaid tuition plan?
Yes. You will need to set up a separate prepaid tuition plan for each child.

Can I change the beneficiary of a prepaid tuition plan?
Typically, yes, but it depends on the plan's terms.

If I change my mind or need the money, can I withdraw funds from a prepaid tuition plan?
It depends on the plan's terms. Bear in mind that if you claim a state tax deduction or tax credit for contributions to a prepaid tuition plan, you may have to repay that tax break if you withdraw funds from the plan.

Tax Benefits of Prepaid Tuition Plans

Are investments in a prepaid tuition plan tax deductible for federal tax purposes?
No. Contributions to a prepaid tuition plan are made in after-tax dollars, not pretax dollars.

What are the tax benefits of investing in a prepaid tuition plan?
With the exception of the Massachusetts U.Plan Prepaid Tuition Program, all prepaid tuition plans are organized under Section 529 of the Internal Revenue Code, which means they qualify for the same tax benefits as 529 savings plans (see pages 113 through 114 above).

If you invest in a 529 prepaid tuition plan, you won't owe any federal taxes on the differential between what you paid for tuition at the time of your investment and the cost of tuition at the time your child is ready for college. Depending on where you live, you may also be able to claim an annual state tax deduction or tax credit for contributions to a 529 prepaid tuition plan. (See the chart on page 303.)

If you are a Massachusetts resident, you will not have to pay state income tax on contributions to the U.Plan

Prepaid Tuition Program. This is because U.Plan tuition certificates represent interests in Massachusetts state bonds, which are exempt from state income taxes.

Financial Aid Impact of Prepaid Tuition Plans

Will a prepaid tuition plan affect my child's eligibility for financial aid? Yes, to a limited extent. Prepaid tuition plans organized under Section 529 of the Internal Revenue Code are considered parent assets rather than student assets under the Free Application for Federal Student Aid (FAFSA) formula, which most colleges use as a starting point for determining your Expected Family Contribution (EFC) toward your child's college expenses. Based on current guidelines, the FAFSA formula will take up to 5.64 percent of the value of parent assets into account when calculating your EFC. (Child assets are assessed at a much higher rate of 20 percent.)

The FAFSA formula counts all Section 529 prepaid tuition plans, including those established for your other children, as parent assets for financial aid purposes. Let's suppose you have three Section 529 prepaid tuition plans, one for each of your three children. When your first child is ready for college, the federal financial aid formula would factor in the value of all three Section 529 prepaid tuition plans when determining your child's financial aid eligibility.

Grandparent-owned Section 529 prepaid tuition plans don't count for FAFSA purposes. If a grandparent sets up a Section 529 prepaid tuition plan naming your child as a beneficiary, the federal financial aid formula will not factor in the value of the plan when calculating your child's financial aid eligibility. However, redemptions of a grandparent-owned Section 529 prepaid tuition plan count as student income and have a significant impact on financial aid eligibility under the FAFSA formula.

A prepaid tuition plan could affect your child's eligibility for **state** *financial aid.* Check the details of the plan you are considering.

Will my child's financial aid be reduced once I start using my 529 prepaid tuition plan to pay for tuition and expenses?

Under the FAFSA formula, redemptions of a 529 prepaid tuition plan do not count as parent or student income for purposes of your child's financial aid eligibility for the following year. This means that using a 529 prepaid tuition plan to pay for your child's college expenses should not impact your child's financial aid package for future years. Bear in mind, however, that different schools use different financial aid methodologies.

Unlike redemptions of parent-owned 529 prepaid tuition plans, redemptions of grandparent-owned 529 prepaid tuition plans count as student income under the FAFSA formula. The FAFSA formula takes 50 percent of student income into account (after certain allowances) when determining your expected family contribution. Once a grandparent begins using a 529 prepaid tuition plan to pay for your child's education, your child's financial aid eligibility for the following year could be reduced by 50 percent of the amount of those redemptions.

Gift Tax Consequences of Prepaid Tuition Plans

Will I owe federal gift taxes on contributions to my child's prepaid tuition plan?

Most parents won't have to worry about federal gift tax consequences when contributing to a prepaid tuition plan. Every year, you can contribute up to the annual gift tax exclusion amount ($14,000 in 2015) to your child's prepaid tuition plan without gift tax consequences.

The gift tax exclusion applies per parent and per child. If you are married with two children, you and your spouse could have contributed $28,000 in 2015 gift-tax free to each child's 529 prepaid tuition plan—for a total of $56,000 in contributions.

Special gift tax rules apply for extra-large 529 prepaid tuition plan contributions. Let's suppose you win the lottery, and you'd like to invest a large percentage of your winnings in your child's 529 prepaid tuition plan. The federal gift tax rules allow you to make a lump-sum contribution to your child's 529 prepaid tuition plan equivalent to five times the gift tax exclusion in a single year. Your lump-sum contribution will be treated as though you had made the gift over a five-year period. As long as you don't make any further contributions to your child's 529 prepaid tuition plan during that five-year period, you won't have to worry about gift taxes.

Choosing a Prepaid Tuition Plan

What questions should I ask before investing in a prepaid tuition plan?
Make sure you thoroughly understand the terms and conditions before investing in a prepaid tuition plan. Here are a few questions to consider asking:

- Which colleges and universities participate in the prepaid tuition plan? How does pricing differ at the various schools covered by the plan?
- Does the plan pricing reflect a premium to account for inflation or tuition increases? If so, how much is this premium?
- Is there a finance charge or any other fees associated with investing in the plan?
- Does the plan apply to tuition only, or does the plan also cover required fees?
- What is the refund policy?
- Can you change the beneficiary of the prepaid plan?
- What happens if your child chooses to attend a school that does not participate in the plan?
- What happens if your child decides not to attend college at all?
- If your family moves out of state, will you be charged out-of-state tuition rates for the first year of college (or longer)? Will you be

responsible for the difference between in-state and out-of-state tuition?

- Can you use the funds in the plan to pay for graduate school tuition as well as college tuition?
- What percentage of the plan is funded for future payouts?
- Is the plan guaranteed by the full faith and credit of the state that sponsors the plan? If so, what are the terms of the guarantee?
- Can you claim a state tax deduction or tax credit for contributions to the plan?
- How will investments in a prepaid tuition plan impact your child's eligibility for state financial aid?
- Is there a minimum initial contribution? Is there a minimum amount for future contributions once you have set up the account?
- What is the maximum amount you can invest in the plan?
- Can you set up automatic payroll deductions or monthly contributions from your savings or checking account?
- Can family and friends contribute directly to your child's prepaid tuition plan?

Setting Up a Prepaid Tuition Plan

I've decided to invest in a prepaid tuition plan. How do I set up an account?

Once you've selected a plan, you may be able to set up an account online directly from the plan's website. You can find links to prepaid tuition plan websites at savingforcollege.com and also at the College Savings Plan Network's site (collegesavings.org).

For More Information

Where can I learn more about prepaid tuition plans?

You can learn more about prepaid tuition plans, including the latest plan news, at savingforcollege.com. Another useful resource is collegesavings.org.

If you are interested in the Private College 529 Plan, you can find out more at privatecollege529.com.

Coverdell Education Savings Accounts

A Coverdell education savings account (Coverdell ESA) is a tax-advantaged investment account that allows you to save up a limited amount per year ($2,000 in 2015) to pay for your child's education. Coverdell ESA investments grow tax deferred for federal tax purposes, and you won't have to pay federal taxes on Coverdell ESA investment earnings provided you use the funds to pay for eligible educational expenses. Most states exempt Coverdell ESA investment earnings used for qualifying expenses from state income taxes as well.

One of the major advantages of investing in a Coverdell ESA is the option to use the funds to pay for elementary, middle, and high school expenses such as private school tuition and academic tutoring. You can also use Coverdell ESA funds to cover college and postsecondary school costs.

To invest in a Coverdell ESA your income must fall below certain limits. In 2015, these limits were $110,000 for single taxpayers and $220,000 for married taxpayers filing jointly.

Coverdell ESA Basics

Am I eligible to open a Coverdell ESA?

You can open a Coverdell ESA if your modified adjusted gross income (MAGI) is below certain limits. In 2015, the limit was $110,000 for single taxpayers and $220,000 for married taxpayers filing jointly.

> A B C *Your MAGI is your adjusted gross income for federal tax purposes, plus certain add-ons.* Different rules apply when calculating your MAGI for different tax benefits. For details on calculating your MAGI for purposes of eligibility to open a Coverdell ESA, check IRS Publication 970 entitled "Tax Benefits for Education," available at irs.gov.

How much can I contribute to a Coverdell ESA?

In 2015, each child was eligible to receive up to $2,000 per year in Coverdell ESA contributions.

ABC *Coverdell ESA contribution limits apply per child, not per family.* If you and your child's other parent both establish Coverdell ESAs for your child, the total amount contributed to *both* accounts cannot exceed the annual limit ($2,000 in 2015).

Not everyone can contribute to a Coverdell ESA. The amount you are permitted to contribute to your child's Coverdell ESA depends on your modified adjusted gross income (or MAGI). You can only contribute the maximum amount each year ($2,000 in 2015) to your child's Coverdell ESA if your MAGI falls below certain limits. In 2015, this limit was $95,000 for single taxpayers and $190,000 for married taxpayers filing jointly.

ABC *Coverdell ESA contribution limits phase out for higher-income earners.* Depending on how much you earn, you may not be eligible to contribute the maximum amount to a Coverdell ESA. For details on calculating reduced Coverdell ESA contribution limits for higher-income earners, turn to IRS Publication 970 entitled "Tax Benefits for Education," available at irs.gov.

Can I choose the investments in a Coverdell ESA?

Yes. You can usually invest Coverdell ESA funds in any stock, bond, mutual fund, or other investment option offered by the financial institution at which you open your account.

If I change my mind or need the money, can I withdraw funds from a Coverdell ESA?

No. Once you establish a Coverdell ESA, you cannot withdraw funds from the account for your own benefit. All distributions from the account must go to the beneficiary of the account.

Who controls the funds in a Coverdell ESA?

A child's parent or legal guardian must serve as the "responsible individual" for the account. The responsible individual controls the funds in a Coverdell ESA and makes all investment and withdrawal decisions.

What happens to the funds in a Coverdell ESA when my child turns eighteen?

It depends on the terms of the trust agreement with the financial institution where you set up your child's Coverdell ESA. Under some plans, your child may become the responsible individual for the account when your child reaches the age of majority under state law (eighteen in most states). This means that your child would then have the authority to make investment and withdrawal decisions on the account.

Read the fine print when you set up a Coverdell ESA. Most financial institutions provide you with the option to remain on as the responsible individual for the account even after your child reaches the age of majority under state law. All you have to do is check a box on the account agreement making that election.

What happens if my child receives more than the annual limit in Coverdell ESA contributions for the year?

Your child will have to pay a 6 percent excise tax to the IRS on the excess contribution. To avoid the excise tax, you can distribute the excess contribution before June 1 of the following tax year (provided you are a calendar-year taxpayer). However, your child will still have to pay taxes *and* a 10 percent penalty on the earnings portion of the excess contribution.

Are there any age limits for Coverdell ESA beneficiaries?

Yes. You can only contribute to a Coverdell ESA for your child if your child is eighteen years of age or younger.

A Coverdell ESA can only be maintained for a beneficiary under the age of thirty. Once your child reaches age thirty, all of the funds in the account must be distributed to your child outright. Your child will then have to pay taxes *and* a 10 percent penalty on the investment earnings.

Coverdell ESA age limits do not apply to children with special needs. If your child has special needs, you can continue contributing to a Coverdell ESA even after your child reaches age eighteen, and there is no mandatory distribution of the account balance when your child reaches age thirty.

If I have more than one child, do I need more than one Coverdell ESA?
Yes. You will need to set up a separate Coverdell ESA for each of your children.

The more children you have, the more you can contribute to Coverdell ESAs. If you have three children, for example, you can open three separate Coverdell ESAs. Depending on your income, you would have been able to contribute a total of up to $6,000 in 2015 to those accounts.

Can I change the beneficiary of a Coverdell ESA?
Yes. If you establish a Coverdell ESA for your child, you can change the beneficiary to a different member of your family at any time, as long as the new beneficiary is younger than age thirty. Bear in mind that you will only be able to make further contributions to the Coverdell ESA if the new beneficiary is eighteen years of age or younger.

My income is too high for me to open a Coverdell ESA for my child. Can I gift money to my child so that my child can open her own Coverdell ESA?
Yes. It is best to transfer the money formally to your child first. One way to do this is through a custodial account (see pages 155 through 162 below). You can then use the money in your child's custodial account to fund a Coverdell ESA for the benefit of your child. On the

account application forms, make sure to name your child as both the depositor of the funds and the designated beneficiary of the account. You can still maintain control over the account by naming yourself as the responsible individual for the account.

> *You will not be able to change the beneficiary of the Coverdell ESA if you gift the money to your child first.* Once you gift the funds for a Coverdell ESA to your child, you cannot later change the beneficiary to someone other than your child. Check with a financial professional for more details.

Can grandparents or other family members establish a Coverdell ESA for my child?
Yes. However, only a child's parent or legal guardian may serve as the responsible individual on a Coverdell ESA. Let's suppose, for example, that your mother would like to establish a Coverdell ESA for your son. Your mother could name you (but not herself) as the responsible individual on the account. You, rather than your mother, would then have decision-making authority with respect to the account.

> *Contributions to Coverdell ESAs established by relatives and friends count against the maximum contribution limit permitted per child per year.* For example, let's suppose your father established a Coverdell ESA for your daughter and contributed $1,000 to that account in 2015. If you also opened a Coverdell ESA for your daughter that same year, you could have contributed a maximum of $1,000 to that account in 2015.

Tax Benefits of Coverdell ESAs

Are Coverdell ESA contributions tax deductible for federal tax purposes?
No. Contributions to a Coverdell ESA are made in after-tax dollars, not pretax dollars.

What are the tax benefits of investing in a Coverdell ESA?
Coverdell ESA investments grow tax deferred for federal income tax purposes. You will not have to pay federal income taxes on Coverdell ESA investment earnings provided you use the funds to pay for eligible educational expenses. Most states mirror the federal tax treatment of Coverdell ESA earnings, and do not tax Coverdell ESA earnings provided the funds are used for qualifying educational expenses.

Eligible Educational Expenses for Coverdell ESAs

What educational expenses can I pay for using a Coverdell ESA?
You can use the funds in a Coverdell ESA to pay for the following elementary, middle, and high school expenses:

- tuition and fees;
- books, supplies, and equipment;
- academic tutoring;
- computer technology and Internet access;
- extended day programs and other school-provided "supplementary items and services";
- uniforms;
- transportation to and from school;
- room and board (if your child attends boarding school); and
- special needs services.

You can also use Coverdell ESA funds to pay for the following college and postsecondary school expenses:

- tuition and fees;
- books, supplies, and equipment;
- room and board (provided your child is enrolled in school at least half time); and
- special needs services.

Can I use the funds in a Coverdell ESA to pay for preschool tuition?
No. Coverdell ESA funds can only be used for educational expenses

from elementary school onward.

Can I use the funds in a Coverdell ESA to pay for extracurricular activities or summer camp?

With the exception of academic tutoring, you can only use Coverdell ESA funds to pay for extracurricular activities that are "required or provided by" your child's school. For example, you can use Coverdell ESA funds to pay for an after-school art class offered by your child's school but you can't use Coverdell ESA funds to pay for ballet lessons provided by a non-school-related dance company.

Can I use the funds in a Coverdell ESA if my child decides to study abroad?

If your child attends a foreign university, you may still be able to use Coverdell ESA funds to pay for your child's education.

Eligibility depends on whether a school participates in the U.S. Department of Education's Federal Student Aid (FSA) program. Many international schools participate, including Oxford University in England and McGill University in Canada. You can find a complete list of participating institutions at the Federal Student Aid website (studentaid.ed.gov) by searching for "international schools that participate in the federal student loan programs." (The Federal Student Aid website maintains a spreadsheet of participating schools that it updates regularly.)

Using Coverdell ESA Funds for Other Purposes

What happens if I withdraw the funds in a Coverdell ESA for something other than eligible educational expenses?

If you withdraw money from a Coverdell ESA for anything other than eligible educational expenses, your child will have to pay taxes *and* a 10 percent penalty on your investment earnings. However, your child will not owe any taxes on your Coverdell ESA contributions because Coverdell ESA contributions are made in posttax dollars, not pretax dollars.

You cannot withdraw contributions only from a Coverdell ESA. For tax purposes, every withdrawal from a Coverdell ESA includes a prorated portion of the account's investment earnings. For example, let's suppose you have $10,000 in a Coverdell ESA, of which $2,500 represents investment earnings. If you withdraw $1,000 from the Coverdell ESA, then the IRS will consider $250 of that amount to represent investment earnings.

The funds in a Coverdell ESA belong to the beneficiary of the account. Once you establish a Coverdell ESA naming your child as the beneficiary, you cannot later withdraw funds from that account for your own use.

Coverdell ESA "What Ifs"

What if my child receives a college scholarship?

If your child receives a college scholarship, your child can withdraw the funds in a Coverdell ESA without paying a 10 percent penalty on the investment earnings. (The IRS provides an exemption from the 10 percent penalty for scholarship recipients.) However, your child will still have to pay taxes on Coverdell ESA investment earnings.

To avoid paying taxes on Coverdell ESA investment earnings, you could use the funds for a different child or family member by changing the beneficiary of the Coverdell ESA or rolling over the funds to a different Coverdell ESA. (The new beneficiary must be younger than thirty years of age.) Another option is to save the Coverdell ESA funds to pay for your child's graduate school expenses.

Bear in mind that if your child receives a scholarship, you will still likely have to pay for room and board, as well as books and supplies. You can make tax-free withdrawals of Coverdell ESA funds to cover these expenses, which can add up quickly.

What if my child decides not to go to college?

If your child decides against college, your child may choose to attend some type of postsecondary education—like culinary school or an art institute. You can use Coverdell ESA funds to pay for educational expenses at most vocational schools in the United States.

Of course, your child may decide not to pursue any type of postsecondary education. In that case, you can change the beneficiary of the Coverdell ESA to another child or family member or roll over the funds to a different family member's Coverdell ESA, provided that the new beneficiary is under the age of thirty.

If all else fails you can simply withdraw the funds from the Coverdell, subject to taxes and a 10 percent penalty on the investment earnings. (There is no exemption from the 10 percent penalty for children who simply decide not to attend postsecondary school.)

Financial Aid Impact of Coverdell ESAs

Will a Coverdell ESA affect my child's eligibility for financial aid for college or postsecondary school?

Yes, to a limited extent. Coverdell ESAs are considered parent assets rather than child assets under the Free Application for Federal Student Aid (FAFSA) formula, which most colleges use as a starting point for determining your Expected Family Contribution (EFC) toward your child's college expenses. This is true even if you first gifted the funds to your child and had your child establish the Coverdell ESA, provided your child is your dependent for tax purposes.

Based on current guidelines, the FAFSA formula will take up to 5.64 percent of the value of parent assets into account when calculating your EFC. (Child assets are assessed at a much higher rate of 20 percent.)

The FAFSA formula counts all Coverdell ESAs, including those established for your other children, as parental assets for financial aid purposes. Let's suppose you have three Coverdell ESAs, one for each of your three children. When your first child is ready for college, the federal financial aid formula would factor in the value of all three Coverdell ESAs when determining your child's financial aid eligibility.

Will my child's financial aid be reduced once I start withdrawing Coverdell ESA funds to pay for tuition and expenses?
Under the FAFSA formula, withdrawals from a parent-owned or child-owned Coverdell ESA do not count as parent or student income for purposes of your child's financial aid eligibility for the following year. This means that Coverdell ESA withdrawals should not impact your child's financial aid package for future years. Bear in mind, however, that different schools use different financial aid methodologies.

Setting Up a Coverdell ESA

I want to invest in a Coverdell ESA. Where do I start?
You can open a Coverdell ESA at just about any financial institution in the country. For convenience, it may make sense to set up a Coverdell ESA at a financial institution that you already use for banking or brokerage services. Your financial institution can give you more details on the process of opening a Coverdell ESA.

My financial institution has asked me to complete a Coverdell ESA account application. Can you give some guidance on completing the application?
When completing a Coverdell ESA account application, you should list your child as the designated beneficiary. You should list yourself (or your child's other parent) as the responsible individual for the account. You should also list yourself as the "depositor" if you are the one contributing the funds for the account. However, if you first gifted the funds to your child to allow your child to set up the account on his or her own behalf, then you should list your child as the depositor.

The "custodian" will be a representative of the financial institution at which you open your Coverdell ESA.

Coverdell ESA applications typically offer you the option to make two very important elections:

- First, you can opt to allow the responsible individual to maintain decision-making authority on the account even after your child

reaches the age of majority. Be sure to check "yes" to this option.
- Second, you can opt to give the responsible individual the authority to change the beneficiary to another member of the beneficiary's family. Be sure to check "yes" to this option as well, unless you first gifted the funds to your child to allow your child to set up the account on his or her own behalf.

For More Information

Where can I learn more about Coverdell ESAs?

You can find helpful information on Coverdell ESAs at savingforcollege.com.

If you would like details on the tax rules governing Coverdell ESAs, consult IRS Publication 970 entitled "Tax Benefits for Education," available at irs.gov.

Roth IRAs

A Roth IRA is an individual retirement account that effectively allows you to save for retirement and college expenses at the same time. Contributions to a Roth IRA are not tax deductible, but the earnings are tax free provided you withdraw the earnings for retirement expenses.

While the IRS has strict requirements in place for withdrawing earnings from a Roth IRA, you can withdraw your contributions at any time and for any reason. Withdrawals are not prorated between contributions and earnings. Instead, the IRS considers every dollar you withdraw from a Roth IRA to be a refund of your original contribution, until you have withdrawn your full contribution amount. Only then do you have to worry about the rules governing Roth IRA investment earnings.

For example, let's suppose you invest $5,000 each year in a Roth IRA, and after five years of investing your Roth IRA grows in value to $40,000. The IRS will allow you to withdraw up to $25,000 from the account at any time, tax free, because that is the total amount of your contributions. You can use the money for anything you wish—including college expenses.

To invest in a Roth IRA, your income must fall below certain limits. In 2015, these limits were $131,000 for single taxpayers and $193,000 for married taxpayers filing jointly.

Roth IRA Basics

Am I eligible to open a Roth IRA?

To open a Roth IRA, you must meet two eligibility requirements.

First, you must have earned income from working (taxable compensation). Wages, salaries, tips, bonuses, and money you earn from running a business all count as taxable compensation. But passive earnings—like interest, dividends, and rental income—generally do not count as taxable compensation. If you are fortunate enough to be able to live off your investment earnings, you won't be able to contribute to a Roth IRA.

> *An exception applies for nonworking spouses.* If you don't work outside the home but your spouse does, you may qualify to open a Roth IRA based on your spouse's earned income. (See page 146 below for details.)

Second, your modified adjusted gross income (MAGI) must fall below certain limits.

> *Your MAGI is your adjusted gross income for federal tax purposes, plus certain add-ons.* Different rules apply when calculating your MAGI for different tax benefits. For details on calculating your MAGI for purposes of eligibility to open a Roth IRA, check IRS Publication 590 entitled "Individual Retirement Arrangements," available at irs.gov.

In 2014, the MAGI limit was $131,000 for single taxpayers, $193,000 for married taxpayers filing jointly, and a mere $10,000 for married taxpayers filing separately who lived together at any time during the year.

How much can I contribute to a Roth IRA?

In 2015, the maximum amount you could contribute to any IRA—including a Roth IRA—was $5,500 per year for anyone under age fifty. The IRS provides higher IRA contribution limits for individuals closer to retirement age. In 2015, the maximum contribution amount was $6,500 for anyone fifty years of age or older.

Depending on how much you earn, you may not be eligible to contribute the maximum amount to a Roth IRA. In 2015, for example, reduced Roth IRA contribution limits applied to married taxpayers filing jointly with a MAGI of more than $183,000 but less than $193,000. For details on calculating reduced IRA contribution limits for higher-income earners, turn to IRS Publication 590 entitled "Individual Retirement Arrangements," available at irs.gov.

> *You cannot contribute more than your taxable compensation (or your spouse's taxable compensation) for the year.* For example, let's suppose that you are single and you earn $3,000 a year from a part-time babysitting job. In that case, you could not contribute more than $3,000—the amount of your taxable compensation—to a Roth IRA.

Can I choose the investments in a Roth IRA?

Yes. You can usually invest Roth IRA funds in any stock, bond, mutual fund, or other investment option offered by the financial institution at which you open your account.

If I change my mind or need the money, can I withdraw funds from a Roth IRA?

You can withdraw your contributions at any time and for any reason. However, you can only withdraw your Roth IRA investment earnings tax free if you are at least 59.5 years old *and* the account has been open for five years or more. If you don't meet these criteria, you will owe taxes and a 10 percent penalty on your investment earnings unless an exception applies.

Can my spouse and I each contribute to our own separate Roth IRAs?
Yes, as long as at least one of you earned income from working during the year *and* your combined modified adjusted gross income (MAGI) falls within the applicable limits.

For example, let's suppose that you are a dental hygienist and your spouse is a magazine editor. Let's further suppose that in 2015 the two of you together earned a MAGI of $125,000. You and your spouse could *each* have contributed $5,500 to a Roth IRA that year—bringing your total Roth IRA contributions to $11,000.

If my spouse does not work, can my spouse still contribute to a Roth IRA?
Yes, as long as you earned income from working during the year and your modified adjusted gross income (MAGI) falls within the applicable limits.

For example, let's suppose that you are a lawyer and your MAGI was $103,000 in 2015. Let's further suppose that your spouse does not work outside the home. Your spouse could have contributed $5,500 to a Roth IRA in 2015 even though your spouse did not have any earned income. This is because the IRS takes a working spouse's earned income into account when determining whether a nonworking spouse is eligible to contribute to a Roth IRA.

> *The working spouse needs to have earned enough income to cover both spouses' Roth IRA contributions.* For example, let's suppose you are married and your spouse does not work outside the home. Let's further suppose that you earn most of your income from rental income, but you also draw a small salary of $8,000 from working part-time as a superintendent for your rental properties. Because you only earn $8,000 in taxable compensation from working (rather than investing), you and your spouse together cannot contribute more than $8,000 to Roth IRAs. If you invested $5,500 in your Roth IRA in 2015, then your spouse could only have invested $2,500 in a Roth IRA that same year.

What happens if I invest more than my maximum contribution limit in a Roth IRA?

You will owe a 6 percent excise tax on the amount that exceeds your Roth IRA contribution limit for the year. If you mistakenly invest more than you should, you can avoid the excise tax by simply withdrawing your excess contributions before you file your tax return for the year.

Can I contribute to both a traditional IRA and a Roth IRA?

Yes, but your total IRA contributions cannot exceed the annual contribution limit. For example, let's suppose you were eligible to contribute $5,500 to a Roth IRA in 2015. If you invested $3,000 in a traditional IRA, you would then only have been able to contribute $2,500 to a Roth IRA that same year.

Can I contribute to both a 401(k) plan and a Roth IRA?

Yes. Your contributions to a 401(k) plan or other employer-sponsored retirement plan have no impact on the amount you can contribute to a Roth IRA. If you can afford it, you can contribute the maximum to both a 401(k) plan and a Roth IRA.

Is there an age limit for contributing to a Roth IRA?

No. You can contribute to a Roth IRA no matter how old you are.

Is there an age at which I will have to take mandatory distributions from a Roth IRA?

No. You won't have to take any required distributions from a Roth IRA during your lifetime. (With a traditional IRA, on the other hand, mandatory distributions apply after a certain age.)

Tax Benefits of Roth IRAs

Are Roth IRA contributions tax deductible for federal tax purposes?

No. Contributions to a Roth IRA are made in after-tax dollars, not pretax dollars.

Don't confuse Roth IRAs with traditional IRAs. If you invest in a traditional IRA, rather than a Roth IRA, your contributions may be tax deductible depending on your income.

What are the tax benefits of investing in a Roth IRA?

Roth IRA investments grow tax deferred for federal income tax purposes. You will not have to pay taxes on your Roth IRA investment earnings as long as you withdraw those earnings when you are 59.5 years or older *and* your Roth IRA has been open for five years or more.

Withdrawing Roth IRA Funds to Pay for Educational Expenses

Do I have to wait until I am 59.5 years old before I can withdraw funds from a Roth IRA to pay for educational expenses?

No. You can withdraw your contributions at any time to pay for your child's educational expenses (or for any other reason).

Will I owe taxes or penalties if I withdraw funds from a Roth IRA to pay for college or other educational expenses?

As long as you don't withdraw more than the total amount you contributed to your Roth IRA, you won't owe any taxes or penalties on your Roth IRA withdrawals.

For example, let's suppose you have $100,000 saved in a Roth IRA by the time your child is ready for college. Let's further suppose that $65,000 of that amount represents your contributions and the remaining $35,000 represents investment earnings. Because the IRS considers every withdrawal from a Roth IRA to constitute a refund of contributions until the contributions are depleted, you would be able to withdraw up to $65,000 from your Roth IRA without paying any taxes or penalties.

You can withdraw Roth IRA contributions to pay for elementary and secondary school expenses as well as college expenses. There are no restrictions on how you can spend withdrawals of your Roth IRA contributions. For example, you can use withdrawals of your Roth IRA contributions to pay for private high school or summer camp.

Will I owe taxes or penalties if I withdraw my Roth IRA investment earnings to pay for college expenses?
Provided your Roth IRA has been open for five years or longer, you won't owe a 10 percent penalty on early withdrawals of Roth IRA investment earnings if you use those earnings to pay for college or postsecondary school expenses. You will still need to pay taxes on the investment earnings, however.

> *You can use Roth IRA investment earnings to pay for a broad range of college and postsecondary school expenses.* The exception from the 10 percent penalty on Roth IRA investment earnings applies to college and post-secondary school tuition, fees, books, and even room and board for students enrolled at least half time.

Financial Aid Impact of Roth IRAs

Will a Roth IRA affect my child's eligibility for financial aid for college or postsecondary school?
It depends. If you do not make any withdrawals from your Roth IRA to pay for your child's education, then your Roth IRA will not count as a parent asset under the Free Application for Federal Student Aid (FAFSA) formula, which most colleges use as a starting point for determining your Expected Family Contribution (EFC) toward your child's college expenses. (Bear in mind, however, that different colleges use different financial aid methodologies.)

If you withdraw your Roth IRA funds to pay for your child's education, however, the *entire* amount of your withdrawal counts as parent income under the FAFSA formula. This will have a sizable impact on your child's financial aid eligibility.

> *A Roth IRA can still be a smart college savings option even if you think your child may need financial aid.* There are ways to structure your Roth IRA withdrawals to

minimize the impact on your child's financial aid application. One option is to take out a loan to pay for your child's tuition, and then to pay back the amount of that loan using funds in your Roth IRA after your child has submitted his or her financial aid application for the last year of college. Talk to a financial professional to learn more.

Setting Up a Roth IRA

I want to invest in a Roth IRA. Where do I start?

You can open a Roth IRA at just about any financial institution in the country. For convenience, it may make sense to set up a Roth IRA at a financial institution that you already use for banking or brokerage services. Your financial institution can give you more details on the process of opening a Roth IRA.

For More Information

Where can I learn more about Roth IRAs?

You can find answers to frequently asked questions about Roth IRAs, as well as the latest information on income and contribution limits, at RothIRA.com. For detailed information on the tax treatment of Roth IRAs, turn to IRS Publication 590 entitled "Individual Retirement Accounts," available at irs.gov.

Education Savings Bonds

If you want guaranteed investment returns without the restrictions that come with a prepaid tuition plan, you may want to consider purchasing federal government-issued education savings bonds. The returns are fairly small relative to other investment options. Series EE bonds are guaranteed to double in value in twenty years, while Series I bonds earn an inflation-adjusted rate of return (1.48 percent in April 2015). However, you won't have to worry about the ups and downs of the market.

When you invest in education savings bonds, you won't have to pay federal taxes on the bond interest if you use the bond proceeds to pay for college or postsecondary school tuition or fees. You also won't owe state taxes on the bond interest because federal government bond interest is always state-tax exempt.

Not everyone can take advantage of the education savings bond program. You can only claim the bond interest exemption for education-related expenses if your modified adjusted gross income (MAGI) falls below certain limits at the time you redeem the bonds (not the time you purchase the bonds). In 2014, these income limits were $91,000 for single taxpayers and $143,950 for married taxpayers.

Education Savings Bond Program Basics

Am I eligible to purchase education savings bonds?

You can purchase education savings bonds as long as you have a Social Security number and you are either a citizen or a resident of the United States.

To qualify for the interest exclusion for education savings bonds, however, a few more requirements apply. First, you must be at least twenty-four years old when you purchase the bonds. Second, if you are married, you must file your taxes jointly with your spouse in the year you redeem the bonds. Finally, your modified adjusted gross income (MAGI) must be below certain limits *at the time you redeem the bonds* (not at the time you purchase the bonds).

> A B C *Your MAGI is your adjusted gross income for federal tax purposes, plus certain add-ons.* Different rules apply when calculating your MAGI for different tax benefits. For details on calculating your MAGI for purposes of eligibility to participate in the education savings bond program, check IRS Publication 970 entitled "Tax Benefits for Education," available at irs.gov.

In 2014, the MAGI limit was $91,000 for single taxpayers and $143,950 for married taxpayers filing jointly. Depending on how much you earn, you may not be eligible to exclude all of your bond interest from your income. For details on calculating the reduced tax exclusion for higher-income earners, check IRS Form 8815, available at irs.gov.

Do all treasury bonds qualify for the education savings bond program?
No. Only Series EE and Series I bonds issued after December 31, 1989, qualify for the education savings bond program.

Series EE bonds earn a fixed rate of return and are guaranteed to double in value in twenty years. In April 2015, the interest rate on Series EE bonds was 0.10 percent.

Series I bonds earn an inflation-adjusted rate of return. In April 2015, the interest rate on Series I bonds was 1.48 percent.

Is there a limit on how many education savings bonds I can buy?
Yes. You can purchase $10,000 worth of Series EE bonds and $10,000 worth of Series I bonds per year. There is no limit on the total number of education savings bonds you can buy over your lifetime.

The limit applies per person, not per couple. This means that you and your spouse can each purchase up to $10,000 of Series EE bonds and up to $10,000 of Series I bonds.

If I change my mind or need the money, can I cash out my education savings bonds?
Yes, as long as it has been at least twelve months since you purchased the bonds. If you cash out your savings bonds within five years of purchase, however, you will forfeit the most recent three months of interest. You will also owe federal income taxes on any bond interest you did not forfeit regardless of how long you have held the bonds (unless you use the interest to pay for qualifying educational expenses).

I expect my income will be higher than the income limits for the education savings bond program when I redeem the bonds. Can I gift money to my child so that my child can purchase education savings bonds in her own name?
No. Education savings bonds must be purchased by someone twenty-four years of age or older in order for the interest exclusion to apply.

Tax Benefits of Education Savings Bonds

Are investments in education savings bonds tax deductible for federal tax purposes?
No. You purchase education savings bonds using after-tax dollars, not pretax dollars.

What are the federal tax benefits of investing in education savings bonds?
You will not have to pay federal income taxes on the interest you earn on education savings bonds provided you redeem the bonds to pay for eligible college and postsecondary school expenses.

Are there any state tax benefits for investing in education savings bonds?
Yes. Education savings bonds (like all treasury bonds) are exempt from state income taxes.

Eligible Educational Expenses for the Education Savings Bond Program

What educational expenses can I pay for using education savings bonds?
You can only use education savings bonds to pay for college or post-secondary school tuition and fees. You cannot use education savings bonds to pay for books, supplies, or room and board.

> *If you want more flexibility, you can redeem your education savings bonds and invest the proceeds in a Coverdell ESA or a 529 savings plan.* Contributions to Coverdell ESAs (see pages _ through __ above) and 529 plans (see pages __ through __ above) count as eligible educational expenses for purposes of the education savings bond program. Check with a financial professional for more details.

Using Education Savings Bonds for Other Purposes

What happens if I redeem education savings bonds and use the funds for something other than eligible educational expenses?
If you use the bond proceeds for anything other than college or post-secondary school tuition or fees, you will owe federal taxes on the bond interest. However, you will not owe state taxes on the bond interest because treasury bonds are always exempt from state taxes.

Financial Aid Impact of Education Savings Bonds
How will purchasing education savings bonds affect my child's eligibility for financial aid?

Because you must purchase education savings bonds in your name rather than your child's name, the bonds will count as parent assets rather than child assets under the Free Application for Federal Student Aid (FAFSA) formula, which most colleges use as a starting point for determining your Expected Family Contribution (EFC) toward your child's college expenses.

Based on current guidelines, the FAFSA formula will take up to 5.64 percent of the value of parent assets into account when calculating your EFC. (Child assets are assessed at a much higher rate of 20 percent.) Bear in mind that different colleges use different financial aid methodologies.

Purchasing Education Savings Bonds

I want to invest in education savings bonds. Where do I start?
You can purchase education savings bonds online from the U.S. Department of Treasury's website (treasurydirect.gov).

For More Information

Where can I learn more about education savings bonds?
The best place to learn more about education savings bonds is the U.S. Department of Treasury's website (treasurydirect.gov). A particularly useful resource is PD P 0051, entitled "Using Savings Bonds for Education," also available at treasurydirect.gov.

The UTMA and UGMA Custodial Accounts

If you want to set up an investment account in your child's name, you may want to consider a custodial account under either the Uniform Gift to Minors Act (UGMA) or the Uniform Transfers to Minors Act (UTMA).

As a general rule, minor children cannot own more than a nominal amount of assets outright. Instead, a child's assets must typically be held in trust for the benefit of the child. The UTMA/UGMA custodial accounts are essentially simplified trusts that allow children to own assets in their own names. While you usually need a lawyer to set up a formal trust, you can establish an UTMA/UGMA custodial account entirely on your own at just about any financial institution.

Once you transfer money or assets to your child's custodial account, those assets will permanently belong to your child. If you appoint yourself as the custodian of the account, however, you can manage the investments and spend the funds in an UTMA/UGMA custodial account for your child's benefit until your child reaches the legal age of majority under your state's UTMA or UGMA law. There are no major restrictions on how you can use the money in an UTMA/UGMA custodial account, as long as you use the funds for your child's benefit. You can spend the money on anything from horseback riding lessons to college tuition.

There are two major drawbacks to investing in an UTMA/UGMA custodial account. First, the IRS essentially penalizes parents who attempt to transfer investment income to their children. If a child's unearned income exceeds a certain limit ($2,100 in 2015), the federal government will tax that excess at the parent's marginal tax rate. Second, a child gains complete control over the funds in an UTMA/UGMA custodial account once the child reaches the age of majority under your state's UTMA or UGMA law (twenty-one in most states). At that point, the child is free to spend the assets in any way he or she pleases.

Basics of UTMA/UGMA Custodial Accounts

What is the difference between an UGMA account and an UTMA account?

If you open an UGMA custodial account for your child, you can only transfer bank deposits, securities (including mutual funds), and life insurance policies. However, you can transfer just about any kind of asset, including real estate, to an UTMA custodial account.

If you live in South Carolina or Vermont, you may only open an UGMA custodial account. Neither South Carolina nor Vermont has adopted UTMA.

Am I eligible to open an UTMA/UGMA custodial account for my child?

Yes. There are no income limits or eligibility restrictions for opening an UTMA/UGMA custodial account for your child. Grandparents, aunts and uncles, and even generous friends can establish an UTMA/UGMA custodial account for the benefit of your child.

Who owns the funds or property in an UTMA/UGMA custodial account?

If you set up an UTMA/UGMA custodial account and name your child as the beneficiary, your child will be the legal owner of the funds or property in the account.

Who controls the funds or property in an UTMA/UGMA custodial account?

The custodian of an UTMA/UGMA custodial account has full authority to manage and spend the assets in the account until the child reaches the legal age of majority under your state's UTMA or UGMA law. You can name yourself as the custodian of an UTMA/UGMA account you establish for your child's benefit.

What happens to the funds in an UTMA/UGMA custodial account once my child reaches the age of majority under my state's UGMA or UTMA law?

Once your child reaches the age of majority in your state under your state's UGMA or UTMA law (twenty-one in most states), your child will have complete access to and full control over the funds in an UTMA/UGMA custodial account. (See the chart on page __ to learn the age of majority under your state's UGMA or UTMA law.) Your child will then be able to spend the funds in the account any way he or she pleases. Your child could opt to use the funds to pay for college tuition. But it would also be perfectly legal for your child to liquidate the account and use the money to pay for a year-long cross-country road trip on a brand new motorcycle. To avoid scenarios like this, many parents choose to spend down the assets in an UTMA/UGMA custodial account before the child reaches the age of majority.

> *If you are investing a large sum of money, consider a trust rather than an UTMA/UGMA custodial account.* The UTMA/UGMA custodial accounts make the most sense when you are gifting a modest amount of money to your child. But if you anticipate that there will be a sizable sum of money left in the account when your child reaches the age of majority under your state's UTMA/UGMA law, you may want to work with a lawyer to set up a trust fund instead. With a trust fund, you can place restrictions on how and when your child can access the funds.

How much can I contribute to an UTMA/UGMA custodial account?
There is no limit on the amount you can contribute to an UTMA/UGMA custodial account.

Can I choose the investments in an UTMA/UGMA custodial account?
Yes. You can usually invest the funds in an UTMA/UGMA custodial account in any stock, bond, mutual fund, or other investment option offered by the financial institution at which you open your account.

If I have more than one child, do I need more than one UTMA/UGMA custodial account?
Yes. You will need to set up a separate UTMA/UGMA custodial account for each child.

If I change my mind or need the money, can I withdraw funds from an UTMA/UGMA custodial account?
No. Once you set up an UTMA/UGMA custodial account for your child, any funds or property you deposit into that account is an *irrevocable* gift to your child. You cannot later reclaim the funds or property in an UTMA/UGMA custodial account.

Can I change the beneficiary of an UTMA/UGMA custodial account?
No. Because an UTMA/UGMA transfer is an irrevocable gift to your child, you cannot later transfer the funds to a different beneficiary.

Can grandparents or other family members establish an UTMA/UGMA custodial account for my child?
Yes. Anyone can establish an UTMA/UGMA custodial account for your child.

Tax Benefits of UTMA/UGMA Custodial Accounts

Are contributions to an UTMA/UGMA custodial account tax deductible for federal tax purposes?
No. Contributions to an UTMA/UGMA custodial account are made in after-tax dollars, not pretax dollars.

How are investment earnings in an UTMA/UGMA custodial account taxed?
A three-tiered tax structure applies to a child's investment earnings, or "unearned income." In 2015, the first $1,050 of a child's investment earnings were tax free for federal income tax purposes.

The second $1,050 of a child's investment earnings were taxed at the child's tax rate.

To the extent a child's investment earnings exceeded $2,100 in 2015, that additional amount was taxed at the parent's marginal tax rate, which is the highest tax rate applicable to the parent's earnings. Often referred to as the "kiddie tax," the high tax rate on a child's investment earnings is designed to prevent parents from attempting to avoid taxes on investment earnings by transferring assets to their children.

In addition to federal taxes, your child may also have to pay state taxes on the income earned from an UTMA/UGMA custodial account.

The kiddie tax applies to children under the age of twenty-four. However, if your child is eighteen or older and your child pays for at least half of his own support using his earned income, then the kiddie tax will not apply.

Do the tax rules governing a child's investment earnings apply per child or per UTMA/UGMA custodial account?

The tax rules governing a child's investment earnings apply per child, not per account. For example, suppose your child has two custodial accounts, one established by each set of grandparents. If your child earned $2,050 in investment income from each account in 2015, for a total of $4,100 in investment earnings, your child would have had to pay taxes at your marginal tax rate on $2,000 of that income.

The tax rules governing a child's unearned income are complicated. You can find more information in IRS Publication 929 entitled "Tax Rules for Children and Dependents," available at irs.gov. It's wise to check with a financial advisor before transferring income-generating assets (like stocks that pay high dividends) to an UTMA/UGMA custodial account for your child's benefit.

I want to set up an UGMA/UTMA custodial account for my child, but I would like to keep the tax bill low. How can I minimize taxes?

To keep the tax bill on your child's UTMA/UGMA custodial account as low as possible, you can use the same tax-minimizing strategies that you would use for any other investment account. For example, you can choose stocks from companies that reinvest their profits rather than paying dividends to shareholders. You can hold on to stocks for the long term, instead of selling appreciated stocks each year. You can also invest in tax-free municipal bonds.

Another option is to set up a custodial 529 savings plan. As long as you use the investment earnings to pay for qualifying college or secondary school expenses, your child will not owe any taxes on those investment earnings.

Most of the rules governing 529 savings plans (see pages __ through __ above) also apply to custodial 529 plans. However, you cannot change the beneficiary of a custodial 529 plan, because the funds in an UTMA/UGMA custodial account are considered an irrevocable gift to your child. For the same reason, you cannot withdraw the funds from a custodial 529 plan for any purpose other than to benefit your child.

If your child already has an UTMA/UGMA custodial account, you can liquidate the assets and reinvest the proceeds in a custodial 529 plan. However, your child will owe taxes on investment earnings when you liquidate an existing UTMA/UGMA custodial account. Talk to a financial professional if this is something you may want to consider.

Eligible Expenses for an UTMA/UGMA Custodial Account

What types of expenses can I pay for using the funds in my child's UTMA/UGMA custodial account?

One of the major advantages of investing in an UTMA/UGMA custodial account is spending flexibility. If you are the custodian of your child's UTMA/UGMA account, you can use the funds in that account to pay for just about any expense that will benefit your child.

You can use the funds in the account to pay for a broad range of educational expenses, from preschool costs to private school tuition to college fees. You can also use the funds in an UTMA/UGMA custodial account to pay for extracurricular expenses like tennis lessons or summer camp. You can even withdraw funds from your child's UTMA/UGMA account to pay for braces, a new computer, or even a new car once your child is old enough to drive.

A B C *You must spend the money prudently.* The custodian of an UTMA/UGMA account has an obligation to manage and spend the money in a reasonable manner. For example, you probably shouldn't use the funds in an UTMA/UGMA custodial account to buy your seventeen-year-old a brand new Ferrari.

Financial Aid Impact of UTMA/UGMA Custodial Accounts

How will an UTMA/UGMA custodial account affect my child's eligibility for financial aid?

The funds in an UTMA/UGMA custodial account are considered child assets rather than parent assets under the Free Application for Federal Student Aid (FAFSA) formula, which most colleges use as a starting point for determining your Expected Family Contribution (EFC) toward your child's college expenses. Based on current guidelines, the FAFSA formula will take 20 percent of the value of an UTMA/UGMA custodial account in your child's name when determining your EFC. Put simply, the assets in an UTMA/UGMA custodial account will negatively impact your child's eligibility for financial aid under the FAFSA formula.

How can I minimize the financial aid impact of an UTMA/UGMA custodial account?

The simplest way is to spend down the funds in an UTMA/UGMA custodial account well before your child's financial aid application is due. Instead of saving the funds in an UTMA/UGMA custodial account for college expenses, use the money to pay for things like summer camp, braces, and piano lessons.

Another option is to liquidate the funds in an UTMA/UGMA custodial account and reinvest the proceeds in a custodial 529 savings plan. The 529 savings plans, including custodial 529 savings plans, are considered parent assets rather than child assets under the FAFSA formula. The difference in treatment can be significant. For example, if your child has $100,000 in a standard UTMA/UGMA custodial account, the FAFSA formula will assume that your family can contribute 20 percent of that amount (or $20,000) toward college expenses. But if your child has $100,000 in a custodial 529 savings plan, then the FAFSA formula will assume that your family can contribute up to 5.64 percent of that amount (or a maximum of $5,640) toward college expenses.

> *Your child may owe taxes on investment earnings if you transfer funds from an UTMA/UGMA custodial account to a custodial 529 savings plan.* Because you can only fund a 529 savings plan with cash, you will need to liquidate the assets in an UTMA/UGMA custodial account before reinvesting the proceeds in a custodial 529 savings plan. Your child will then have to pay taxes on the investment earnings. Check with a financial professional for more details.

Setting Up an UTMA/UGMA Custodial Account

I want to establish an UTMA/UGMA custodial account for my child. Where do I start?

You can open an UTMA/UGMA custodial at just about any financial institution in the country. For convenience, it may make sense to set up an UTMA/UGMA custodial account at a financial institution that you already use for banking or brokerage services. Your financial institution can give you more details on the process of opening an UTMA/UGMA custodial account.

For More Information on Education Savings Plans

If you'd like to learn more about education savings plans, there are plenty of resources available. An excellent place to start is savingforcollege.com. In addition, here are a couple of books that can help you understand your options:

- *Savingforcollege.com's Family Guide to College Savings* by Joseph F. Hurley (Savingforcollege.com Publications, 2014).
- *The Forbes Guide to Paying for College* by Jennifer Eum (Forbes Media, 2014).

CHAPTER 5

Life and Disability Insurance

WHEN you are starting a family, the last thing you want to think about is the possibility that you might not be around to watch your little ones grow up. But part and parcel of being a good parent is making sure that your family's needs will always be met, even if you die prematurely. Having a good life insurance policy in place can help you sleep better at night because you'll know that your family will be protected regardless of what the future holds.

Along with life insurance, you should also consider investing in long-term disability insurance, which will provide you with monthly payments in the event that you cannot work because of an illness or an injury. Long-term disability insurance is effectively income protection insurance.

In this chapter, you'll learn everything you need to know to make smart decisions about life and disability insurance coverage. We cover:

- The basics of life insurance. You'll learn how life insurance works and how much it costs. We'll also help you determine whether you need life insurance and how much coverage to buy.
- Choosing a life insurance policy. We'll help you decide between

term life insurance and permanent life insurance. You'll also learn about the different types of policy provisions (or *riders*) you can add on to enhance your policy.
- Shopping for life insurance. We'll tell you what to expect with the application process and help you decide whether to buy life insurance through an agent or directly from an insurance company.
- Naming a life insurance beneficiary and life insurance-related tax issues. You'll learn how to name a minor child as the beneficiary of a life insurance policy. We'll also explain the tax treatment of life insurance policies.
- The basics of long-term disability insurance. We'll help you understand how long-term disability insurance works and whether it is something you should consider to protect your family. We'll also give you some guidance on choosing a long-term disability insurance policy.

Many thanks to insurance experts Lawrence B. Keller and Jennifer Fitzgerald for reviewing this chapter. Lawrence B. Keller is a CERTIFIED FINANCIAL PLANNER™ professional and the founder of Physician Financial Services (physicianfinancialservices.com), a New York-based company dedicated to the financial needs and concerns of medical professionals. Jennifer Fitzgerald is the founder and CEO of PolicyGenius (policygenius.com), a user-friendly website that makes it almost effortless to purchase life and disability insurance.

Life Insurance 101

What is life insurance and how does it work?

Life insurance is a contract pursuant to which an insurance company agrees to pay a certain amount of money to the person you name as the *beneficiary* of your policy if you die while your policy is in effect. For example, let's suppose you purchase a $250,000 term life insurance policy and name your spouse as the beneficiary. If you die during the policy term, the insurance company will pay your spouse $250,000 in death benefits.

I'm young, healthy, and in good shape. Do I really need life insurance?

When deciding whether to buy life insurance, it doesn't really matter how old or healthy you are. What matters for life insurance purposes is whether your family would suffer financially without your income. Ask yourself what would happen if you died tomorrow. Would your family have the resources to pay the rent or mortgage, cover the day-to-day bills, and pay for future college and retirement expenses? If the answer is no, then you need to protect your family's financial future by purchasing life insurance.

> *The younger you are when you purchase life insurance, the less you will pay in premiums.* Here's another good reason to purchase life insurance when you are young and healthy: you'll pay less! Life insurance companies set premiums based on the likelihood that you will die during the policy term and collect on the policy. The younger and healthier you are when you purchase life insurance, the lower your premiums.

I'm a single parent. Do I need life insurance?

If you are a single parent, it is especially important to protect your family with life insurance, particularly if there is no other parent or family member who could step in and provide for your family's needs in the event of your death.

I'm a stay-at-home parent. Do I need life insurance?

It depends. Remember that even if you are not working outside the home, there is an economic value to caring for a child and running a home.

Think about what would happen if you died next week. Who would take care of your child? Would you want your child's other parent or someone else in your family to stop working outside the home or take a less demanding (and less lucrative) job in order to care for your child? Would your family have to hire a nanny or pay for day care? Would your family have to pay for additional household help, like hiring a housekeeper?

Life insurance can help with all of these different needs. If you die prematurely, your family can use the proceeds of your life insurance policy to care for your child and keep your home running smoothly.

How much life insurance should I buy?

The answer depends on your personal financial situation. One rule of thumb is to purchase at least seven to ten times your gross income, but you may need to purchase much more (or much less) than that amount.

When deciding how much life insurance to buy, you should consider:

- *Your existing coverage under an employer-sponsored life insurance plan.* You may already have some amount of life insurance coverage through your employer. Bear in mind, however, that you may not be able to maintain employer-sponsored life insurance if you switch jobs. Moreover, employer-sponsored life insurance typically covers only one to two times your annual salary—which is probably far less coverage than you need.
- *Your debt.* Do you have an outstanding mortgage, a high credit card balance, or other loans that your family might have to pay if you die?
- *Your expenses.* Approximately how much does your family spend each month? Think about housing, child care, transportation, food, and clothing. Also consider your family's other expenses, like travel and home maintenance costs.
- *Your family's income.* Does your family have any other income besides your income? If your spouse or partner works outside the home, or if you have rental or investment income, you should take this income into account when determining your life insurance needs.
- *Your child's education.* How much will your family need to pay for

your child's educational and extracurricular expenses from preschool tuition and swimming lessons all the way through college?

- *Saving for retirement and other goals.* You may want to consider purchasing enough life insurance to ensure that your spouse or partner has enough money for retirement. You may also have other financial goals for your family—like paying for weddings and bar mitzvahs, or leaving a legacy for your child.

In addition you should bear in mind that your family will incur a variety of final expenses if you die, including funeral and burial costs and the costs of settling your estate.

Life insurance calculators can help you estimate your needs. There are plenty of helpful calculators available online that you can use to determine how much life insurance to buy. Life Happens, a nonprofit organization dedicated to helping Americans take financial personal financial responsibility for themselves, offers a particularly easy-to-use life insurance calculator at lifehappens.org/insurance-overview/life-insurance/calculate-your-needs/. Term for Sale, a website that provides term life insurance comparisons, also provides a useful calculator at term4sale.com/life-insurance-calculator.php.

Don't scrimp on life insurance. To be on the safe side, buy a little more life insurance than you think your family might need. While an additional 10 percent in coverage might cost you a few extra dollars today, that extra coverage could prove to be an invaluable financial cushion for your family if the worst comes to pass.

How much does life insurance cost?

The amount you'll pay for life insurance each year (your *annual premiums*) depends on the type of insurance you buy, the benefit amount, and the length of coverage. A term life insurance policy that insures your life for a set number of years costs much less than a permanent life insurance policy. When it comes to term life insurance policies, the details matter. A $500,000 policy for a term of fifteen years is much less expensive than a million-dollar policy with a thirty-year term.

A basic term life insurance policy is cheaper than you might think. If you are a healthy thirty-year-old man, for example, you could purchase a $500,000 twenty-year-long term life insurance policy for less than $25 per month.

You may be surprised to learn that you will not pay the same premiums as your friend or neighbor, even if you buy the exact same amount and type of coverage. Life insurance pricing is highly personalized, based on an insurance company's assessment of the likelihood that you will die during the coverage period. Factors a life insurance company will consider include:

- *Your age.* The younger you are when you purchase life insurance, the lower your premiums will be.
- *Your health.* The insurance company will want to know whether you are overweight, for example, or whether you suffer from any medical conditions like diabetes or heart disease.
- *Your family health history.* You may not qualify for the best rates if one of your close family members suffers from heart disease or cancer, for example.
- *Your lifestyle.* The insurance company will consider lifestyle factors such as whether you smoke and how often you drink.
- *Your occupation.* You'll generally pay less if you are in a low-risk occupation. Insurance companies love teachers, for example.
- *Your hobbies.* If you skydive in your spare time, for example, you'll likely pay more for life insurance than someone who spends her free time organizing her rock collection.

I have a fair bit of money in savings, and my family is in good financial health overall. Do I still need to consider life insurance?

Even if you have a comfortable amount in savings, you should still give serious thought to purchasing life insurance because it offers a few unique benefits.

One of the major advantages of life insurance is that the proceeds pass according to the terms of your beneficiary designation rather than by will. Unless you name your estate as your life insurance beneficiary, a court will not distribute your life insurance proceeds through probate, the time-consuming legal process that takes place after someone dies. Rather, the insurance company will pay your beneficiary directly in the event of your death. Your family will gain access to your life insurance proceeds soon after your death, and will be able to use these funds to pay your final expenses and cover basic living expenses until your estate is settled.

Another major benefit of life insurance is that the proceeds are not subject to federal income taxes. For example, let's suppose you purchased a one-million-dollar life insurance policy and designated your spouse as the beneficiary. If you died during the policy term, the insurance company would pay your spouse one million dollars in death benefits. Your spouse would not owe a single dollar in federal income taxes on that money.

> *Your family may owe estate taxes on life insurance proceeds.* Unless your spouse is the beneficiary of your life insurance policy, your life insurance proceeds will count as part of your estate for federal estate tax purposes. Depending on the size of your estate, your family may have to pay federal estate taxes on your life insurance proceeds. An exception applies if you do not own the policy at the time of your death. (For more information on this exception, see pages 189 through 190 below.)

I have life insurance through my employer. Do I need to buy additional life insurance?

It depends on the amount of coverage you have under your employer-sponsored plan. In most cases, the amount of coverage available under an employer-sponsored plan is not enough to cover a growing family's needs. You should give some thought to purchasing additional life insurance coverage to supplement your employer-sponsored policy.

While you may be able to purchase supplemental insurance coverage through your employer, you will generally pay less if you purchase a term insurance policy on your own. The rates on employer-sponsored supplemental life insurance are usually higher than the rates on individual term life insurance policies.

Be careful of relying exclusively on employer-sponsored life insurance. Remember that you may not always work for the same employer. If you change jobs, you will likely lose your employer-sponsored life insurance. You might then have to purchase life insurance privately. Depending on your age and your health at the time you change jobs, your life insurance premiums could be substantially higher than they would be if you purchased additional insurance today.

I often see advertisements for life insurance coverage for children. Should I buy life insurance for my child?
As a general rule, you only need life insurance coverage if someone else depends on you for financial support. Unless your new baby is helping to pay the mortgage (perhaps with a lucrative baby modeling career), you do not need to buy life insurance for your child.

Choosing a Life Insurance Policy

What are the different types of life insurance policies?
There are two main types of life insurance:

- *Term life insurance*, which insures your life for a set period of time, or *term* (typically five to thirty years). Term life insurance has no cash value and only provides your family with benefits if you die during the policy term. (See pages 172 through 177 for more information on term life insurance.)

- *Permanent life insurance (also known as cash-value insurance)*, which provides you with insurance coverage for your entire lifetime. When you purchase a permanent insurance policy, a portion of your premiums is invested on your behalf in a tax-deferred account. Your policy's cash value grows over time. You can borrow against the value of your policy or surrender your policy for its cash value. (See pages 177 through 180 for more information on permanent life insurance.)

Should I buy term life insurance or permanent insurance?

For most young parents, term life insurance is the far better choice. Term life insurance is *much* less expensive than permanent life insurance. For example, let's suppose you are a healthy forty-year-old man and you want $500,000 worth of insurance coverage. You could purchase a twenty-year-level term life insurance policy for about $350 a year. If you wanted a permanent insurance policy, however, you would spend approximately $3,000 a year for the same amount of coverage.

When deciding whether to buy term life insurance or permanent insurance, keep your family's needs in mind. You will probably only need insurance coverage for the years when your family depends on your income. Chances are you won't be supporting your children twenty-five years from now. A term life insurance policy provides ample coverage for most families.

Having said that, permanent life insurance may be a good choice if you need lifelong insurance coverage—for example, if you have a child with special needs—or if you simply want life insurance with an investment component. Permanent life insurance can act as a forced savings vehicle, which can be helpful if you are worried you might not have the discipline to save and invest on your own. Some families also like the fact that the investment portion of a permanent life insurance policy grows tax deferred and may be creditor-protected under state law.

Pay attention to fees and expenses when investing in a permanent life insurance policy. Financial advisors frequently advise families against investing in permanent life insurance policies because the fees and expenses are often much higher than other investment options.

Consider a term policy that is convertible. If you're torn between the low cost of term life insurance and the lifetime coverage of permanent life insurance, you may want to purchase term life insurance that is convertible into a permanent policy for a fee. This convertibility feature is built into most term life insurance policies.

Term Life Insurance

What is the term of a life insurance policy?

The *term* is the amount of time that a life insurance policy remains in effect. A life insurance company will only pay out the benefit amount if you die during the policy term. The shorter the term, the cheaper the policy because the chances that you will die during the policy term are lower.

If I buy term life insurance, how long should the term of coverage be?

If you are a new parent, you should probably buy a policy with a term of at least twenty years. This way, your family will be protected all the way through your child's elementary, middle, and high school years. You may want an even longer term of twenty-five or thirty years of coverage if you plan on having more children down the line.

Don't buy a policy with too short of a term. It can be tempting to save a few dollars by buying a policy with a shorter term (perhaps fifteen years instead of twenty). But bear in mind that the cost of insurance is closely tied to your health. Ten years from now you may not be quite as healthy as you are today. If you decide to purchase additional life insurance coverage at that point, you will probably pay much more than you would if you purchased a policy with a longer term today.

You can always cancel your policy if you decide you no longer need coverage. Suppose you buy a twenty-five-year term policy, but you decide twenty years from now that you have sufficient savings to meet your family's needs without relying on life insurance. You can always cancel the policy at that point and you won't owe any further premiums.

Should I opt for the longest term that the insurance company offers?
Probably not. The longer the term, the more expensive your annual premiums will be. Your best bet is to buy only the amount of insurance coverage that you actually need. If your family only needs life insurance coverage for twenty years, for example, then you don't need to buy a policy with a thirty-year term.

Consider laddering two term life insurance policies. Depending on your personal financial situation, you may need more life insurance over the next twenty years than you will once your child has graduated from college. In that case, it can be cost effective to buy two policies—one policy for a thirty-year term, and another policy for a twenty-year term. If you die in the next twenty years, then your family will collect the proceeds of both policies. But if you die twenty-five years from now, your family will only collect the proceeds of the policy with the thirty-year term. A laddering strategy can be a cost-effective way to tailor your life insurance plan to your family's needs. Talk to a life insurance agent for more details.

Will the premium for my term life insurance policy increase every year?
No. As long as you purchase a *level premium term* policy, you will pay the same annual premium every year that the policy is in effect.

For example, let's say you purchase a twenty-year-level term policy with an annual premium of $500 a year when you are thirty years old. You will still pay the same premium of $500 a year when you are forty-five years old. (When you buy a level term policy, the insurance company averages out the premiums that you would owe during the entire policy, so you get the peace of mind that comes with a fixed-rate guarantee.)

I think term life insurance coverage will be enough to protect my family, but what happens if I end up needing lifelong insurance coverage?
For most families, term life insurance provides more than adequate coverage. But there are situations where permanent life insurance becomes a necessity—for example, if you have a special needs child who will depend on your financial support for the duration of his or her life. Just in case your family's needs change, it's best to purchase a term life insurance policy that is convertible into a permanent policy. (This feature is built into most term life insurance policies.)

I want to keep my life insurance costs as low as possible. Should I consider renewable term life insurance?
A *renewable term* life insurance policy provides you with life insurance coverage for a set number of years (often as short as one year), with the option to renew your policy at the end of that time period without having to go through a medical examination and the insurance application process all over again. Renewable term life insurance can seem like a smart option because the initial premiums are very low. However, you will likely end up paying more in the long run because your premiums will increase (often substantially) every time you renew the policy. With a standard-level term policy, on the other hand, your premiums remain the same every year.

I hate the idea of wasting money on life insurance. Should I consider return of premium term life insurance?
If you buy term life insurance with a *return of premium* feature, you will get a refund of your premiums at the end of the policy term (as long as you do not die during the policy term). Return of pre-

mium term life insurance can seem like a smart investment because it sounds as if there is no way to lose—either you die during the policy term and the insurance company pays death benefits on your behalf, or you outlive the policy and you get a refund of your premiums. However, you will pay dramatically more (around 200–300 percent extra) for return of premium life insurance as compared to standard term life insurance. The "guarantee" is simply not worth the cost.

Can I cancel my term life insurance policy at any time?
Yes. If you choose return of premium term life insurance, however, you will not receive a refund of your premium payments unless you keep the policy in effect for the complete length of the term.

Think twice before canceling a term life insurance policy. You usually cannot reinstate a canceled term life insurance policy simply by resuming payment. If you change your mind and decide you want life insurance coverage after all, you will have to go through the insurance application all over again. Depending on your age and your health at the time you reapply, you may have to pay more to obtain the same amount of coverage.

Can I take out a loan against my term life insurance policy?
No. Term life insurance is not an asset and it has no cash value. You cannot borrow money from or invest money in a term life insurance policy.

Term Life Insurance Riders and Features

What is a rider?
A *rider* is an insurance policy provision that provides you with additional insurance coverage or a unique insurance coverage feature. Typically, you will pay a bit more for your insurance policy for every rider you add—so don't buy more riders than you need.

Don't be afraid to ask your insurance agent to explain the riders on your policy. There are many other types of riders besides the ones we mention below. Before buying an insurance policy, make sure you aren't paying for unnecessary riders or missing important ones.

What is a term conversion feature?

A *term conversion* feature gives you the option to convert your term life insurance policy into a permanent life insurance policy if your family's needs change down the line. This option is built into most term life insurance policies.

What is an accelerated death benefits rider?

An *accelerated death benefits* rider provides that an insurance company will pay all or part of your death benefits to you during your lifetime if you develop a terminal illness (one in which you have twelve months or less to live) while the policy is in effect. Insurance companies typically do not charge for this rider.

Some insurance companies also offer a rider that accelerates death benefits in the event of a chronic illness or disability. Check with your insurance agent for more details.

What is an accidental death & dismemberment (AD&D) rider?

With an *accelerated death & dismemberment* (AD&D) rider, the insurance company will pay substantially more in death benefits if you die in an accident (for example, a car crash) rather than as a result of illness or disease. An AD&D rider may also provide that the insurance company will pay benefits if you survive an accident but lose a limb or a key faculty (like your eyesight or hearing). The AD&D riders are tremendously expensive, and generally not worth the cost.

What is a waiver of premium rider?

A *waiver of premium* rider provides that your insurance policy will remain in effect even if you cannot afford to pay your annual premiums because of a long-term disability. These riders are very pricey, and generally not worth the added expense.

> *Consider protecting your family with disability insurance.* If you worry that you won't be able to afford your life insurance premiums and other bills in the event of a serious injury or illness, then chances are you need a comprehensive disability insurance policy in addition to life insurance. (See pages 190 through 198 below to learn more about long-term disability insurance.)

Permanent Life Insurance

There are so many different types of permanent life insurance. Can you help me understand my options?

There are three main types of permanent life insurance, each of which combines insurance coverage with a savings feature.

Whole life. With a whole life policy, you pay level premiums in exchange for a fixed-death benefit. Part of your premiums pay for the cost of your insurance coverage, and the remainder is invested in the insurance company's general account. The insurance company guarantees that your policy will have a certain cash value. However, your policy's cash value—and your death benefit—may be higher than the guaranteed amount if the insurance company pays dividends.

Universal life. When you invest in a universal life policy, part of your premiums pay for the cost of a fixed amount of insurance coverage while the remainder is invested in an account that earns at least a guaranteed minimum interest rate. You cannot choose your investments with a universal life policy. However, you will have the flexibility to vary the amount and frequency of your premium payments.

Variable universal life. With a variable life policy, there is no guaranteed death benefit or cash value. Part of your premiums pay for the cost of your insurance coverage while the remainder is invested. You can allocate your investments in stocks, bonds, and money market funds. There are risks and rewards associated with variable life policies: the savings portion of your variable universal life policy can benefit from market upswings, and suffer from market downturns. It's especially important that you request and carefully review a prospectus, which will provide complete plan information, before investing in a variable universal life policy.

In addition to these three main types of permanent life insurance, there are various subcategories of permanent life insurance with different features.

> *Read the fine print carefully before investing in a permanent life insurance policy.* Make sure you fully understand the policy terms, including the extent to which the savings component of your permanent life insurance plan will be subject to market fluctuations. Otherwise, you might eventually find that the cash value of your life insurance policy is far less than you had expected.

My insurance agent is encouraging me to consider purchasing permanent life insurance. Is permanent life insurance a smart investment?
Probably not. Financial experts generally agree that permanent life insurance is a poor investment choice for young families, even though the savings account component of permanent life insurance grows tax deferred. First, the insurance coverage protection you buy with a permanent life insurance policy is much more expensive than term life insurance. Second, the investment component of a permanent life insurance policy is heavily weighted down by annual investment fees (often 3 percent or more) and marketing and sales commissions. You will almost always do better financially if you keep your insurance coverage and your investments separate. Purchase term life insurance and invest the extra amount that you would have paid for permanent life insurance in tax-favored investments instead.

> *Insurance agents earn more selling permanent life insurance policies rather than term life insurance policies.* Insurance companies pay insurance brokers a percentage of your first year's premium as a commission. Because the premiums for permanent life insurance policies

are much higher than the premiums for term life insurance policies, it is in the insurance agent's best interest to sell you permanent life insurance. So take your insurance agent's advice on permanent life insurance with a grain of salt.

If I buy permanent life insurance, can I cancel my policy at any time?
Yes, but it will cost you. With most permanent insurance policies, you will not break even until you have had the policy for at least ten years. If you cancel the policy before that point, the cash value will almost certainly be substantially less than what you have paid in premiums.

Even with the downsides, I'm still interested in considering permanent life insurance. What questions should I ask my insurance agent before making my decision?
You should be very careful to do your homework before investing in a permanent life insurance policy. Here are a few questions to ask:

- How much is the annual investment management fee?
- How much is the annual mortality and expense charge?
- What were the average returns for the investment portion of the same type of policy over the past five years? How do those returns compare to similar investments and the overall market performance?
- How much of your premium payments will be allocated to your investment account in the first five years that you own the policy?
- How long will it be before you can expect to generate significant positive returns on your investment?
- What is the surrender charge? Are there any other restrictions on your ability to cancel the policy?

Consult with an independent financial advisor before making your decision. Instead of leaping headfirst into a permanent life insurance policy, you may want to talk to a financial expert who does not sell permanent life insurance—like a fee-only CERTIFIED FINANCIAL PLANNER™ professional or a certified public accountant—to help you understand the pros and cons.

Shopping for Life Insurance

When you have figured out what type of life insurance policy you would like to buy, as well as the amount and length of coverage, the next step is to start shopping around for the best coverage at the best price.

I just want to get a sense of how much life insurance will cost me. Can I get life insurance quotes online?
Yes. There are a number of online sites that can provide you with quick quotes. A particularly useful and easy-to-use site is policygenius.com. Other sites include term4life.com, selectquote.com, and iquote.com.

> *Your actual life insurance quote might be substantially higher than your preliminary quote.* The insurance company will price your policy based on the unique details of your health and lifestyle that it uncovers during the underwriting process. Depending on your personal risk profile, you may not qualify for the lowest insurance rates—and this could make your final quote higher than your preliminary quote.

Will it cost me more to buy life insurance if I use an insurance agent instead of shopping for insurance on my own?
No. Insurance companies pay insurance agents commissions for every policy they sell. Your insurance policy won't cost more if you buy coverage through an agent, and you won't owe the agent any fees or commissions.

Is it a smart idea to buy life insurance through an insurance agent?
Life insurance is a complicated financial product, so you might benefit from the expert guidance of an insurance agent or broker. An agent can streamline the process for you by helping you to shop around for

the best coverage and by tailoring the policy provisions to your family's needs.

Working with an insurance agent is a particularly good idea if any aspect of your health or lifestyle puts you in a high-risk category. For example, if you have been a smoker for the past decade, or you are a professional stunt double, you might have trouble finding adequate and affordable coverage on your own. A quality insurance agent will be familiar with the best insurance companies and policy options for individuals with your type of risk profile.

> *Even if you buy insurance online, you will probably go through an insurance agent without even realizing it.* Most insurance is sold through agents, even insurance that is sold online. Since you will almost certainly be purchasing insurance through an agent (even if it seems as though you are purchasing insurance directly), you may as well work with an individual agent who can provide you with customized advice.

How can I find a good insurance agent?

You can get referrals from family and friends, or use the agent locator tool at Life Happens (www.lifehappens.org/agent-locator) to find an insurance agent who belongs to the National Association of Insurance and Financial Advisors.

Before deciding on an insurance agent, you should find out whether the agent works for just one insurance company or whether the agent sells policies from various companies. An agent who works for just one company may be able to offer competitive pricing on that company's policies, but your options will be limited. An independent agent might be able to provide more options from different companies, but may not be able to offer the same type of discounted pricing.

You should also check the insurance agent's credentials. Find out whether the agent has any particular certifications, such as Chartered Life Underwriter (CLU) or Chartered Financial Consultant (ChFC). Ask how long the agent has been in the business of selling insurance and the number of insurance companies with which the insurance agent works. If you think you may fall into a high-risk insurance category (for example, if you have diabetes or heart disease), find out whether the insurance agent specializes in high-risk coverage.

Can you tell me about the life insurance application process?

You will first have to complete a formal application that provides the insurance company with basic information about your health history, employment status, and personal details.

You will then need to undergo a basic medical examination paid for and arranged by your life insurance company. Typically, a technician will visit you at your home or office. He or she will get your height and weight measurements, and check your blood pressure and pulse. The technician may also take blood and urine samples.

Finally, you will have a telephone interview with someone from the insurance company who will ask you questions about your lifestyle, your health history, and your family health history.

The insurance company will use all of the information from the application process, as well as the results of its own investigation, to determine whether to offer you coverage and at what price.

> *Some companies have a simplified underwriting process for certain levels of coverage.* Depending on the amount of insurance coverage you need, you may be able to qualify for an insurance policy without a medical examination or an extensive application process. Ask your insurance agent for more information.

What happens if I lie (or just stretch the truth a little) on my insurance application?

Any misstatements on your insurance application can jeopardize your entire insurance policy. Life insurance policies typically come with a two-year *contestability period.* If you die during the contestability period, the insurance company has the right to challenge its obligation to pay death benefits based on inaccuracies in your insurance application. A little white lie on an insurance application could leave your family with absolutely no insurance coverage.

Insurance companies will investigate the statements you make on your application. If you think you can get away with fudging the truth on an insurance application, think again. Insurance companies have access to personal information about you from a wide range of sources, and conduct comprehensive investigations both during the underwriting process and in the event that a claim under the policy is made. When it comes to life insurance, honesty really is the best policy.

Should I buy the cheapest insurance coverage that meets my basic requirements?

Not necessarily. One of the things you'll want to consider when buying insurance is the quality and financial stability of the insurance company. If an insurance company becomes insolvent, it may be unable to pay death benefits—so your coverage could be worthless.

The federal government does not guarantee insurance policies. While many states offer insurance guarantee funds, there is no fail-safe government program that will pay your benefits in full and on time if your insurance company goes under. Protect yourself by choosing the most stable insurance company you can.

Before deciding on an insurance policy, find out how the company scored with the major insurance company rating services. (Your insurance agent or an insurance company representative can give you the company's "report card.") The best grades from the major rating services are:

- AM Best: A++ and A+
- Standard & Poor's: AAA and AA+
- Moody's Investors Service: Aaa, Aa1, Aa2, Aa3
- Fitch Ratings: AAA, AA

You should also check the policy details very carefully before making your decision. Even though two policies may offer the same amount and length of coverage, one policy might have more exclusions or limitations. A good insurance agent can help you make an apples-to-apples comparison of different policy quotes.

What questions should I be sure to ask before purchasing a life insurance policy?

Before signing on the dotted line, you should ask your insurance agent or insurance company representative a few final questions:

- *How long is the contestability period?* A *contestability period* is the time during which your insurance company can refuse to pay claims under your policy based on misstatements on your insurance application. Contestability periods usually last for two years.
- *Is there an incontestability provision?* An incontestability provision ensures that an insurance company cannot cancel your coverage based on misstatements in your insurance application after the contestability period ends.
- *What are the policy exclusions?* Every insurance policy has limits on the circumstances under which death benefits will be owed. Almost every policy contains a suicide exclusion, which means that the insurance company will not have to pay benefits if you kill yourself during the policy period. Your policy may also contain an illegal activity exclusion, which means that your family will not receive any benefits if you die while committing a crime. Make sure you understand the policy exclusions before finalizing your policy.
- *How long is the grace period?* If you miss a premium payment on your insurance policy, the insurance company has the right to cancel your insurance policy completely. Most insurance companies offer a *grace period* (typically thirty days beyond the premium due date). As long as you pay your premium during the grace period, you won't have to worry about policy cancellation. A generous grace period can come in handy if your premium check gets lost in the mail, or if you run into a temporary cash crunch when your premium payment is due.

- *Is there a reinstatement clause? If so, what are the terms?* If your policy lapses for nonpayment of premiums, the insurance company may permit you to reinstate your policy within a certain amount of time and for a certain fee.

Naming a Life Insurance Beneficiary

Once you have a life insurance policy in place, you will need to name a *beneficiary* (the person who will receive the benefit amount in the event of your death).

How do I designate a beneficiary for my life insurance policy?
You will need to complete a *beneficiary designation form* and submit it to your life insurance company. You should be able to obtain a copy of the beneficiary designation form directly from your insurance company or insurance agent, or from your insurance company's website.

What is the difference between a primary beneficiary and a contingent beneficiary?
A *primary beneficiary* is the person who will receive your life insurance proceeds in the event of your death. A *contingent beneficiary* is the back-up beneficiary. The contingent beneficiary of your life insurance policy will only receive benefits if the primary beneficiary of your insurance policy is no longer alive at the time of your death.

Should I name my spouse or partner as the beneficiary of my life insurance policy?
Yes. Most people who are married or in a committed relationship name their spouse or partner as the beneficiary of their life insurance policy.

Can I name my child as the beneficiary of my life insurance policy?
Naming a child as the beneficiary of a life insurance policy presents unique issues because minor children cannot own more than a nominal amount of property in their own names. Generally, an adult

guardian must be responsible for managing any property owned by a minor child.

If you name your child as the beneficiary of your life insurance policy, you will need to: (1) appoint a guardian to manage the insurance proceeds on your child's behalf, and (2) set up a management structure to hold your child's insurance proceeds. Fortunately, this is not quite as complicated as it sounds.

The easiest option is to name a custodian under the Uniform Transfers to Minors Act (UTMA) to hold your child's insurance proceeds in a custodial account. A custodial account is a simplified trust that you can establish on your own at any financial institution without the assistance of a lawyer. With an UTMA account, an adult you name as the custodian will be responsible for managing the funds in the account until your child reaches the age specified by your state's UTMA law (twenty-one in most states, but up to twenty-five in a few states). The custodian of the UTMA account will have full authority to invest and spend the funds in the account on your child's behalf while your child is below the legal age.

It's easy to use UTMA to name your child as the beneficiary of your life insurance policy. Using UTMA to name a child as the beneficiary of a life insurance policy is a fairly standard practice, so insurance companies have forms available that let you do this. You will have to name both your child and the custodian in the beneficiary designation, using wording along the lines of the following: "Mark Smith, custodian for Sarah Doe, under the Uniform Transfers to Minors Act (UTMA)."

If you live in South Carolina or Vermont, you cannot use UTMA to name your child as a beneficiary of your life insurance policy. Neither South Carolina nor Vermont has adopted UTMA. If you live in one of these states, your best option may be to leave your life insurance proceeds to a trust for the benefit of your child. Speak to an experienced trusts and estates attorney for more information.

While UTMA accounts are an attractive option because of their simplicity and affordability, a major drawback is that your child will gain complete access to and control over the funds in the account when he or she reaches the age of majority specified under your state's UTMA law. (See page 306 of Appendix D to learn the UTMA age of majority in your state.) This is not too worrisome if the amount of your insurance proceeds is small enough that the custodian will likely spend down most of the proceeds for your child's benefit before your child reaches the age of majority. But if your insurance proceeds will be sizable, then you may want to consider establishing a customized trust with restrictions on how and when your child can access the funds. A trust may be particularly important to have in place if life insurance proceeds will make up the bulk of your child's inheritance.

If you want to leave life insurance proceeds in a trust for your children, one option is to set up a *living trust* and name the trustee of that trust as the beneficiary of your life insurance proceeds. A living trust is a trust that is in existence while you are still alive. An advantage of using a living trust is that the life insurance proceeds will then pass by will rather than by probate (the legal process in which the court allocates the property in your estate). The trustee of a living trust will be able to access your life insurance proceeds soon after your death, which can be helpful if the money will be needed as early as possible to cover your child's expenses.

Another option is to establish a trust in your will (known as a *testamentary trust*), and name the trustee of that trust as the beneficiary of your life insurance policy. If you name a testamentary trust as the beneficiary of your life insurance policy, the trustee will not receive the life insurance proceeds until the probate process is complete.

A B C *Consider consulting with an experienced trusts and estates attorney to understand your options for leaving life insurance proceeds to your child.* (You can also learn more about trusts and estate planning in Chapter 7.)

What happens if I name my child as the beneficiary of my life insurance policy without naming a trustee or custodian to manage the funds on my child's behalf?
In that case, a court will only release the insurance proceeds to your child after it has appointed a property guardian to manage the insurance proceeds on your child's behalf. If you have not named a property guardian for your child's assets in your will, then the court will have full discretion over whom to appoint. The process of appointing a guardian is time consuming, administratively burdensome, and expensive. What's more, the court could even appoint a complete stranger to manage the funds for your child. (See pages 255 through 262 of Chapter 7 for more information on property guardianship.)

I have three children. Can I name all three children as equal beneficiaries of my life insurance policy?
Yes. Life insurance beneficiary designation forms allow you to name multiple beneficiaries and to allocate the percentage of your life insurance proceeds that should go to each beneficiary.

Can I change my life insurance beneficiary down the line?
Yes. You can change your beneficiary designations at any time, unless you designate a beneficiary as an *irrevocable* beneficiary (a beneficiary that cannot be changed without the beneficiary's consent).

> A B C *Keep your life insurance beneficiary designations up to date.* If there is any major change in your life, like an addition to your family or a divorce, make sure you update your life insurance beneficiary designations to reflect those changes.

What happens if I die without a beneficiary designation on file?
If you die without naming a beneficiary, the proceeds of your life insurance policy will be paid to your estate. Your estate will go through the probate process, and your life insurance proceeds will be then be distributed according to the terms of your will. If you die without a will, your insurance proceeds will be distributed according to state

law governing *intestate succession*. (For more information on how the assets will be distributed in the event of your death, see Chapter 7.)

Life Insurance-Related Tax Issues

One of the best features of life insurance is that your family will receive the money free of income tax. Depending on your personal financial situation, however, your family may owe estate taxes on life insurance proceeds.

Are life insurance premiums tax deductible?
No. You pay life insurance premiums in after-tax dollars, not pretax dollars.

Will my family have to pay income taxes on life insurance proceeds?
No. The proceeds of a life insurance policy are not considered income for federal tax purposes.

> *Check with a tax specialist if you have a permanent life insurance policy.* If you have a permanent life insurance policy, then your family may owe taxes on the interest or income portion of the savings component of your permanent life insurance policy.

Will my family have to pay estate taxes on life insurance proceeds?
Probably not, but it depends on whom you name as the beneficiary of your life insurance policy and the size of your estate.

If your spouse is the beneficiary of your life insurance policy, then no estate taxes will be owed regardless of the size of your estate because transfers between spouses are exempt from estate taxes.

If you name someone other than your spouse as the beneficiary of your life insurance policy, then your family may owe estate taxes on your life insurance proceeds if the total amount of your estate *including* the proceeds of your insurance policy exceeds the estate tax exemption. (In 2015, the estate tax exemption was $5.43 million.)

Life insurance proceeds do not count as part of your estate if you transfer ownership of your life insurance policy more than three years before you die. You can exclude life insurance proceeds from your taxable estate by naming someone else as the owner of your life insurance policy or by transferring your policy to a life insurance trust more than three years before you die. If you are concerned that your life insurance proceeds may subject your family to estate taxes, you may want to talk to an experienced trusts and estates attorney about transferring ownership of your life insurance policy.

Long-Term Disability Insurance 101

What is long-term disability insurance and how does it work?
Long-term disability insurance is a contract pursuant to which an insurance company agrees to pay you a percentage of your income (60 percent is typical), up to a maximum monthly benefit amount, if you are unable to work for more than a few months because of an illness or injury.

Long-term disability insurance will not cover short illnesses or medical conditions. If you cannot work for a couple of months due to a short-term condition, like pregnancy-related bed rest, then you may be eligible for short-term disability benefits under a state program or as part of your employee benefits package.

I am young and healthy. Do I really need long-term disability insurance?
It depends on your personal financial situation. Ask yourself what would happen if you were unable to work for two or three years because of a major illness or injury. How would your family pay for basic living expenses? Do you have enough savings to cover your rent or mortgage, as well as the many other costs of day-to-day life? If

the answer to these questions is no, as it is for most people, then you probably need long-term disability insurance coverage.

If you need life insurance, you almost certainly also need long-term disability insurance. As a general rule, the same considerations that go into determining whether you need life insurance also apply to long-term disability insurance. The key question for both life insurance and long-term disability insurance is whether your family would suffer financially without your income.

Will long-term disability insurance cover my medical bills in the event of a major illness or injury?

No. Long-term disability insurance is income replacement insurance, not health insurance. However, you can use the benefits you receive from a long-term disability insurance policy to pay for any medical expenses that your health insurance does not cover (like out-of-network fees and prescription drug co-pays).

How much does long-term disability insurance cost?

It depends on your age, your health, and the amount and length of coverage, among other factors. As a general rule of thumb, disability insurance will cost you somewhere between 1 percent and 3 percent of your annual salary.

Can I buy long-term disability insurance that covers 100 percent of my current salary?

No. You generally cannot buy a long-term disability insurance for anything more than 80 percent of your current salary. A typical long-term disability insurance policy will cover 60 percent of your current salary, up to a maximum monthly benefit.

Will I owe federal income taxes on my disability insurance benefits?

If you purchase an individual long-term disability insurance policy and you pay the premiums yourself, then you will owe no federal income taxes on your disability insurance benefits. Thanks to this favorable tax treatment, 60 percent of your salary in tax-free disability insurance proceeds will be roughly equivalent to 100 percent of your salary in taxable income.

If you have employer-sponsored long-term disability insurance, however, the federal income tax treatment of your disability insurance premiums depends on who pays the premiums and how. If your employer pays the policy premiums and does not add that amount back to your income, then your benefits will be taxable as income. Similarly, if you pay the premiums using pretax dollars, then your benefits will be subject to income tax. However, if you pay the premiums on an employer-sponsored long-term disability insurance policy using after-tax dollars, then any benefits you receive will be tax free.

A B C *The IRS applies a three-year look-back period when determining whether or not to tax disability insurance benefits from an employer-sponsored plan.* If you receive disability benefits, the IRS will look at how you paid your premiums for the three prior years when deciding whether your benefits are taxable.

Make your employer-sponsored long-term disability insurance elections wisely. If your employer offers the option and you can afford it, it's a smart idea to pay the premiums on your employer-sponsored long-term disability insurance policy with after-tax dollars instead of pretax dollars. The few extra dollars you spend now could save you thousands of dollars in taxes if you suffer a long-term disability down the line.

I have long-term disability insurance through my employer. Do I still need to purchase an individual disability insurance policy?

It depends. The first thing to consider is the extent of coverage under your employer-sponsored insurance plan. Is there a cap on the monthly benefits under your employer-sponsored plan? Is there a limit to the number of months or years of coverage?

The next question is whether your employer pays the premiums for the policy and does not add that amount back to your income for tax purposes. If so, then any disability benefits you receive will be taxable. Let's suppose, for example, that your employer-sponsored disability insurance plan will provide you with benefits equivalent to 60 percent of your current salary. If you have to pay taxes on that benefit amount, you will be left with far less than half of your current salary in long-term disability benefits. This may be dramatically insufficient to meet your family's financial needs.

Finally, you need to think about what will happen if you change jobs or lose your job. Remember that employer-sponsored long-term disability insurance is generally not portable. Moreover, the older you are when you apply for long-term disability insurance, the higher your premiums will likely be.

> *Employer-sponsored disability insurance policies are governed by the federal Employee Retirement Income Security Act (ERISA), which limits your rights in the event of a coverage dispute with your insurer.* With an individual disability insurance policy, however, you have a broad range of legal options available to you if your employer refuses to pay benefits under your policy for any reason.

I don't work in a risky job or have any dangerous hobbies. What are the chances that I will suffer a long-term disability?

The chances are much higher than you might think. For example, a twenty-eight-year-old man has a one in four chance of getting a long-term disability, and chances are that the disability will last a little longer than two years. (To figure out the odds that you will suffer a long-term disability, use the odds calculator at PolicyGenius, available at policygenius.com/long-term-disability-insurance/guide/disability-odds-calculator.)

Won't Social Security or workers' compensation provide me with benefits in the event that I suffer a long-term disability?

Probably not. Workers' compensation will only provide you with coverage if you suffer a work-related accident or injury, and you meet all the requirements for coverage. You might be surprised to learn that work-related injuries are responsible for only 5 percent of long-term disabilities. Non-work-related medical conditions, like arthritis and cancer, cause the vast majority of long-term disabilities.

As to Social Security, the process of getting benefits is long and complex. You will only qualify for benefits if you are unable to work at *any* occupation, not just your own occupation. Moreover, the majority of Social Security claims (nearly 65 percent) are denied. If you do manage to qualify, the average monthly benefit is only about $1,000 per month.

I am a stay-at-home parent. Should I consider long-term disability insurance?

No. You can only purchase long-term disability insurance if you have an income to replace. If you are not working right now, you do not qualify for long-term disability insurance.

I am ready to look into purchasing long-term disability insurance. Where should I start?

You should reach out to a reputable insurance agent (see page __ above for tips on choosing an insurance agent). Alternatively, you can use an online insurance site such as policygenius.com.

Issues to Consider before Purchasing Long-Term Disability Insurance Coverage

Will I be eligible for long-term disability insurance benefits as soon as I suffer an illness or injury that makes it impossible for me to work?

No. There is typically a waiting period, or *elimination period*, of three to six months before you are eligible for long-term disability insurance benefits.

Will the premiums for my long-term disability insurance policy increase every year?

If you opt for a *noncancelable* and *guaranteed renewable* policy, then the insurance company cannot increase your premiums or change the scope of your coverage as long as you pay the annual premium.

> *Think twice before purchasing a "conditionally renewable" or "optionally renewable" disability insurance policy.* Under these types of policies, insurers may retain the right to increase premiums, change the terms of coverage, or refuse to renew your coverage. Moreover, if you purchase a "guaranteed renewable" policy (rather than a "noncancelable and guaranteed renewable" policy), then your insurance company can increase your premiums under certain conditions.

I work at a very specialized job. What if I suffer an injury that makes it impossible for me to do my current job (but not any job)?

If you have a job that requires very specific physical skills—for example, if you are a hand surgeon or a renowned violinist—then *own occupation* is the best coverage for you. You will be eligible for benefits under an *own occupation* policy if you cannot work in your chosen occupation because of an illness or injury, even if you can still work in some other capacity. Standard long-term disability insurance, on the other hand, will only provide you with benefits if you cannot work at *any* other occupation for which you are reasonably suited based on your experience, education, and training. For most people, "own occupation" coverage is the better choice, even though it is a more expensive form of coverage.

> *Pay careful attention to the terms of the policy's own occupation coverage.* Make sure the policy language accurately describes the nature of your work, so there can be no room for dispute down the line as to what constitutes working in your own occupation. Also determine how long the own occupation coverage lasts. Some policies will provide you with own occupation coverage for a set period of time, and after that point you will receive benefits only if you cannot work in any occupation for which you are reasonably suited.

What if I suffer an illness or injury that forces me to work part time rather than full time?

If you opt for a policy with *residual disability coverage*, then you will be eligible for partial disability insurance benefits in the event that you suffer an illness or injury that interferes with your ability to work full time. Your benefit amount will be proportionate to your loss of income.

> *Give serious thought to adding a residual disability rider to your disability insurance policy.* There are many types of injuries and illnesses that could limit, but not completely eliminate, your ability to work in your chosen profession. If you suffer a disability that forces you to reduce your workload, residual disability insurance coverage can help you make up for your loss of income.

What happens if my income increases substantially after I purchase my disability insurance policy?

If you opt for a policy with a future increase option, you can increase the amount of your disability insurance benefits without going through the application process all over again. To bump up the amount of your benefits, you'll need to provide the insurance company with verification that your income has increased. You will also have to disclose any other individual or employer-sponsored disability insurance coverage you may have in place at the time. If your application is approved, you will pay higher premiums because you'll have greater insurance coverage.

I have a history of heart disease. Will my long-term disability insurance policy provide me with benefits if I cannot work because of my heart condition?

Insurance companies typically exclude long-term disability coverage for *preexisting conditions* (health problems that you had at the time you applied for insurance). Your insurance company may issue an exclusion rider specifically disclaiming coverage for illnesses or injuries relating to a specific preexisting medical condition you may have. Check with your insurance agent to learn more about what your policy will (and won't) cover.

If I suffer a debilitating illness or injury, will I be eligible to receive long-term disability insurance benefits for the rest of my life?

No. You will only receive benefits for the length of time specified in your policy (typically somewhere between age sixty-five and age seventy, although a couple of companies offer lifetime benefits).

What questions should I ask before purchasing a long-term disability insurance policy?

A quality insurance agent can help you understand the scope of your long-term disability insurance policy and make sure that you are getting the right type of coverage for your needs. Before signing on the dotted line, here are a few questions to ask:

- What percentage of your current income will the policy pay you in benefits? What is the maximum monthly benefit that you will be eligible to receive?
- Is the policy an own occupation policy? If so, how does the policy define the term own occupation?
- Does the own occupation coverage last for the duration of the policy, or does coverage drop down to any occupation coverage after a certain period of time?
- Is the policy noncancelable and guaranteed renewable? In other words, does the insurance company retain the right to cancel the policy, raise your premiums, or change the terms of coverage?
- How long is the elimination period?
- Until what age will you receive benefits under the policy if you are permanently unable to work?
- What exclusions and/or limitations apply? For example, does the policy exclude preexisting conditions? Will the policy provide coverage if you suffer from a mental health issue, such as an anxiety disorder?
- Does the policy include residual disability benefits? If so, what are the terms of coverage?

- Does the policy include a future increase option that allows you to purchase additional disability coverage if your income increases?
- Does the policy include a cost of living adjustment that automatically increases the amount of your disability insurance benefits to reflect inflation?
- What happens if you qualify for benefits through Social Security or workers' compensation? Will the insurance company offset those benefits against the amount of your benefits under your long-term disability insurance policy?

You can learn more about life insurance and long-term disability insurance, and also apply for insurance, at policygenius.com. PolicyGenius is a fun and friendly website that takes complex insurance issues and makes them easy to understand. You can find out more about your coverage needs, and apply for insurance, with the click of a few buttons.

CHAPTER 6

Tax Breaks for New Parents

WITH the many expenses that come with having a new baby, you will probably want to stretch each dollar as far as it can go. One of the best ways to save money after you have a baby is to take advantage of every opportunity to trim your tax bill.

In this chapter, you'll learn about the many different federal income tax breaks you may be eligible for after your baby arrives. Some of the tax breaks we discuss are specific to parents (like the child care credit), while others (like employer-sponsored health care flexible spending accounts) can also be used by people who don't have any children.

This chapter covers:

- The basics of the federal income tax system, in case you need a quick refresher course on how the federal income tax system works.
- The dependent exemption and the child tax credit, two tax breaks that can save you a bundle after baby arrives.
- Tax breaks on child care expenses. We'll address the child care credit, as well as employer-sponsored dependent care flexible spending accounts.

- Tax breaks on health care costs. We'll cover employer-sponsored health care flexible spending accounts, health savings accounts, and the tax deduction for health care expenses that exceed a certain percentage of your taxable income.
- Tax breaks for adoptions. We'll help you understand the ins and outs of the adoption tax credit, as well as the exclusion for employer-provided adoption assistance.
- Tax breaks for single parents. We'll help you determine whether you qualify to save taxes by filing as "head of household."
- Tax breaks for low-income parents. You'll learn about the earned income credit, which could provide you with a valuable tax refund come tax time.

Many thanks to tax expert David Spitzkoff for reviewing this chapter. David is a certified public accountant with Spitzkoff & Associates (spitzkoff.com), a New York-based firm that has been providing tax, bookkeeping, and business advisory services in the tri-state area since 1968.

To qualify for child-related tax breaks, you will need a Social Security number for your child. If you are in the process of a domestic adoption, you can use an Adoption Taxpayer Identification Number (ATIN) instead. (You can learn more about obtaining a Social Security number or an ATIN for your child on pages 45 through 48 of Chapter 2.)

In addition to federal tax breaks, you may qualify for state tax breaks when you have a new baby. Check with a tax professional or consult your state's tax laws for more details.

Consider investing in an education savings plan to save even more in taxes. If you are ready to start saving for your child's future educational costs, you can avoid paying taxes on your investment income provided you use a qualifying education savings plan. (You can learn more about education savings plans in Chapter 4.)

Federal Income Taxes 101

If you're not a financial professional, the federal income tax system can be very difficult to understand—especially since the rules change every single year. Here we'll answer some of the basic questions you might have on the federal income tax system.

Do I owe federal income taxes on every dollar of income that I earn? No. Every taxpayer is entitled to a *standard deduction* that is not subject to federal income taxes. The amount of your standard deduction depends on your tax filing status. In 2015, the standard deduction was $12,600 for married couples filing jointly and $9,250 for single parents filing as head of household.

> *Some taxpayers choose to itemize their deductions instead of claiming the standard deduction.* There are a wide range of other tax deductions available—including a deduction for home mortgage interest and a deduction for charitable contributions. You can either take the standard deduction or claim the various other deductions, but you cannot do both. If the total amount you can claim using the various other deductions exceeds the standard deduction, then it probably makes sense for you to itemize your deductions on your tax return.

In addition to the *standard deduction*, you can claim a *personal exemption* for yourself and for your spouse, as well as a *dependent exemption* for each of your children. In 2015, these exemption amounts were $4,000 per person.

The personal and dependent exemptions phase out for high earners. In 2015, married couples filing jointly with an adjusted gross income of more than $432,400 lost the per-person exemption entirely.

Do I owe the same tax rate on all of my income?

No. The federal government applies a progressive tax system under which each level of income is taxed at a certain fixed rate. Think of it like a staircase: the first chunk of your income is taxed at one rate, the second chunk of your income is taxed at a higher rate, and so on. The tax rate that applies to the top chunk of your income is called your *marginal tax rate*. The specific tax rates that apply to each chunk of your income depend on your tax filing status.

Suppose, for example, that you and your spouse had $200,000 in taxable income in 2015. Let's further suppose that you filed your taxes jointly. You would fall into the tax bracket for married couples filing jointly with taxable income between $151,201 and $230,450. In 2015, couples in this tax bracket owed $29,387.50 in federal income taxes *plus* 28 percent of their taxable income over $151,200. The *marginal tax rate* for couples in this tax bracket was 28 percent.

In our hypothetical, you and your spouse would have owed $43,051.50 in federal income taxes. You would not have owed 28 percent of your whole taxable income of $200,000 (which would work out to $56,000) because the marginal tax rate only applies to the top chunk of your income.

What is the alternative minimum tax (AMT)?

The alternative minimum tax (AMT) system is a parallel tax system that Congress devised to prevent wealthy taxpayers from using itemized deductions to lower their tax bills. The AMT system comes with its own set of tax rates and exemptions. Many of the deductions and tax credits that apply under the standard tax system—including the personal and dependent exemptions—do not apply under the AMT system.

While the AMT was originally designed to target the very wealthy, the AMT casts a very wide net and forces many middle class and upper-middle class taxpayers to pay higher taxes than they would owe under the normal tax system.

It's not easy to predict whether or not you will be subject to the AMT system, but one of the major risk factors is claiming a large amount in tax deductions (for example, a high state tax deduction) or exemptions (for example, if you have several children).

A B C *To find out whether you are subject to the AMT, you have to calculate your taxes under both the standard system and the AMT system and pay the higher amount.* You have to complete both your regular tax return *and* IRS Form 6251, the return for the AMT (available at irs.gov). If the amount you owe under the AMT system is higher, then you are subject to the AMT and must pay taxes according to your AMT return.

What is the difference between a tax deduction and a tax credit?

A tax deduction lets you subtract a certain dollar amount from your taxable income. In effect, a tax deduction protects some of your income from federal income taxes.

A tax credit is a dollar-for-dollar reduction of your tax bill. It is much more valuable than a tax deduction because every dollar of a tax credit is a dollar more in your pocket.

What does it mean if a tax break "phases out" for higher-income earners?

Many of the best tax breaks are only available to taxpayers whose income falls below certain limits. These tax breaks often "phase out" for higher-income earners, which means that if your income is above certain limits, you can only claim a portion of the tax break. The higher your income, the less of the tax break you can claim. If your income is above a certain level, you may not be able to claim the tax break at all.

What is my adjusted gross income (AGI)?

Your adjusted gross income is your total income for the year, minus certain deductions. You can find your adjusted gross income on line 38 of your Form 1040, or line 22 of your Form 1040A.

For some tax breaks, the IRS uses your modified adjusted gross income (MAGI) rather than your adjusted gross income (AGI). Your MAGI is your AGI, plus certain add-ons. The MAGI is calculated differently for different tax breaks. To learn how the IRS calculates your MAGI for purposes of a particular tax break, refer to the IRS publication governing that particular tax break.

If you want more information on the basics of federal income taxes, turn to IRS Publication 17 entitled "Tax Guide for Individuals," available at irs.gov.

Tax Breaks for Having a Child

There are two tax breaks that you may qualify for simply by having a baby: the dependent exemption and the child tax credit. With the dependent exemption, you may be able to claim a sizable annual tax deduction (up to $4,000 in 2015) beginning in the year your child is born. With the child tax credit, you may be eligible to trim a big chunk of change ($1,000 in 2015) from your tax bill each year—a nice little baby gift from Uncle Sam!

You can claim both the dependent exemption and the child tax credit. As long as you meet the eligibility requirements, you can claim both the dependent exemption and the child tax credit for each child.

Give yourself a "raise" after your baby arrives. Having a new baby means that you can claim one more withholding allowance on your W-4 form. Once your baby is born or adopted, ask your employer if you can file a new W-4 form to change your withholdings. Your employer will then be able to decrease your tax withholdings in each paycheck—putting more money in your pocket each month.

The Dependent Exemption

What is the dependent exemption?
The dependent exemption is a tax deduction you may be able to claim if you have a child who lives with you and depends on you for support.

How much is the dependent exemption worth?
In 2015, the dependent exemption provided a tax deduction of $4,000 per child.

Do I qualify to claim the dependent exemption?
Probably, but it depends on your income. The dependent exemption phases out for higher-income earners. In 2015, married couples filing jointly with an adjusted gross income of more than $309,900 could only claim a portion of the dependent exemption. The dependent exemption disappeared completely in 2015 for married couples filing jointly with an adjusted gross income (AGI) of more than $432,400, and for single parents filing as head of household with an AGI of more than $406,550.

To learn more about the income-based eligibility requirements for the dependent exemption and the phase-out rules, turn to IRS Publication 501 entitled "Exemptions, Standard Deduction, and Filing Information," available at irs.gov.

Do I have to itemize my tax deductions in order to claim the dependent exemption?
No. You can claim the dependent exemption regardless of whether or not you itemize your deductions.

I am subject to the alternative minimum tax (AMT). Can I claim the dependent exemption?
No. Under the AMT system, you cannot claim either a personal exemption or a dependent exemption. (See page 202 above to learn more about the AMT system.)

I have two children. Can I claim two dependent exemptions?
Yes. You can claim a dependent exemption for each of your children, as you long as you meet the income-based eligibility requirements for the dependent exemption.

My child was born in December. Can I claim the full amount of the dependent exemption for this tax year?
Yes. You can claim the full amount of the dependent exemption for any child born during the tax year, no matter how late in the year your child was born.

Can I claim the dependent exemption for an adopted child?
Yes, but your child must meet certain residency requirements. For domestic adoptions, your adopted child must have lived with you for more than half the year. For foreign adoptions, your adopted child must have lived with you for the entire year if your child is not a United States citizen. Check with a tax professional for details on the residency requirement as it applies to your adoption.

A B C *You may be able to claim the dependent exemption even if your adoption is not yet final.* A child who is legally placed with you for adoption is considered your adopted child for tax purposes.

My child's other parent and I are divorced. Can we both claim the dependent exemption for our child?
No. Only one parent can claim the dependent exemption.

As a general rule, the custodial parent is entitled to claim the dependent exemption. However, there are some instances in which it makes more financial sense for the noncustodial parent to claim the dependent exemption. In that case, the custodial parent can assign the dependent exemption to the noncustodial parent using IRS Form 8332, available at irs.gov.

My child does not live with me, but I pay for most of my child's expenses. Can I still claim the dependent exemption for my child?
Probably not. In order to claim the dependent exemption, you must have lived with your child for more than half of the year. An exception applies if your child lives with the other parent and the other parent assigns the dependent exemption to you using IRS Form 8332, available at irs.gov.

My child has a large trust fund that I use to pay most of my child's expenses. Can I still claim the dependent exemption?
No. You cannot claim the dependent exemption if your child provided more than half of his or her own support during the year.

Can I claim the dependent exemption every year until my child goes off to college?
Yes. In fact, you may even be able to claim your child as a dependent during the years when your child is in college.

You can claim the dependent exemption for your child every year as long as the following requirements are met:

- Your child is under age nineteen *or* your child is a student under age twenty-four.
- Your child lives with you for more than half the year. The IRS considers education-related absences to be "temporary absences" that do not count against the residency requirement. So if your child attends college in a different state, the IRS still counts your child as living with you for more than half the year.
- Your child does not provide more than half of his or her support for the year. Once your child starts earning enough to pay his or her own bills, you can no longer claim your child as your dependent for tax purposes.

How do I claim the dependent exemption?

Claiming the dependent exemption is easy. All you have to do is provide your child's name and Social Security number (or Adoption Taxpayer Identification Number) on line 6C of your Form 1040 or 1040A.

To learn more about the dependent exemption, turn to IRS Publication 501 entitled "Exemptions, Standard Deduction, and Filing Information," available at irs.gov.

The Child Tax Credit

What is the child tax credit?

The child tax credit is a tax credit you may be able to claim if you have a child who lives with you and depends on you for support.

How much is the child tax credit worth?

In 2015, the child tax credit was $1,000 per child.

Do I qualify to claim the child tax credit?

It depends on your income. The child tax credit phases out for higher-income earners. For married couples filing jointly in 2014, the phase out began at a modified adjusted gross income (MAGI) of $110,000. The phase out began for single parents filing as head of household at a modified adjusted gross income of $75,000.

To learn more about the phase-out rules for the child tax credit, turn to IRS Publication 972 entitled "Child Tax Credit," available at irs.gov.

I am subject to the alternative minimum tax (AMT). Can I claim the child tax credit?

No. Under the AMT system, you cannot claim many of the deductions and credits available under the standard tax system, including the child tax credit. (See page __ to learn more about the AMT system.)

ABC *The AMT system only applies to higher-income earners.* If you are subject to the AMT, you probably don't qualify for the child tax credit.

I have two children. Can I claim two child tax credits?
Yes. You can claim a child tax credit for *each* of your children, as you long as you meet the income-based eligibility requirements. (The child tax credit phases out for higher-income earners.)

My child was born in December. Can I claim the full amount of the child tax credit for this tax year?
Yes. You can claim the full amount of the child tax credit for any child born during the tax year, no matter how late in the year your child was born.

Can I claim the child tax credit for an adopted child?
Yes, but your child must meet certain residency requirements. For domestic adoptions, your adopted child must have lived with you for more than half the year. For foreign adoptions, your adopted child must have lived with you for the entire year if your child is not a United States citizen. Check with a tax professional for details on the residency requirement as it applies to your adoption.

ABC *You may be able to claim the child tax credit even if your adoption is not yet final.* A child who is legally placed with you for adoption is considered your adopted child for tax purposes.

My child's other parent and I are divorced. Can we both claim the child tax credit for our child?
No. Only the parent who claims the dependent exemption may claim the child tax credit. (See page 206 for rules on which parent may claim the dependent exemption when the child's parents are divorced.)

My child does not live with me, but I pay for most of my child's expenses. Can I still claim the child tax credit for my child?

Probably not. In order to claim the child tax credit, you must have lived with your child for more than half of the year *and* you must claim your child as a dependent on your tax return. An exception applies if your child lives with the other parent and the other parent assigns the dependent exemption to you using IRS Form 8332, available at irs.gov.

My child has a large trust fund that I use to pay most of my child's expenses. Can I still claim the child tax credit?

No. You cannot claim the child tax credit if your child provides more than half of his or her own support.

Can I claim the child tax credit every year until my child goes off to college?

Almost. You can claim the child tax credit for your child every year as long as the following requirements are met:

- your child is under age 17,
- your child lives with you for more than half the year, and
- your child does not provide more than half of his or her support for the year.

> *The child tax credit is more restrictive than the dependent exemption.* Unlike the child care credit, you may be able to continue claiming the dependent exemption for your child even after your child starts college. (See page __ above for eligibility requirements for the dependent exemption.)

How do I claim the child tax credit?

You must first determine the amount of the credit you are eligible to claim by completing the child tax credit worksheet in IRS Publication 972 entitled "Child Tax Credit," available at irs.gov. You will then need to list this amount on line 52 of your Form 1040, or line 35 of your Form 1040A.

You can only claim the child tax credit if you are also claiming the dependent exemption. Be sure to check the child tax credit box on line 6c of your Form 1040 or 1040A for each child for whom you are claiming the child tax credit.

Is the child tax credit refundable?

Yes. If the total amount of your federal income tax liability is less than the amount of your child tax credit, you may be eligible to receive a partial cash refund of the child tax credit from the federal government. To claim your refund you will need to complete IRS Schedule 8812, available at irs.gov, and submit it along with your Form 1040 or Form 1040A.

You cannot obtain a refund of the child tax credit if you have no taxable income for the year. To qualify for a refund, you must have a certain minimum amount of earned income during the year. (This amount was $3,000 in 2014.)

To learn more about the child tax credit, turn to IRS Publication 972 entitled "Child Tax Credit," available at irs.gov.

Tax Breaks on Child Care Costs

As a new parent, child care may be one of your biggest expenses. Fortunately, there are two tax breaks that can save you money on child care costs. First, with the child care credit, you may be eligible for a dollar-for-dollar reduction in your tax bill for a certain percentage of your child care expenses each year. Second, if your employer offers you the option of contributing to a dependent care flexible spending account (dependent care FSA), you may be able to pay for some of your child care expenses with pretax dollars rather than posttax dollars.

You may be able to claim the child care credit even if you use a dependent care FSA to pay for some of your child care costs. The only catch is that you can't "double dip" by claiming the child care credit for the same child care costs that you paid for using the funds in your dependent care FSA.

Contribute the maximum to your dependent care FSA if you have one. As a general rule, you'll save far more in taxes using a dependent care FSA than you will with the child care credit.

The Child Care Credit

How much is the child care credit worth?
It depends on the number of children you have, your adjusted gross income (AGI), and your out-of-pocket child care expenses.

The amount you can claim as a tax credit is based on a percentage of your eligible child care expenses, up to a certain limit. In 2014, you could have claimed a child care credit on a percentage of up to $3,000 in eligible child care expenses if you had one child, and up to $6,000 in eligible child care expenses if you had two or more children.

The percentage that applies when calculating your tax credit depends on your adjusted gross income. If your adjusted gross income was more than $43,000 in 2014, then you would have been eligible for a credit of 20 percent of your qualifying child care expenses.

There are no income-based limitations on claiming the child care credit. The amount you earn affects only the percentage of child care expenses you can claim for purposes of the credit, not whether or not you can claim the credit.

For example, let's suppose you and your spouse have two children. Let's further suppose that in 2014 you had an adjusted gross income of $80,000 and you spent $8,000 on day care costs. Your child care credit would have been based on $6,000 in child care expenses—the maximum limit for a family with two or more children. Based on your adjusted gross income, you would have been able to take a tax credit of 20 percent of that amount—which would have worked out to a tax credit of $1,200.

For more information on calculating your child care credit, use the worksheet in IRS Publication 503 entitled "Child and Dependent Care Expenses," available at irs.gov.

Do I qualify to claim the child care credit?

To take advantage of the child care credit, you must have earned income from working during the year. (Exceptions apply if you are looking for work or if you are a full-time student.) If you are married, you and your spouse must file your taxes jointly to claim the credit.

You can claim the child care credit regardless of your income. Unlike many other tax breaks, the child care credit does not phase out completely for higher-income earners.

See page __ below for answers to frequently asked questions about whether you qualify to claim the child care credit. (The eligibility requirements for the child care credit are the same as the eligibility requirements for dependent care FSAs.)

What counts as an eligible child care expense for purposes of the child care credit?

Eligible child care expenses include day care costs, the salary for a nanny or au pair, and before and after school care for a school-aged child. The child care costs must be for a child under the age of thirteen.

See page __ below for answers to frequently asked questions about eligible child care expenses for the child care credit. (The eligible child care expenses for the child care credit are the same as the eligible child care expenses for dependent care FSAs.)

Do I have to itemize my deductions to claim the child care credit?
No. You can claim the child care credit regardless of whether you itemize your deductions.

I am subject to the alternative minimum tax (AMT). Can I still claim the child care credit?
No. Under the AMT system, you cannot claim many of the deductions and credits available under the standard tax system, including the child care credit. (See page 202 above to learn more about the AMT system.)

I contribute to an employer-sponsored dependent care FSA. Can I still claim the child care credit?
Yes. However, you must subtract the amount you contribute to your dependent care FSA from the dollar limit on eligible child care expenses that you can claim for purposes of calculating the child care credit.

For example, let's suppose you are married, you have five-year-old twins, and you spent $10,000 on day care in 2014. Let's further suppose that you contributed $5,000 to an employer-sponsored dependent care FSA. You would ordinarily have been entitled to claim a percentage of up to $6,000 in eligible child care expenses under the child care credit. However, because of your dependent care FSA contributions, you would only be able to claim a percentage of $1,000 under the child care credit.

How do I claim the child and dependent care credit?
You will have to complete IRS Form 2441, available at irs.gov. You will need to provide the name, address, and Social Security number or Employer Identification Number of your child care provider, as well as the exact amount you paid in child care expenses to that provider during the tax year.

If your child care provider is a tax-exempt organization, you do not have to provide an Employer Identification Number (EIN). You can simply write the words "tax exempt" in the box where you would otherwise provide the child care provider's EIN.

You will also need to enter the amount of the child care credit you can claim on line 49 of your Form 1040 or line 31 of your Form 1040A.

For more information on the child care credit, including details on how to calculate and claim the credit, turn to IRS Publication 503 entitled "Child and Dependent Care Expenses," available at irs.gov.

Dependent Care Flexible Spending Accounts

What is a dependent care flexible spending account (FSA)?
A dependent care flexible spending account (dependent care FSA) is a savings account that allows you to set aside pretax dollars from your paycheck to pay for child care expenses. You can only invest in a dependent care FSA if your employer offers one as part of your benefits package.

What taxes can I save using a dependent care FSA?
You will not owe federal income taxes, or the 7.65 percent tax for Social Security and Medicare, on your dependent care FSA contributions. Depending on your state's tax laws, your dependent care FSA contributions may also be exempt from state income taxes.

Do I qualify to claim a tax break for contributions to a dependent care FSA?
To claim a tax break for contributions to a dependent care FSA, you must have earned income from working during the year. (Exceptions apply if you are looking for work or if you are a full-time student.) If you are married, you and your spouse must file your taxes jointly to claim this tax break.

You can contribute to a dependent care FSA regardless of how much you earn. Unlike many other tax breaks, there is no income-based limitation on dependent care FSAs.

See page 217 below for answers to frequently asked questions about whether you qualify to contribute to a dependent care FSA. (The eligibility requirements for dependent care FSAs are the same as the eligibility requirements for the child care credit.)

What counts as an eligible child care expense for purposes of a dependent care FSA?

Eligible child care expenses include day care costs, the salary for a nanny or au pair, and before and after school care for a school-aged child. The child care costs must be for a child under the age of thirteen.

See page 221 below for answers to frequently asked questions about child care expenses eligible for reimbursement using a dependent care FSA. (The eligible child care expenses for dependent care FSAs are the same as the child care expenses eligible for the child care credit.)

How much can I contribute to a dependent care FSA?

The federal government sets limits on how much you can contribute to a dependent care FSA each year. In 2015 the maximum contribution was $5,000 for single taxpayers or married taxpayers filing jointly, and $2,500 for married taxpayers filing separately.

However, employers can choose to set limits that are lower than these maximum amounts. For example, it would have been perfectly legal for your employer to allow you to contribute no more than $2,000 to your dependent care FSA in 2015.

You cannot contribute more than your earned income for the year or your spouse's earned income, whichever is lower. If your spouse does not have earned income from working during the year, then you are not eligible to contribute to a dependent care FSA.

My spouse and I both work for employers that offer dependent care FSAs. Can we each contribute to our own separate dependent care FSAs?

Yes. However, your total contributions cannot add up to more than the maximum amount allowed under the tax laws. (In 2015, the limit was $5,000 for married taxpayers filing jointly.)

Contributing to two separate dependent care accounts can be a smart idea if the maximum contribution allowed under each plan is less than the maximum allowed under the federal tax laws. For example, let's suppose that in 2015 you and your spouse both worked for employers that allowed you to set aside up to $2,500 per year in a dependent care FSA. You could each have contributed $2,500 to your own dependent care FSAs, bringing your total dependent care FSA contributions to $5,000 (the maximum allowed under the federal tax laws).

I am subject to the alternative minimum tax (AMT). Can I still benefit from contributing to a dependent care FSA?

Yes. While you cannot claim many of the usual deductions and tax credits (like the child care credit) under the AMT system, you only owe the AMT on your adjusted gross income. Contributions you make to a dependent care FSA lower your adjusted gross income for tax purposes, which in turn lowers the taxes you owe under both the AMT and the usual tax system.

If I contribute to a dependent care flexible FSA, can I still claim the child care credit?

Yes. However, you must subtract the amount you contribute to your dependent care FSA from the dollar limit on eligible child care expenses you can claim for purposes of calculating the child care credit.

For example, let's suppose you are married, you have five-year-old twins, and you spent $10,000 on day care in 2014. Let's further suppose that you contributed $5,000 to an employer-sponsored dependent care FSA. You would ordinarily have been entitled to claim a percentage of up to $6,000 in eligible child care expenses under the child care credit. However, because of your dependent care FSA contributions, you would only have been able to claim a percentage of $1,000 under the child care credit.

How can I enroll in a dependent care FSA?
Check with your benefits administrator about how and when to enroll. You can usually enroll in a dependent care FSA when you first start your job or during your annual benefits open enrollment period.

You may also be able to enroll in a dependent care FSA during a special enrollment period after your baby is born or adopted. Depending on the terms of your employer's benefits plan, you may be able to make changes to your benefits outside of your annual benefits open enrollment period within a month or two after the birth or adoption of a child. Check with your benefits administrator for more details.

How do I make deposits in a dependent care FSA?
You make contributions to a dependent care FSA through paycheck deductions (similar to how you fund a 401[k] plan).

How can I withdraw funds from a dependent care FSA to cover child care costs?
You will need to submit a claim form, along with a receipt for your child care expenses, to your plan administrator. Check with your benefits administrator for more details on how to get reimbursed for eligible child care expenses.

You can only obtain reimbursement for child care expenses once you have accumulated enough funds in your dependent care FSA to cover those expenses. For example, let's suppose that you elect to contribute $2,500 to your dependent care FSA in monthly increments of a little over $200. Let's further suppose that you pay your day care provider $400 in January. You will need to wait until at least the end of February—when you would have contributed more than $400 to your account—to claim reimbursement of the $400 you paid to your day care provider in January.

You may have until March 15 of the following tax year to claim reimbursements from your dependent care FSA. Most plans give you a few extra months to claim your dependent care FSA reimbursements.

What happens if I contribute more to my dependent care FSA than my eligible child care expenses for the year? Can I get a refund of my contributions?

Unfortunately not. Dependent care FSAs work on a "use it or lose it" basis. If you contribute more to your account than you ultimately spend in child care expenses, you will forfeit the money. So be careful not to contribute more than you think you will actually spend on qualifying child care expenses during the year.

How do I claim a tax break on contributions to my dependent care FSA?

The amount you contribute to your dependent care FSA will appear in box 10 of the Form W-2 that you will receive from your employer come tax time. In order to exclude dependent care benefits from your taxable income, you will need to complete and submit Parts I and III of Form 2441, available at irs.gov, along with your tax return.

If you are claiming the child care credit in addition to an exclusion for your dependent care FSA contributions, you will also need to complete Part II of Form 2441. Remember that you cannot "double dip" by claiming both tax breaks for the same child care expense.

Qualifying for the Child Care Tax Breaks

I work full time, but my spouse works only part time. Do we still qualify for the child care tax breaks?

Yes. However, you cannot claim more in child care expenses than your earned income for the year or your spouse's earned income for the year, whichever is smaller. For example, let's suppose you work full time as an accountant but your spouse works only occasionally as a freelance book editor. If your spouse only earned $2,500 in the entire tax year, then you cannot claim more than $2,500 in eligible child care expenses, even if your actual child care expenses exceeded $2,500.

I do not work outside the home, but I do use a babysitter once a week so that I can run errands and have a little time to myself. Do I qualify for the child care tax breaks?

No. In order to qualify for the child care tax breaks, you must have earned income from working outside the home during the year. If you are married, you can only claim the child care tax breaks if both you and your spouse work outside the home.

> *Exceptions apply if you are looking for work or if you are a full-time student.* (See page 221 below for more details.)

I am not working right now, but my child is in day care because I am actively looking for a job. Do I qualify for the child care tax breaks?

Yes, provided you ultimately find a job and earn income from working during the tax year.

> *The amount you can claim in eligible child care expenses is limited to your earned income for the year.* If you end up finding a job late in the year, you may not be able to claim the full amount of the child care tax breaks.

I leave my child with a sitter a few days a week to attend graduate school classes. Do I qualify for the child care tax breaks?
Yes, provided you are a full-time student for some part of at least five months during the year.

> *You do not need to attend classes and do schoolwork for forty hours a week to qualify as a full-time student.* Rather, you simply have to be enrolled at a school for the number of hours or classes that the school considers a full-time course load.

I am divorced, and my child does not live with me. Do I qualify for the child care tax breaks?
No. You can only claim the child care tax breaks if your child lives with you for more than half the year. Even if you are entitled to claim the dependent exemption for your child pursuant to the terms of a divorce decree or settlement, you cannot claim the claim the child care tax breaks if you are not your child's custodial parent.

Eligible Child Care Expenses

I pay my nanny off the books. Can I still claim the child care tax breaks?
No. You can only claim the child care tax breaks for a nanny you hire and pay legally. (For more information on hiring and paying a nanny legally, see Chapter 3.)

> *If you attempt to claim the child care tax breaks for an off the books nanny, you risk penalties from the IRS for noncompliance with the tax laws governing household employers.* To claim the child care tax breaks, you will need to provide the IRS with your nanny's name and Social Security number. The IRS could quickly cross-reference your tax return against your nanny's tax return (if she filed one) to determine whether you both reported your nanny's wages and paid all taxes due. If the IRS finds a discrepancy, it may

penalize both you and your nanny for failing to comply with the tax laws.

My child attends a family day care program that is not officially licensed. Can I claim the child care tax breaks for my day care costs?
Probably not. You can only claim the child care tax breaks if your day care provider gives you a completed Form W-10 entitled "Dependent Care Provider's Identification and Certification." Your child's day care provider will likely be unwilling to provide you with this form if the provider is unlicensed.

Can I claim the child care tax breaks for preschool tuition?
Yes. For purposes of the child care tax breaks, the IRS counts preschool tuition as a child care expense rather than an educational expense.

Can I claim the child care tax breaks for private school tuition?
No. Beginning with kindergarten, the IRS considers private school tuition to be an educational expense rather than a child care expense.

Can I claim the child care tax breaks for the costs of before- and after-school programs?
Yes. Before- and after-school programs for a child under the age of thirteen count as eligible child care expenses.

Can I claim the child care tax breaks for the costs of summer camp?
Yes. Believe it or not, summer camp costs for a child under the age of thirteen are eligible child care expenses.

You cannot claim the child care tax breaks for sleep-away summer camp. If you want to claim the child care tax breaks, send your child to day camp instead.

I have a housekeeper who cares for my children after school. Can I claim the child care tax breaks for my housekeeper's salary?
Yes. As long as your housekeeper's duties include caring for a child

under the age of thirteen and you pay your housekeeper on the books, you can claim the child care tax breaks on your housekeeper's wages.

My child is permanently disabled and may never be able to care for herself. Can I claim the child care tax breaks for her care after she reaches age thirteen?
Yes. The age limit for eligible child care expenses does not apply for a child who is not physically or mentally able to care for herself.

For more information on the child care tax breaks, turn to IRS Publication 503 entitled "Child and Dependent Care Expenses," available at irs.gov.

Tax Breaks on Health Care Costs

Even if you have excellent health insurance coverage, you may still end up spending a fair bit of money each year on unreimbursed health care expenses like copayments for prescription medications and dentist bills. You may be able to cover some of these costs using an employer-sponsored health care flexible spending account (health care FSA). Alternatively, if your only insurance is a high-deductible plan, you may be able to save a substantial amount on your out-of-pocket health care costs by investing in a health savings account (HSA). Finally, for the occasional years when your unreimbursed health care expenses are unusually high, you may be able to claim a tax deduction to the extent those expenses exceed 10 percent of your adjusted gross income.

Health Care Flexible Spending Accounts

What is a health care flexible spending account (health care FSA)?
A health care flexible spending account (FSA) is a savings account that allows you to set aside pretax dollars from your paycheck to pay for out-of-pocket health care expenses. You can only contribute to a health care FSA if your employer offers one as part of your benefits package.

What taxes can I save using a health care FSA?

You will not owe federal income taxes, or the 7.65 percent tax for Social Security and Medicare, on your health care FSA contributions. Depending on your state's tax laws, your health care FSA contributions may also be exempt from state income taxes.

I have comprehensive health insurance. Should I still consider contributing to a health care FSA?

Even if you have good health insurance, there are many health-related expenses that your insurance plan probably does not cover—like the cost of a good pair of prescription sunglasses or out-of-network physician fees. A health care FSA can save you money by letting you pay for these out-of-pocket expenses with pretax dollars.

What out-of-pocket health care expenses can I pay for using the funds in a health care FSA?

You can use the funds in your health care flexible spending account to pay for a wide range of medical and dental expenses for yourself, your spouse, or your child, including:

- copayments for physicians or other health care providers;
- deductibles under your health insurance plan;
- prescription medication;
- dental x-rays, fillings, and root canals;
- orthodontics;
- eye exams, eyeglasses, and contact lenses;
- fertility treatment, such as in vitro fertilization procedures; and
- breast pumps and lactation supplies.

You can find a list of qualifying health care expenses in IRS Publication 502 entitled "Medical and Dental Expenses," available at irs.gov.

Can I use the funds in my health care FSA to pay for my health insurance premiums?

Unfortunately not, even though health insurance premiums are probably your largest out-of-pocket health care expense.

Are there any other health-related expenses that I cannot pay for using the funds in a health care FSA?

There are limits to the types of health care expenses that you can pay for with the funds in a health care FSA. As a general rule, the IRS has made it clear that the expenses "must be primarily to alleviate or prevent" a health condition.

You cannot use a health care FSA to pay for:

- the cost of staying in good health, like health club dues, vitamins, and nutritional supplements;
- cosmetic procedures, like teeth whitening or electrolysis;
- weight loss programs (unless your weight loss treatment is for a specific disease diagnosed by a physician); or
- diet food or beverages.

You cannot use the funds in a health care FSA to pay for nonprescription drugs and medicines, like aspirin or ibuprofen. An exception applies if you have a prescription from your physician for over-the-counter medication.

If you're not sure whether a particular expense is covered, check IRS Publication 502 entitled "Medical and Dental Expenses," available at irs.gov.

Are there any eligibility requirements for contributing to a health care FSA?

No. The only requirement is that you must work for an employer that offers you the option of contributing to a health care FSA.

How much can I contribute to a health care FSA?

In 2015, the maximum amount you could contribute to a health care FSA was $2,550. (The government adjusts the maximum limits annually for inflation.) However, your employer may have lower limits for your plan. For example, your employer may only allow you to contribute a maximum of $1,500 to your health care FSA.

My spouse and I both work for employers that offer health care FSAs. Can we each contribute the maximum amounts under our own health care FSAs?

Yes. You and your spouse may each contribute the maximum amount allowed under your respective plans, even if you both work for the same employer.

> *Only contribute the amount that you will likely spend the following year on eligible out-of-pocket health care expenses.* You cannot carry over health care FSA contributions from year to year. If there is any money left in your health care FSAs at the end of the year, you will forfeit those funds.

I am subject to the alternative minimum tax (AMT). Can I still benefit from contributing to a health care FSA?

Yes. While you cannot claim many of the usual deductions and tax credits (like the child and dependent care credit) under the AMT system, you only owe the AMT on your adjusted gross income. Contributions you make to a health care FSA lower your adjusted gross income for tax purposes, which in turn lowers the taxes you owe under both the AMT and the usual tax system.

How can I enroll in a health care FSA?

Check with your benefits administrator about how and when to enroll. You can generally enroll in a health care FSA when you first start your job, or during your annual benefits open enrollment period.

> *You may also be able to enroll in a health care FSA during a special enrollment period after your baby is born or adopted.* Depending on the terms of your employer's benefits plan, you may be able to make changes to your benefits outside of your annual benefits open enrollment period within a month or two after the birth or adoption of a child.

Check with your benefits administrator for more details.

How do I make deposits in a health care FSA?
You make contributions to a health care FSA through paycheck deductions (similar to how you fund a 401[k] plan).

How can I withdraw funds from a health care FSA to cover health care costs?
Depending on the terms of your plan, you may be able to obtain a debit card that you can use to pay for your out-of-pocket health care expenses. If your company does not offer this option, then you may need to submit a claim form, along with a receipt for your health care expenses, to your plan administrator. Check with your benefits administrator for more details on how to get reimbursed.

You may be able to access the full amount of your annual contribution on the first day of the year. Depending on your benefit elections, it may take you the entire year to fund your health care FSA. However, you may be able to obtain reimbursement for health care expenses for the full amount of your annual contribution at the start of the year—before you have funded your account through paycheck contributions. Check with your benefits administrator for more details.

You may have until March 15 of the following tax year to claim reimbursements from your health care FSA. Most plans give you a few extra months to claim your health care FSA reimbursements.

What happens if I contribute more to my health care FSA than my eligible health care expenses for the year? Can I get a refund of my contributions?
No. However, your plan may offer one of two options that could help if you find yourself in this situation:

- the option to carry over $500 of your health care FSA contributions to the following tax year *or*
- a grace period of an extra two and a half months in the following tax year to use the funds in your health care FSA.

Your best bet, however, is to estimate your health care expenses conservatively. If you contribute more to your account than you ultimately spend in eligible health care expenses, you risk forfeiting the money.

How do I claim a tax break on contributions to my health care FSA?
Fortunately, you don't have to do anything to claim a tax break on contributions to your health care FSA. Contributions to your health care FSA will not be included as part of your taxable wages on your W-2, so you won't pay any federal income taxes or Social Security and Medicare taxes on those contributions.

Health Savings Accounts

If you have a high-deductible health insurance plan, you may be eligible to invest in a tax-advantaged health savings account (HSA). An HSA allows you to pay for your family's eligible health care expenses using pretax dollars.

What is a health savings account (HSA)?

A health savings account (HSA) allows you to save and invest pretax dollars to pay for your family's future health care expenses. While a health care FSA works like a checking account at a bank, an HSA is more like a brokerage account or 401(k) plan because you can invest the funds you save.

Can I choose the investments in my HSA?
Yes. You can invest your HSA contributions in any mutual fund or other investment option offered by the financial institution at which you open your account.

What are the tax advantages of investing in an HSA?
First, you won't have to pay income taxes or Social Security and Medicare taxes on your HSA contributions. Second, your HSA investments grow tax deferred. Finally, you won't owe any taxes on the money you withdraw from an HSA as long as you use those funds to pay for qualifying health care expenses.

Am I eligible to invest in an HSA?
You can invest in an HSA if your family is *only* covered by a high-deductible health insurance plan. To qualify, your family's high-deductible health insurance plan must have an annual deductible that meets or exceeds certain minimum requirements. (In 2015, the minimum deductible for a qualifying family health insurance plan was $2,600.)

This minimum annual deductible must apply to all health care costs under the plan (except for preventative care, which all health care plans must cover without first applying the deductible). If your high-deductible health insurance plan applies a lower deductible to prescription drug benefits than other health care costs, for example, then you are not eligible to invest in an HSA.

Your family's high-deductible health insurance plan must also have limits on your annual out-of-pocket expenses. (In 2015, the maximum out-of-pocket expenses under a qualifying high-deductible health insurance plan could not have exceeded $12,900.)

If you are not sure whether your health insurance plan is a high-deductible health insurance plan, check IRS Publication 969 entitled "Health Savings Accounts and Other Tax-Favored Health Plans," available at available at irs.gov. You can also check with your benefits administrator.

How much can I invest in an HSA?
In 2015, a family with a high-deductible health insurance plan could have invested up to $6,650 in an HSA.

Older parents have higher contribution limits. If you were age fifty-five years or older, you could have invested an additional $1,000 per year in an HSA in 2015.

You have until April 15 of the following tax year to make your HSA contributions for the year.

I am subject to the alternative minimum tax (AMT). Can I still benefit from contributing to an HSA?

Yes. While you cannot claim many of the usual deductions and tax credits (like the child care credit) under the AMT system, you only owe the AMT on your adjusted gross income. Contributions you make to an HSA lower your adjusted gross income for tax purposes, which in turn lowers the taxes you owe under both the AMT and the usual tax system.

My employer contributes to my HSA. Do my employer's contributions affect the amount I can invest in my HSA?

Yes. Your employer's contributions count against the maximum you may invest in your HSA each year. For example, let's suppose your family was eligible to invest $6,650 in an HSA in 2015. If your employer contributed $3,000 to your HSA that year, then you would only have been able to invest $3,650 in your account that year.

Can my spouse and I invest in our own separate HSAs? If so, can we each invest up to the maximum family contribution limit?

You and your spouse can establish separate HSAs, but your total contributions cannot exceed the family contribution limit for the year. For example, let's suppose your family was eligible to contribute $6,650 in an HSA in 2015. If your spouse contributed $2,000 to an HSA that year, then you would only have been able to invest $4,650 in your HSA that same year.

Can I invest in both an HSA and a health care FSA?

As a general rule, you cannot invest in an HSA if you also contribute to a standard health care FSA (see pages 223 through 228 above). However, you may be still be eligible to invest in an HSA if you also contribute to a *limited-purpose* or *postdeductible* health care FSA. As the name suggests, you can use a limited-purpose health care FSA to pay for a narrow range of unreimbursed health care costs (typically dental and vision expenses). You can only use a postdeductible health care FSA to pay for out-of-pocket medical expenses you incur after you have already met your annual deductible.

If your spouse invests in a standard health care FSA, then you cannot invest in an HSA. This is true even if your family's only health insurance coverage is a high-deductible health insurance plan.

What out-of-pocket health care expenses can I pay for using the funds in an HSA?

You can use the funds in an HSA to pay for a wide range of medical and dental expenses for yourself, your spouse, or your child, including:

- deductibles under your health insurance plan;
- copayments for physicians or other health care providers;
- prescription medication;
- dental x-rays, fillings, and root canals;
- orthodontics;
- eye exams, eyeglasses, and contact lenses;
- fertility treatment, such as in vitro fertilization procedures; and
- breast pumps and lactation supplies.

You can find a list of qualifying health care expenses in IRS Publication 502 entitled "Medical and Dental Expenses," available at irs.gov.

Can I use the funds in my HSA to pay for my health insurance premiums?

As a general rule, you cannot use your HSA to pay for health insurance premiums. (A couple of narrow exceptions apply.)

What happens if I use the money in my HSA for something besides health care expenses?
You'll pay a steep price if you use the money in your HSA on anything other than eligible health care expenses. Not only will you owe income taxes on your withdrawal, but you will also owe the federal government a 20 percent penalty on that amount.

Do I have to spend all the money in my HSA every year?
No. Unlike health care FSAs, HSAs don't have any built-in time limits on when you must spend the money. There is no "use it or lose it" rule with an HSA. Any money you do not spend simply stays invested in your HSA from year to year.

Can I keep my HSA if I switch jobs?
Yes. The HSAs are portable, which means that you take them with you even if you switch employers down the line.

What happens to my HSA if I get a job with an employer that offers comprehensive health insurance coverage instead of a high-deductible plan?
If you switch to a job that offers comprehensive health insurance coverage rather than high-deductible health insurance coverage, you will no longer be eligible to contribute to your HSA. However, you can still withdraw the funds in your HSA for eligible health care expenses tax free.

How can I enroll in an HSA?
You can open an HSA at any financial institution that offers these accounts. You can find a list of participating financial institutions (known as "HSA administrators" or "HSA providers") at hsasearch.com. As with any investment account, you should pay careful attention to the account management fees as well as the available investment options before making your decision.

If your employer has a relationship with a particular HSA administrator, then it probably makes sense to open your HSA with that HSA administrator. You may only be eligible to receive employer contributions to your HSA if you use your employer's preferred HSA administrator. There may be other benefits as well, like a streamlined claims-paying process.

How do I withdraw money from my HSA?
You can make withdrawals from an HSA the same way you would make withdrawals from any investment account. Depending on your plan's features, you may be able to use a debit card or checkbook linked to your HSA to pay for eligible health care expenses.

How do I claim a tax deduction for my HSA contributions?
You will need to complete Form 8889, available at irs.gov, and submit it along with your tax return. Enter the amount from line 13 of your Form 8889 on line 25 of your Form 1040 or Form 1040NR.

How do I claim a tax break on my HSA withdrawals?
You will need to complete Part II of Form 8889, available at irs.gov, and submit it along with your tax return.

> *For more information about the rules governing HSAs, turn to* IRS Publication 969 entitled "Health Savings Accounts and Other Tax-Favored Health Plans," available at irs.gov.

Tax Deduction for Health Care Expenses

Depending on the scope of your health insurance coverage and the health issues your family faces, there may be years when you have unusually large medical or dental bills. You may be eligible to claim a tax deduction for your unreimbursed medical or dental expenses, but only to the extent those expenses exceed 10 percent of your adjusted gross income. As a practical matter, only families with extraordinary health care costs are eligible to take this deduction.

Am I eligible to claim a deduction for my unreimbursed health care expenses?

You can claim a tax deduction for your out-of-pocket medical and dental expenses provided two conditions are met: (1) your unreimbursed health care expenses exceed 10 percent of your adjusted gross income, and (2) you itemize your deductions on your tax return.

How much can I claim as a tax deduction for my unreimbursed health care expenses?

You can claim a tax deduction for the amount that your unreimbursed health care expenses exceed 10 percent of your adjusted gross income. For example, let's suppose that your adjusted gross income was $100,000 in 2015. Let's further suppose that you spent $15,000 on an experimental cancer treatment that year. Provided you itemized your deductions, you would have been eligible to claim a tax deduction of $5,000 (the amount of your unreimbursed health care expenses that exceeded 10 percent of your adjusted gross income).

> *Special rules apply if you are age sixty-five or older.* In that case, you can claim a tax deduction to the extent that your unreimbursed health are expenses exceed 7.5 percent of your adjusted gross income.

I am subject to the alternative minimum tax. Can I still claim a tax deduction for my unreimbursed health care expenses?

No. Under the alternative minimum tax (AMT) system, you cannot claim many of the deductions and tax credits available under the standard tax system—like the deduction for health care expenses. (See page 202 above for more information on the AMT system.)

What types of health care expenses can I deduct?

You can deduct a broad range of medical and dental expenses for yourself, your spouse, or your child. Qualifying expenses include your out-of-pocket costs for:

- copayments for physicians or other health care providers;

- deductibles under your health insurance plan;
- prescription medication;
- dental x-rays, fillings, and root canals;
- orthodontics;
- eye exams, eyeglasses, and contact lenses;
- fertility treatment, such as in vitro fertilization procedures; and
- breast pumps and lactation supplies.

You can claim a deduction for your health insurance premiums. While you cannot obtain reimbursement under a health care FSA or an HSA for your health insurance premiums, you can claim a tax deduction for your health insurance premiums.

You can find a list of qualifying health care expenses in IRS Publication 502 entitled "Medical and Dental Expenses," available at irs.gov.

Bear in mind that you can only deduct expenses that you actually pay during the tax year. Also, if you pay for any of your out-of-pocket health care expenses using a health care FSA (see pages 222 through 228 above) or an HSA (see pages 228 through 233), then you cannot claim a tax deduction for those same expenses.

How do I claim a tax deduction for my unreimbursed health care expenses?

You will need to complete Items 1 through 4 of Schedule A of Form 1040, available at irs.gov, and submit it along with your tax return.

You do not need to provide the IRS with receipts for your unreimbursed health care expenses. However, you should keep the receipts in your files in case of an audit.

To learn more about the deduction for health care expenses, turn to IRS Publication 502 entitled "Medical and Dental Expenses," available at available at irs.gov.

Tax Breaks for Adoptions

The costs of adopting a child can be staggering. When you add up agency fees and attorney's fees, as well as the many incidental expenses of adoption, you could easily spend upward of $25,000 to welcome a new addition to your family. Thankfully, the federal government offers two valuable tax breaks that can ease the financial burden for adoptive parents. First, the adoption tax credit provides eligible parents with a substantial dollar-for-dollar reduction in tax liability for adoption-related expenses. Second, the federal government provides a tax exclusion for employer-provided adoption assistance. Depending on your income and your adoption-related expenses, you may qualify for both tax breaks.

Adoptive parents also qualify for the same tax breaks as all new parents. In addition to the special adoption-related tax breaks, adoptive parents are also eligible for the dependent exclusion, the child care credit, and the child care tax breaks.

Stepparent adoptions do not count. If you are adopting your spouse's child, you are not eligible for either of the adoption tax breaks.

In order to claim the adoption-related tax breaks for a U.S.-based (or domestic) adoption, you will need either a Social Security number for your child or an Adoption Taxpayer Identification Number (ATIN). You can obtain an ATIN by completing IRS Form W-7A, available at irs.gov.

To claim the adoption-related tax breaks for an international adoption, however, you must have a Social Security number for your child. You will only be able to apply for a Social Security number for your adopted child once the adoption is finalized and your child is in the United States. (For more information on applying for a Social Security number for your child, see pages 45 through 48 of Chapter 2.)

The Adoption Tax Credit

What is the adoption tax credit?

The adoption tax credit allows eligible parents to claim a dollar-for-dollar reduction in their tax liability for adoption-related expenses, including adoption agency fees, court costs, attorney's fees, travel expenses, and other adoption-related costs.

How much is the adoption tax credit worth?

In 2015, the adoption tax credit was $13,400 per adoption.

Do I qualify for the adoption tax credit?

You can only claim the full adoption tax credit if your modified adjusted gross income (MAGI) falls below certain limits. In 2015, the full adoption tax credit was only available to taxpayers with a MAGI of less than $201,010.

The adoption credit is phased out for higher-income earners. In 2015, taxpayers with a MAGI of more than $241,010 were ineligible to claim the adoption tax credit.

To determine your MAGI for purposes of claiming the adoption tax credit and to learn more about the phase out of the adoption tax credit, check the instructions for Form 8839, available at irs.gov.

I am subject to the alternative minimum tax (AMT). Can I still claim the adoption tax credit?

Yes. Unlike many other tax credits and deductions, the adoption tax credit is available to taxpayers subject to the AMT.

My adoption-related expenses are less than the adoption tax credit. Can I still claim the adoption tax credit?

Yes, but you can only claim a tax credit for your actual out-of-pocket adoption-related expenses. For example, let's suppose you spent $10,000 in 2015 on a domestic adoption finalized that same year. Let's further suppose that you were eligible to claim the full amount of the adoption tax credit. Because you incurred only $10,000 in adoption-related expenses, you would only have been able to claim an adoption tax credit of $10,000, not $13,400.

> *An exception applies if you adopt a special needs child.* In that case, you can claim the full amount of the adoption tax credit even if you did not have any adoption-related expenses. (See page 240 below for more details.)

I am planning on adopting two children. Can I claim the adoption tax credit for both adoptions?
Yes. The adoption tax credit applies per child, not per family.

My employer has reimbursed me for some of my adoption-related expenses. Can I still claim the adoption tax credit?
Yes, but you must subtract the amount of your employer-provided adoption assistance from your adoption-related expenses when determining your adoption tax credit.

For example, let's suppose that you were eligible to claim the full amount of the adoption tax credit in 2015. Let's further suppose that you spent $15,000 on adoption-related expenses for an adoption that was finalized that same year. If your employer provided you with $7,000 in adoption assistance, then you would only have been able to claim an adoption tax credit for $8,000.

When can I claim the adoption tax credit?
It depends on whether your adoption is domestic or international and whether the adoption is finalized. For domestic adoptions, you can claim the adoption tax credit in the year after you incur the expenses if the adoption is not yet finalized. Alternatively, you can claim the adoption tax credit in the same year you incur the expenses if your domestic adoption is finalized.

For international adoptions, you can only claim the adoption tax credit once your adoption is finalized.

Can I claim part of the adoption tax credit in one tax year and the rest in a different tax year?
For domestic adoptions, you can claim the adoption tax credit piecemeal over two different tax years—the year after you incur the expenses when the adoption is not yet final, and the year the adoption is finalized. Your total adoption tax credit in both years cannot exceed the limit, however.

For international adoptions, you must claim the entire adoption tax credit in the year that your adoption is finalized.

Can I claim the adoption tax credit for adoption-related expenses I incurred in previous years?
Yes. Let's suppose, for example, that you began the international adoption process in 2013. Let's further suppose that you incurred $5,000 in expenses in 2013, another $5,000 in expenses in 2014, and $4,000 in expenses in 2015, when the adoption was finalized. Assuming you met the income-based eligibility requirements, you would have been able to claim an adoption tax credit of $13,400 in 2015, even though you only incurred $4,000 in adoption-related expenses that year because you incurred a total of $14,000 in expenses in connection with that international adoption.

Is the adoption tax credit refundable?
No. If your total tax liability is less than the amount of the adoption tax credit, you will not receive a tax refund for the difference.

If my adoption is unsuccessful, can I still claim the adoption tax credit?
You can claim the adoption tax credit for an unsuccessful domestic adoption, but not for an unsuccessful international adoption.

Claiming the adoption tax credit for an unsuccessful domestic adoption counts against the adoption tax credit you may claim if you later successfully adopt a child in a domestic adoption. Check the instructions for Form 8839, available at irs.gov, for more details.

I am adopting a special needs child. Can I claim the adoption tax credit even if I do not incur any adoption-related expenses?

Yes, as long as the adoption is domestic and your state's adoption agency has specifically designated the child you are adopting as a special needs child.

A child may be considered to have special needs for adoption purposes even if the child does not have a physical or mental disability. What matters for purposes of a special needs designation is whether a state agency determines that the child is difficult to place for adoption. Criteria states use in making this assessment include the child's age, the child's race or ethnicity, and whether the child must be adopted together with one or more siblings.

How do I claim the adoption tax credit?

You will need to complete IRS Form 8839, available at irs.gov, and submit it along with your tax return. Enter the amount on line 16 of Form 8839 on line 54 of your Form 1040, or line 51 of your Form 1040NR.

> A B C *You don't have to submit your adoption documentation with your tax return.* However, you should keep records and receipts of your adoption-related expenses, in case of an audit.

Tax Exclusion for Employer-Provided Adoption Assistance

How does the exclusion for employer-provided adoption assistance work?

Provided you meet the eligibility requirements, you will not have to pay federal income taxes on any employer-provided adoption assistance you receive. However, you will still have to pay Social Security and Medicare taxes on that amount.

How much is the exclusion for employer-provided adoption assistance worth?

In 2015, you could claim a maximum exclusion of $13,400 per adoption.

Do I qualify for the tax exclusion for employer-provided adoption assistance?

You can only claim the full tax exclusion for employer-provided adoption assistance if your modified adjusted gross income (MAGI) falls below certain limits. In 2015, the full exclusion was only available to taxpayers with a MAGI of less than $201,010.

The exclusion for employer-provided adoption assistance is phased out for higher-income earners. In 2015, taxpayers with a modified adjusted gross income of more than $241,010 were ineligible to claim the exclusion.

> *To determine your MAGI for purposes of claiming the adoption tax credit and to learn more about the phase out of the adoption tax credit, check the instructions for* Form 8839, available at irs.gov.

I am subject to the alternative minimum tax (AMT). Can I still claim the tax exclusion for employer-provided adoption assistance?

Yes. Unlike many other tax credits and deductions, the exclusion for employer-provided adoption assistance is available to taxpayers subject to the AMT.

My adoption-related expenses are less than the amount of my employer-provided adoption assistance. Can I still claim an exclusion for my employer-provided adoption assistance?

Yes, but you can only claim an exclusion up to the amount of your actual out-of-pocket adoption-related expenses. For example, let's suppose you spent $5,000 in 2015 for a domestic adoption finalized that same year. Let's further suppose that your employer provided you with $7,000 in adoption assistance and you were eligible to claim the full amount of the exclusion for employer-provided adoption assistance. Because you incurred only $5,000 in adoption-related expenses, you would only have been able to claim an exclusion for $5,000 in employer-provided adoption assistance—even though your employer provided you with $7,000 in assistance.

An exception applies if you adopt a special needs child. In that case, you can claim the full amount of the exclusion for employer-provided adoption assistance even if you do not have any adoption-related expenses. (See page 240 above for more details.)

If I claim the exclusion for employer-provided adoption assistance, can I still claim the adoption tax credit?

Yes, but you must subtract the amount of your employer-provided adoption assistance from your adoption-related expenses when determining your adoption tax credit.

For example, let's suppose that you were eligible to claim the full amount of the adoption tax credit in 2015. Let's further suppose that you spent $18,000 on adoption-related expenses for an adoption that was finalized that same year. If your employer provided you with $7,000 in adoption assistance, then you would only have been able to claim an adoption tax credit for $11,000.

When can I claim the exclusion for employer-provided adoption assistance?

It depends on whether your adoption is domestic or international and whether the adoption is finalized. For domestic adoptions, you can claim the exclusion in the year after you incur the expenses if the adoption is not yet finalized. Alternatively, you can claim the exclusion in the same year you incur the expenses if your domestic adoption is finalized.

For international adoptions, you can only claim the exclusion once your adoption is finalized.

You could incur higher-than-expected tax liability if you receive adoption assistance from your employer in a year in which you are not eligible to claim the exclusion. Let's suppose, for example, that your employer provided you with $5,000 in adoption assistance in 2014 for an international adoption that was not finalized until 2015. You would have had to pay taxes on your employer-provided adoption assistance in 2014; however, you could have claimed the exclusion for that assistance in 2015, when the adoption was finalized.

If my adoption is unsuccessful, can I still claim the exclusion for employer-provided adoption assistance?
You can claim the exclusion for an unsuccessful domestic adoption, but not for an unsuccessful international adoption.

How do I claim the exclusion for employer-provided adoption assistance?
You will need to complete IRS Form 8839, available at irs.gov, and submit it along with your tax return. Enter the amount on line 29 of Form 8839 on line 7 of your Form 1040, or line 8 of your Form 1040NR.

A B C *You don't have to submit your adoption documentation with your tax return.* However, you should keep records and receipts of your adoption-related expenses in case of an audit.

Tax Breaks for Single Parents

If you are a self-supporting single parent, you may be eligible to lower your tax bill by filing your taxes as "head of household" rather than as a single taxpayer.

How can I benefit by filing my taxes using the head of household filing status instead of filing as a single taxpayer?
Filing as head of household generally entitles you to pay a lower

tax rate, and also allows you to claim a higher standard deduction. (A standard deduction is the amount you can subtract from your adjusted gross income when determining your taxable income. The higher your standard deduction, the lower your tax bill.) In 2015, the standard deduction for a single taxpayer was $6,300, while the standard deduction for a taxpayer filing as head of household was $9,250.

Do I qualify to file as head of household?
You can file your taxes as head of household if you meet *all* of the following requirements:

- You are not married *or* you are married but your spouse did not live with you for the last six months of the year.
- You paid more than half the cost of keeping up your home during the year. Home-keeping expenses include the mortgage or rent, utility charges, and grocery bills.
- Your child lived with you for more than half the year.

My spouse was away on business for more than half the year. Do I qualify to file as head of household?
No. You cannot file as head of household if your spouse was only temporarily absent from your home because of a special circumstance, like serving military duty or attending a graduate program in a different state.

My baby was born in October. Can I still file as head of household?
Yes. If your baby was born at any time during the tax year, you may file as head of household.

You cannot file as head of household if your baby did not live with you for more than half of the time after your baby was born. Suppose, for example, that your baby was born in October, but only began living with you in December. You would not be able to file as head of household because your baby did not live with you for more than half of the time that your baby was alive in the tax year.

My child has a large trust fund that I use to pay most of the cost of keeping up our home. Can I still file as head of household?
No. You cannot file as head of household if your child provides more than half of his or her own support.

I receive child support payments. Can I still file as head of household?
If the child support payments cover more than half the cost of keeping up your home during the year, then you cannot file as head of household.

I am divorced, but my ex-spouse claims the dependent exemption pursuant to the terms of our divorce settlement. Can I still file as head of household if I am the custodial parent?
Yes, as long as you meet the requirements for filing as head of household. For purposes of filing as head of household, it does not matter who claims the dependent exemption. What matters is who actually lives with the child and provides more than half the cost of providing a home for the child.

For more information on filing as head of household, turn to IRS Publication 501 entitled "Exemptions, Standard Deduction, and Filing Information," available at irs.gov.

Tax Breaks for Low-Income Parents

If your income falls below certain limits, you may be eligible for a significant dollar-for-dollar reduction in your tax liability through the earned income tax credit.

How much is the earned income tax credit worth?
The amount you can claim as a tax credit depends on your adjusted gross income and the number of children you have. In 2014, a married couple with three children and an adjusted gross income of $35,150 could have qualified for a tax credit of $3,633.

Am I eligible for the earned income tax credit?

Your eligibility depends on your adjusted gross income and the number of children you have, among other requirements. In 2014, a married couple with one child could have claimed the earned income credit if their adjusted gross income was less than $43,941, and a married couple with three children could have claimed the earned income tax credit if their adjusted gross income was less than $52,427.

You can only claim the earned income credit if you earned income during the year. If you did not earn any income from working during the year, then you are not eligible for the earned income credit.

I earned income during the year from dividends and rental income. Do I qualify for the earned income credit?

To qualify for the earned income credit, you cannot have more than a nominal amount in investment income, such as rental income or dividends. In 2014, you would not have qualified for the earned income credit if you had more than $3,350 in investment income.

I am a single parent. Can I claim the earned income credit?

Yes. However, the income limits are lower for single parents than for married couples filing jointly.

The amount of my earned income credit is more than my tax liability for the year. Will I receive a refund of the difference?

Yes. The earned income credit is a refundable credit. This means that if your total tax liability for the year is less than your earned income credit, the government will send you a check for the difference.

To find out whether you qualify for the earned income credit and to figure out the amount of your credit, turn to IRS Publication 596 entitled "Earned Income Credit (EIC)," available at irs.gov.

For More Information

If you want to learn more about tax breaks that could help your family, a useful resource is kiplinger.com. Just click on "Taxes" in the menu bar at the top of the page. Another helpful website is turbotax.intuit.com. Click on the link marked "Tools & Tips" in the menu bar at the top of the page. Of course, you can always go straight to the IRS's website (irs.gov) to get the most up-to-date tax information.

CHAPTER 7

Wills and Estate Planning

IT'S far from easy to consider the possibility that you might die while your child is still very young. Just the thought of missing important milestones, like the first day of kindergarten or high school graduation, keeps many new parents from even beginning the process of preparing a will. But as a parent, one of your most important responsibilities is making sure that your child will always be well cared for, no matter what unpleasant surprises life has in store.

In this chapter, we'll give you the information you need to make important decisions about the care of your child and the management of your child's assets in the event that both you and your child's other parent die while your child is still young. We discuss:

- *Why you need a will.* We'll explain what might happen to your child and your assets if you die without a will.
- *How to choose a guardian for your child.* We'll guide you through the process of selecting a trusted person who can raise your child if you and your child's other parent both die while your child is still young.
- *How to leave assets to your child in your will.* We'll tell you why

you need to name a financial guardian for your child's assets and help you determine whether you should place your child's assets in a custodial account or a trust.

- *The nuts and bolts of preparing a will.* We'll cover the basic requirements for a legally valid will and help you decide whether you need a lawyer to prepare your will.
- *Estate tax basics.* We'll give you a quick overview of the rules governing estate and inheritance taxes.

Many thanks to trusts and estates experts Denis Clifford and Dr. Stephen Maple for reviewing this chapter. Denis Clifford practices trusts and estates law in Berkeley, California. He is the author of several books on wills and estate planning, including *Estate Planning Basics* (Nolo, 2013) and *Plan Your Estate* (Nolo, 2014). Dr. Stephen Maple is a trusts and estates attorney who is now on the faculty at the University of Indianapolis School of Business. He is the author of *The Complete Idiot's Guide to Wills and Estates* (Alpha, 2009).

Why Do You Need a Will?

If you're like many new parents, you may not know exactly what a will is and why you need one. Here we'll help you understand what a will can do for your family. We'll also tell you what will happen if you die without a will.

What is a will?

A will is a legal document that sets forth your final wishes with respect to the disposition of your assets and the care of your children. For parents, a will serves two very important purposes. First, a will allows you to name a *guardian* for your child in the event that both you and your child's other parent die. A guardian is someone who will take care of and raise your child, and assume legal responsibility for your child, if both parents die while your child is still a minor.

Second, a will lets you leave instructions for how you want your assets to be distributed after you die. If you leave any of your assets to your child, you need to name a financial guardian in your will to manage the assets on your child's behalf until your child is old enough to do so. You can also use a will to set up a management structure for your child's assets. For example, you can establish a trust for your child in your will or direct that your child's inheritance be placed in a custodial account for your child's benefit.

> *Wills are not just for wealthy families!* If you are a parent, you need a will—regardless of how much (or how little) you have in the bank.

Who will have custody of my child if I die without a will?
It depends on whether one parent dies or both parents die.

If you die but your child's other parent is still alive, then your child's other parent will automatically have sole custody of your child. Your child will live with the surviving parent and that parent will have complete and exclusive rights to make all decisions concerning the care and upbringing of your child.

> *If your child's other parent is uninvolved in your child's life or unfit to raise your child, then a court will not necessarily give your child's other parent custody of your child in the event of your death.* It is especially important in this situation to have a will in place naming a guardian for your child. You should also include a letter with your will explaining to the court why you believe that your child's other parent should not obtain custody of your child in the event of your death. Speak to an experienced trusts and estates attorney for more information. You may also want to consult with a family law attorney.

If both you and your child's other parent die without wills, then a court will choose a guardian for your child. The court will have complete discretion to name any individual the court deems most appropriate to serve as your child's guardian. The court does not have to appoint a relative as a child's guardian. Depending on the circumstances, the court could select a willing friend or neighbor to serve as your child's guardian.

> *Your family members may disagree on who should have guardianship of your child.* Even if both sides of the family get along perfectly now, death and loss can cause emotions to flare. Relatives from both sides of the family might seek to obtain custody of your child, resulting in a legal dispute with your child caught in the middle. Protect your child by preparing a will that clearly establishes who should have guardianship of your child in the event of your death.

My sister has already agreed to serve as my child's guardian in the event of my death. Do I still need a will naming a guardian for my child?

Absolutely. Even if a relative has agreed to assume guardianship of your child in the event of your death, courts place very little weight (if any) on these types of informal agreements. The only way to ensure that a court will consider your choice of guardian is by naming a guardian in your will.

What will happen to my money, my property, and my other assets if I die without a will?

It depends on the types of assets you own. You might be surprised to learn that a will does not control the distribution of all of your property. Contract law—rather than estate law—determines who receives certain types of assets, including:

- *Joint banking and brokerage accounts.* The assets in a joint banking or brokerage account will pass to your joint account owner in the event of your death. If you have a joint account with your spouse, and your spouse is still alive when you die, your spouse will automatically acquire sole and complete ownership of all of the funds in that account.
- *Real estate you own in joint tenancy.* Property held in joint tenancy will pass to your co-owner in the event of your death. If you and

your spouse own a home together, and both names are on the deed to the property, then your spouse will automatically obtain sole and complete ownership of your home when you die.

- *Retirement accounts, such as 401(k) plans or IRAs.* The funds in your retirement accounts will be distributed to the person you named as the beneficiary of those accounts. If you have a 401(k) plan and you are married, your spouse will be the beneficiary of that account unless your spouse signed a written waiver that is on file with your plan administrator at the time of your death.
- *Life insurance proceeds.* The proceeds of your life insurance policy will be paid to the person you named as the beneficiary of the policy.
- *Funds in a payable-on-death account.* If you have a bank or brokerage account with a pay-on-death designation, then the funds in that account will be distributed in accordance with your pay-on-death designation when you die.
- *Real estate with a transfer-on-death designation.* If you have real estate with a transfer-on-death designation, then that property will be distributed in accordance with your transfer-on-death designation when you die.
- *Assets held in a living trust.* If you established a trust during your lifetime, those assets will remain in trust for the benefit of your designated beneficiaries after your death.

All of your remaining assets will be distributed according to the intestate succession laws of your state. These laws determine who inherits property when there is no will in place. While the intestate succession laws vary from state to state, the intestate succession laws generally provide that your assets will go to your spouse (if you have one) and to your children in the event of your death.

Property you own as a "tenant in common" with someone else will be distributed according to your state's intestate succession laws if you die without a will. Unlike a joint tenant, a tenant in common does not have survivorship rights. For example, let's suppose that you and your brother own a home together as tenants in common. If you were to die without a will, your half of that home would not automatically pass to your brother. Rather, your half of the home would be distributed according to your state's intestate succession laws.

If I die without a will, who will be responsible for managing my child's inheritance?

It depends on whether one parent dies or both parents die.

If you die but your child's other parent is still alive, then your child's other parent will be responsible for managing your child's inheritance.

If both you and your child's other parent die without wills, then a court will appoint an adult to serve as your child's *property guardian.* Your child's property guardian will manage your child's assets until your child reaches the age of majority in your state (in most states, the age of majority is eighteen).

A B C *Under state law, a minor child may not own more than a nominal amount of assets or property in his or her own name.* A child's property must be held in the care of an adult until the child reaches the age of majority under state law.

The court does not have to appoint a relative or a family friend to serve as your child's property guardian. In fact, the court may appoint a complete stranger to serve in this role. A court-appointed property guardian may be completely unfamiliar with your preferences as to how you would like your child's assets to be invested and spent on your child's behalf. Moreover, if the court appoints a financial professional rather than a friend or family member to serve as your child's property guardian, then your child may have to pay annual management and/or administrative fees that will cut into the value of your child's assets. Finally, the court will retain supervisory authority over the management of your child's assets. Your child's property guardian will have to report to the court and may need court approval to make decisions such as selling or investing your child's assets.

The court may appoint one person to serve as your child's legal guardian and another person to serve as your child's property guardian. Depending on the circumstances, a court may decide that it is in your child's best interests to have someone other than your child's legal guardian serve as your child's property guardian. This can add one more layer of complexity to the care and upbringing of your child in the event of your death.

What will happen to my child's inheritance when my child turns eighteen if both parents die without wills?

If both you and your child's other parent die without wills, your child may be able to obtain full access to and control over his or her inheritance once he or she reaches the age of majority in your state (eighteen in most states). Ask yourself whether you think your child will be ready to handle complete financial responsibility at that early age. Will your child be mature enough to make smart financial decisions? Are you confident that your child will use the money wisely to pay for smart investments, like a college education? What will happen if your child squanders the funds rather than saving for the future?

If you want some control over when and how your child can access his or her inheritance, you may want to consider creating a custodial account under the Uniform Transfers to Minors Act (UTMA) or a trust for your child in your will. (To learn more about these options, see pages 272 through 275 below.)

I'm ready to begin the process of creating a will. Where should I start?

Before you can turn to the nuts and bolts of preparing a will, you will first need to make some important decisions. You must:

- choose a guardian for your child,
- decide how you would like your assets to be distributed after your death,
- determine what kind of management structure you would like to use for your child's assets, and

- select a financial guardian to manage your child's assets.

You can find guidance on making each of these decisions in the pages that follow.

Choosing a Guardian for Your Child

Deciding who should care for your child in the event of your death is a purely personal decision. Only you can determine who would be best suited to take your place as your child's caregiver. For many parents, the natural choice is a sibling with similar values. Other parents opt to name a grandparent as the guardian, and some choose to name a close friend. Here we'll answer some of the questions you may have on selecting a guardian and help guide you on making this important decision.

Should I name my child's other parent as my child's guardian?
No. If you die while your child's other parent is still alive, then your child's other parent will in most cases automatically obtain custody of your child. A court will usually only appoint a guardian for your child if both you and your child's other parent die while your child is still a minor.

Only a child's legal parent is entitled to automatic custody in the event of the other parent's death. A stepparent, or the domestic partner of a child's parent, might not be considered the child's parent in the eyes of the law. If your child's other parent is not your child's legal parent, you should consult with an attorney about how to ensure that your child's other parent will have custody of your child in the event of your death.

If your child's other parent is either uninvolved in your child's life or unfit to raise your child, then a court may choose to appoint a guardian for your child (rather than awarding custody to your child's other parent) in the event of your death. Speak to an experienced trusts and estates attorney if this situation applies to you.

If I name a guardian for my child in my will, does a court have to approve my decision?

Yes. A court will determine whether it is in your child's best interests to appoint the guardian you selected. As a practical matter, the court will almost certainly respect your wishes unless there is some glaring problem with your choice. For example, if your chosen guardian has been convicted of a felony or is addicted to drugs, then the court will likely name someone else to serve as your child's guardian. Aside from such extreme circumstances, however, you can generally rest assured that a court will honor your choice of guardian.

What factors should I consider when choosing a guardian for my child?

There are many different factors you might want to consider when selecting a guardian for your child. Here are a few questions you should ask yourself:

- *Whom do you trust the most to step in and serve as a parent to your child?* At the end of the day, this really is the key consideration in naming a guardian.
- *Whose values and parenting style best mesh with your own?* While no two people see eye to eye on every important issue, like education and religion, it's best to name a guardian who shares as many of your values as possible.
- *Who would have the time and energy to care for and raise your child?* For example, you may have a sister who would do anything in the world for your child. But if she has a demanding job that entails long hours and international travel, then your sister might not be the best choice to serve as your child's guardian.
- *How old is the person you have in mind?* If you are considering naming your child's grandparent as guardian, for example, think about whether your child's grandparent might be too old to han-

dle the demands of child rearing over the next couple of decades. Even if your child's grandparent is young and healthy right now, much can change in the span of several years.

- *Does the person you are considering have children of his or her own? Would your child fit well into that person's family?* You may want to think about whether it would be burdensome or difficult for the person you have in mind to raise your child in addition to his or her own children. If you have a brother with two-year-old triplets, for example, it might be hard for him to give your child adequate love and attention.
- *Where does the person you are considering live? Would your child have to move far away from your home and your community?* If you die when your child is a baby or toddler, you don't have to worry too much about the consequences of uprooting your child. But if your child is older and already enrolled in school at the time of your death, then it might be difficult for your child to lose ties to friends and a familiar community.

After thinking it over, you will probably come to the realization that there is no "perfect" person who could step into your shoes and raise your child exactly the way you would. Chances are that there are pros and cons for every person on your list of potential guardians. Ultimately, you'll just have to trust your gut and make the best choice you can. It is far better to name a less-than-perfect guardian in your will than to leave the decision up to a judge.

Do I have to choose a relative as my child's guardian?

No. You can name anyone you feel would be best suited to care for your child in the event of your death. Having said that, most parents do choose a family member—such as an aunt, uncle, or a grandparent—to serve as their child's guardian.

If you name a friend rather than a family member as your child's guardian, consider explaining your decision to your close relatives. To avoid leaving a legacy of hurt feelings, it may be wise to discuss your decision up front with your family members. Otherwise, they may feel slighted and distance themselves from your child in the event of your death. Another option is to leave a letter behind explaining why you chose to leave your child in the care of a friend instead of a family member. A carefully crafted letter of explanation can smooth over possible hurt feelings and help to protect your choice of guardian if your close relatives contest your decision.

Can I name a couple to serve together as my child's guardians?
You are legally permitted to name a couple (like your parents, for example) to serve together as your child's guardians. However, you may want to think twice before doing so. First, there is the possibility that the couple might divorce while they have guardianship of your child. In that case, a court may have to step in to decide which of the two will retain custody of your child. Second, you should think about what might happen if one person in the couple dies. If only one person in the couple is your blood relative, and that person passes away, would you want the other person to raise your child? Finally, having just one guardian (rather than two) can be easier because you won't have to worry about the possibility of differences of opinion on child-rearing issues.

Should I choose a guardian who has the financial know-how to manage my child's inheritance?
While financial savviness is one factor you may wish to consider when naming a guardian, you don't have to name the same person to serve as both your child's legal guardian and your child's financial guardian. For example, if your sister is an accomplished accountant with an uncanny knack for numbers but your brother is a schoolteacher who is terrific with kids, it may make sense to name your brother as your child's guardian and your sister as the manager of your child's inheritance.

Should I name a backup guardian, just in case?
You should definitely name an alternate guardian who can assume

responsibility for your child just in case your first choice is unable or unwilling to serve as your child's guardian in the event of your death. The alternate guardian can also step in to care for your child if your child's guardian becomes injured or ill after he or she has assumed custody of your child.

Do I need to ask permission before naming someone as my child's guardian in my will?

Yes. You should have a frank conversation to make sure that the person you plan to name as your child's guardian would be willing to raise your child in the event of your death. You should also speak to the person you plan to name as your child's alternate guardian.

The guardian you name in your will is not legally required to assume responsibility of your child in the event of your death. He or she can choose to accept or decline the role.

If the person you plan to name as your child's guardian is married, obtain permission from his or her spouse as well. Guardianship is a big responsibility that dramatically changes the lives of everyone in the guardian's family. Check to make sure that your chosen guardian's spouse would be willing to welcome your child into their family in the event of your death.

I have two children. Can I name two separate guardians, one for each child?

Although you can name separate guardians for each child in your will, a court may not be willing to enforce a divided custody arrangement in the event of your death. Courts are generally reluctant to separate siblings unless there is a very good reason for doing so. Before naming different guardians for each child, ask yourself whether it wouldn't be better to have your children grow up in the same household. If you are not there to raise your children, at least they will have one another's companionship and support as they grow up.

I have two children from different marriages. They are far apart in age, and they each have strong relationships with different family members. Can I name two separate guardians, one for each child?
Yes. You clearly have good reasons for believing that naming different guardians for each child would be in your children's best interests. Given the circumstances, you should consider preparing a detailed letter explaining your rationale for naming different guardians for each of your children. Keep the letter with your will. The court can then take your views into account when appointing guardians for your children.

Can I provide for a change in guardianship after a certain number of years?
Sometimes, parents think it might be a good idea for a grandparent to serve as a child's guardian for a set number of years, and then to have an aunt or uncle take over guardianship when the child's grandparent becomes too old to handle the responsibilities of day-to-day child care. While this seems like a smart option in theory, the reality is that stability will be more important than anything else if you die while your child is still young. Setting up a guardianship structure in which your child would eventually have to switch homes, and possibly even schools, is probably not in your child's best interests. What's more, a court may be unlikely to approve a change in guardianship several years after your child has settled down.

What happens if my child's other parent and I cannot agree on a guardian?
Parents often disagree as to who should serve as their child's guardian. Each person typically prefers a relative on his or her own side of the family. Instead of resolving the issue, many parents end up deciding not to decide. They simply don't name a guardian and just cross their fingers and hope that they both stay healthy and live long lives.

The better option, by far, is for one parent to "give in" on the issue. In most cases, it is vastly preferable to name someone from the other side of the family as your child's guardian instead of leaving the guardianship decision in a court's hands. Just think of it as one in a long line of sacrifices you will have to make for your child's benefit.

Don't name different guardians in your wills! If you and your child's other parent cannot agree on a guardian, it might seem like a good idea to name different guardians in your wills. When faced with inconsistent wills, however, a court will have to choose your child's guardian. What's more, there could be a legal dispute between the guardians named in the two wills—the last thing you would want for your child in the event of your death.

If you and your child's other parent cannot come to a resolution on the guardianship issue, a possible "win-win" solution is to name one parent's choice as your child's guardian and the other parent's choice as your child's alternate guardian.

My child's other parent is completely uninvolved in my child's life. Is there anything I can do to prevent my child's other parent from obtaining custody in the event of my death?

It is very difficult to prevent a child's legal parent from obtaining custody if the other parent dies. Unless your child's other parent is truly unfit to care for your child, a court will almost certainly award custody to your child's other parent in the event of your death.

If you are concerned that it would be harmful for your child to live with his or her other parent, then it is especially important in this situation to have a will in place naming a guardian for your child. You should also include a letter with your will explaining to the court why you believe that your child's other parent should not obtain custody of your child in the event of your death. Speak to an experienced trusts and estates attorney for more information. You may also want to consult with a family law attorney to explore your options.

Can I place any rules or restrictions on my child's guardian? For example, can I require my child's guardian to take my child to religious school every Sunday?

No. Your child's guardian will have complete discretion to make all decisions with respect to your child. This is why it is so important to choose someone whose values align closely with your own.

> *Consider writing a letter to your guardian or preparing a video discussing how you wish your child to be raised.* If there are issues that are particularly important to you, like ensuring that your child maintains regular contact with the other side of the family, then you may want to communicate those wishes to your child's guardian through a letter or video. Be sure to keep a copy of the letter, or instructions for finding your video, in the same place as your will.

What happens if I change my mind down the line? Can I amend my will to name a different guardian?

Yes. You can change your will at any time to name a different guardian for your child. Just remember that you will need to fulfill all the requirements for legally changing your will. (For more information on changing your will, see pages 287 through 288 below.)

> *Reevaluate your guardianship decision every couple of years.* It's a smart idea to revisit the question of who should serve as your child's guardian from time to time because relationships and circumstances can change over the years. The person you select as your child's guardian today might not be the ideal candidate five or ten years from now.

Deciding Who Should Inherit Your Assets

Once you have made the difficult decision of who should serve as your child's guardian, you can then turn to the question of who should inherit your assets in the event of your death. For most new parents, this is a fairly straightforward decision. If you are married to or in a committed relationship with your child's other parent, then it probably makes sense to leave most or all of your assets to your spouse or partner and to name your child as the contingent beneficiary under your will. This way, your child will only inherit your assets if both you and your child's other parent die.

For some parents, particularly those with substantial resources, the question of who should inherit which assets is more complicated. If you are married to someone who is not your child's other parent, for example, then you will probably want to leave at least some of your assets directly to your child. If you are a single parent, then you may choose to leave all of your assets to your child. In addition, you may have other goals or obligations, like providing for aging parents or contributing to a charity. Here we'll help you think about how you should divide and distribute your assets in the event of your death.

Do I have to leave some or all of my assets to my child?

No. You might be surprised to learn that you are not legally required to leave any part of your estate to your child. In many cases, it makes more sense to leave assets to your child's other parent, who can then use those assets to care for and raise your child if you die.

I am married to my child's other parent. Can I leave all of my assets to my spouse?

Yes. In fact, this is what most people in your situation do. You can name your child as the contingent beneficiary of your estate, which means that your child will inherit your assets if your spouse dies.

Complications can arise if yours is a blended family. If you or your spouse have children from a prior relationship, then it may not make sense to leave all of your assets to your spouse in the event of your death. You may want to leave some of your assets to your spouse and leave other assets to your children from a prior relationship, or you might want to place all of your assets in trust, for the benefit of your spouse during your spouse's lifetime and then for the benefit of your children after your spouse dies. Because of the complexities involved with estate planning for blended families, you should consult with an experienced trusts and estates attorney for guidance on how to structure your estate.

I am in a committed relationship with my child's other parent. Can I leave all of my assets to my partner?
Yes. You can leave all of your assets to your partner. You can also name your child as the contingent beneficiary of your assets, which means that your child will inherit your assets if your partner dies.

My spouse is not very good at managing money. Does it make sense to leave all of my assets to my spouse?
If you are worried that your spouse will make poor spending or investment decisions, then you may want to consider establishing a trust in your will for the benefit of your spouse instead of leaving your assets to your spouse outright. You can choose a trustee to give your spouse a limited monthly spending allowance, and can manage the assets on your spouse's behalf. After your spouse dies, you can provide that the assets in the trust will go to your child. If you are interested in setting up this type of trust in your will, you will need to consult with an experienced trusts and estates attorney.

I am a single parent. Can I leave all of my assets to my child?
Yes. Just remember that you will need to appoint a financial guardian to manage your child's assets. You should also set up a management structure (a custodial account or trust) to hold your child's assets. (See pages 271 through 272 below for more details.)

I am married, but my spouse is not my child's other parent. Can I leave all of my assets to my spouse?
You can leave all of your assets to your spouse, but you may want to think twice before doing so. Your spouse will have no legal obligation to leave those assets to your child when he or she dies. Remember

that your spouse could remarry and build a new family. In the event of his or her death, your assets could pass to members of that new family instead of going to your child. The safest course of action in this type of situation is to leave your assets in trust. The assets in the trust could be used for the benefit of your spouse while your spouse is alive, and the assets could then pass to your child after your spouse's death. Speak to an experienced trusts and estates attorney for more information.

A useful resource on these issues is Estate Planning for Blended Families: Providing for Your Spouse & Children in a Blended Marriage by Richard E. Barnes (Nolo, 2009).

I am married, but I would like to leave all of my assets to my child. Is this legal?

As a general rule, you cannot completely disinherit your spouse unless your spouse voluntarily agrees to waive his or her share of your assets, either before marriage in a prenuptial agreement or after marriage through a postnuptial agreement. If you live in a community property state, your spouse legally owns half of all assets acquired by either you or your spouse during your marriage. (The community property states are Arizona, California, Idaho, Louisiana, Nevada, New Mexico, Texas, Washington, and Wisconsin.) If you live in any other state, your spouse is generally entitled to a certain portion of your assets (typically half of what you own) in the event of your death. This amount is known as your spouse's *elective share* of your estate.

If you wish to leave all of your assets to your child rather than your spouse, you will need to speak with an experienced trusts and estates attorney. You may also need to consult with a family lawyer experienced in drafting postnuptial agreements.

I have three children. Can I leave all of my assets to be shared among my children, or do I have to divide up my assets?

You can leave your assets to your children collectively by setting up a family "pot trust." With a pot trust, your children's financial guardian (the trustee) can use your assets as he or she sees fit for the benefit of all of your children. It is entirely possible that your children will have different financial needs. One child might decide to attend medical school, for example, while another child might decide to skip college and start a business. A pot trust allows a financial guardian to use his or her discretion to make unequal distributions to your children as needed, just the same way that a parent would.

You can provide that the pot trust will ultimately be terminated and the assets divided equally among your children once certain milestones have been met. For example, you may have the pot trust end once your youngest child reaches age twenty-five, or after your youngest child graduates from college.

I have two children. Do I have to leave them equal shares of my property?

No. It is perfectly legal to leave your children unequal shares of your assets, and there are sometimes good reasons for doing so. For example, if one of your children is disabled and will need financial support for the rest of his or her life, you may wish to leave a much larger portion of your estate to your disabled child in the form of a special needs trust.

Do I have to leave all of my assets to my spouse and my child? Or can I leave some of my assets to other beneficiaries, like my parents or my favorite charity?

As long as you provide your spouse with the legally required portion of your assets (see page 265 above), you can dispose of the rest of your assets however you see fit. It is perfectly legal to leave the bulk of your assets to your spouse and the remainder of your assets to other beneficiaries of your choosing—such as your parents or your favorite charity.

Choosing a Financial Guardian for Your Child's Assets

Even if your will provides that your child will only inherit your assets if both you and your spouse die, you will still need to make arrangements for the management of your child's inheritance. You must appoint a financial guardian to handle your child's assets in case your child inherits your assets while he or she is still a minor. Here we'll help you understand how to choose a financial guardian for your child. In the section that follows, you'll learn about the different management structures you can establish for holding your child's assets.

Your child's financial guardian may be called a "custodian" or a "trustee" depending on the management structure you choose. If you set up a custodial account for your child's inheritance, then your child's financial guardian will be referred to as the "custodian" of your child's account. If you set up a trust for your child's inheritance, then your child's financial guardian will be referred to as the "trustee" of your child's trust.

Why do I need to name a financial guardian to manage my child's inheritance?

As a general rule, a minor child cannot own more than a nominal amount of property (typically nothing more than $5,000) in his or her own name, without adult supervision. If there is a possibility that your child will inherit your assets while he or she is still a minor, you must appoint a financial guardian to manage your child's assets.

Should I name a financial institution or a financial planner to serve as my child's financial guardian?

No, unless your child's inheritance is so large that an expert's services would be absolutely necessary. Banks and financial experts charge significant fees and they won't be able to make personalized decisions based on what they know about your family and your child. In most cases, you should simply name someone you trust to handle your child's assets prudently and carefully.

> *Your child's financial guardian can always hire an expert if needed.* If things get complicated, your child's financial guardian can hire a professional accountant or investment advisor to provide guidance on an as-needed basis.

Must my child's financial guardian be someone with extensive financial expertise?

No. Your child's financial guardian doesn't have to be an expert on money. All that matters is that your child's financial guardian is competent, careful, and committed to your child's best interests.

Should I name the same person as both my child's legal guardian and my child's financial guardian?

If at all possible, you should consider naming the same person as both your child's legal guardian and your child's financial guardian. This is because financial decisions and child-rearing decisions often go hand in hand. For example, your child's legal guardian might decide to send your child to an expensive but enriching summer camp, or purchase a brand new computer for your child when he or she starts high school. If your child's legal guardian is not your child's financial guardian, then your child's legal guardian will constantly need to seek permission and approval from your child's financial guardian when making these types of decisions.

Of course, there are many situations in which the ideal person to serve as your child's legal guardian might not be the right person to serve as your child's financial guardian. In that case, it's perfectly fine to name one person as your child's legal guardian and another person as your child's financial guardian. Just make sure that the two people you choose will be able to communicate effectively and work well together to advance your child's best interests.

Should I name a backup financial guardian, in case the person I name as my child's financial guardian is unable or unwilling to do the job?

Yes. As you've probably already realized, estate planning is a big exercise in "what ifs." It's a wise idea to name an alternate financial guardian just in case your first choice can't do the job for any reason.

You can name your child's backup legal guardian as your child's backup financial guardian. Keep things simple by naming the same individual as both your child's backup legal guardian and your child's backup financial guardian.

If I name a financial guardian in my will, is a court legally required to appoint the financial guardian I choose?

As a general rule, a court will appoint whomever you choose as your child's financial guardian. Courts are much less concerned with money and property than they are with the care and upbringing of young children. While a court might review your choice for your child's legal guardian, a court will almost always appoint whomever you selected in your will to serve as your child's financial guardian.

I have two children. Should I name two different financial guardians, one for each child?

Probably not, unless you have a compelling reason for doing so.

If you name different financial guardians for each child, you may make things unnecessarily complicated for your family. You also run the risk of differences of opinion on financial decisions, which could lead to your children being raised in different ways. For example, one child's financial guardian might be willing to use your child's funds to pay for academic tutors, while the other child's financial guardian might decide that tutoring is a frivolous expense. Keep it simple by naming one financial guardian for all of your children.

If you name different financial guardians for different children, then you will have divide your assets

between your children in the event of your death. What many parents opt to do instead is to create a pot trust, in which all of the assets are held in one combined trust for the benefit of all of their children. (See page 275 below for more information on pot trusts.)

Should I ask permission before naming someone as my child's financial guardian in my will?

Yes. You should make sure that the individuals you plan to name as your child's financial guardian and your child's backup financial guardian are both willing to take on the responsibility of managing your child's assets in the event of your death.

Can I place any rules or restrictions on how my child's financial guardian can spend or invest my child's assets?

It depends on the management structure you choose for your child's assets. If you decide to set up a trust for your child's benefit, then you can establish restrictions on how and when your child's financial guardian (the *trustee* of your child's trust) can spend or invest your child's assets. For example, you can specify that your child's assets may only be invested in diversified mutual funds, rather than more speculative assets. You can also limit your trustee's discretion to spend your child's assets on expenses you might consider wasteful, like international travel or private ping pong lessons.

If you opt to have your child's assets held in a custodial account under the Uniform Transfers to Minors Act (UTMA), then you won't have the same ability to limit your child's financial guardian's ability to invest and spend your child's assets. In that case, the best thing you can do is to draft a letter to your child's financial guardian detailing your wishes when it comes to the management of your child's assets. Keep a copy of the letter in the same place you keep your will.

Establishing a Management Structure for Your Child's Assets

Once you have determined who should manage your child's assets in the event of your death, you then have to decide on a management structure for your child's assets. You have three main choices.

Your first option is to use a custodial account under the Uniform Transfers to Minors Act (UTMA). A custodial account is essentially a simplified trust established under state law. (All states except South Carolina and Vermont offer UTMA custodial accounts.) With an UTMA custodial account, your child's assets will remain in trust until the age of majority under your state's UTMA law. In most states, the age of majority for UTMA purposes is twenty-one. A few states permit the age of majority to be extended to twenty-five. At that point, your child will obtain complete access to and control over his or her assets. (See Appendix D: UTMA Age of Majority by State for more information.)

Your second option is to create a trust to hold your child's assets. You can create a trust in your will (a *testamentary trust*) or you can establish a trust during your lifetime (a *living trust*). A trust gives you far greater control over the management and disposition of your child's assets than a custodial account. However, a trust is significantly more complicated to establish, and requires considerably more effort to manage than an UTMA custodial account.

Finally, you can establish a simple property guardianship in your will. If you opt for a property guardianship, then your child will obtain complete access to and control over his or her assets as soon as your child reaches the legal age of majority in your state (in most states, this is age eighteen).

You can use more than one type of management structure for your child's assets. Depending on your circumstances, you may want to place some of your child's assets in an UTMA custodial account and the remainder of your child's assets in a trust for your child.

You should always establish a property guardianship in your will for "spillover" assets. Even if you provide that your child's assets will be placed in an UTMA custodial account or a trust, you should nevertheless establish a property guardianship in your will. A property guardianship provides a management structure for any assets your child acquires from other sources (like a gift or inheritance from a relative, for example, or income from a part-time job) while your child is under age eighteen.

UTMA Custodial Accounts

What is the Uniform Transfers to Minors Act (UTMA)?

The UTMA is a law established in all but two states that allows you to transfer assets or property to a child. (Neither South Carolina nor Vermont has adopted UTMA.) Assets transferred under UTMA are held by a custodian for the benefit of the child until the child reaches the age of majority under the state's UTMA law.

Why should I consider using an UTMA account for my child's inheritance?

An UTMA account is essentially a simplified trust for your child's assets. You get many of the benefits of a trust without the legal complexities involved in establishing or managing a trust.

The UTMA custodial accounts offer tax advantages over trusts. Trust assets are taxed at a rate that applies specifically to trusts, while assets in an UTMA custodial account are taxed at individual tax rates. This often results in a lower tax rate for assets in UTMA custodial accounts as compared with assets held in trust. Moreover, there are simplified tax reporting requirements for UTMA custodial accounts as compared with trusts. You can learn more about the tax rules governing trusts in the instructions for Form 1041, the U.S. Income Tax Return for Estates and

Trusts, available at irs.gov.

What types of assets can I place in an UTMA custodial account for my child?

You can transfer just about any type of asset—from stocks in a brokerage account to real estate—to an UTMA custodial account for your child.

Who would be responsible for managing the assets in my child's UTMA custodial account?

You choose a custodian to manage the assets in your child's UTMA custodial account. If you set up an UTMA custodial account, you should appoint the person you selected as your child's financial guardian (see pages 267 through 270 above) to serve as your child's UTMA custodian.

What rights and responsibilities does an UTMA custodian have?

Your child's UTMA custodian will have very broad discretion to spend, invest, and manage your child's assets as he or she sees fit. However, your child's UTMA custodian must make prudent decisions and always act in the best interests of your child.

What happens to the assets in an UTMA custodial account once my child reaches the age of majority under my state's UTMA law?

Once your child reaches the age of majority under your state's UTMA law (twenty-one in most states, and up to twenty-five in a few states), then your child will obtain complete access to and control over the assets in his or her UTMA account. At that point, your child will be free to spend the assets however he or she wishes. A studious child might use the assets to pay for college, a more free-spirited child might decide to invest the money in a start-up yoga studio, and an impulsive child might spend all of it on designer clothes and a fancy new car.

To find out the age of majority under your state's UTMA law, check the Appendix C on page 303. Some states allow you or the custodian to designate an age of majority within a certain range. For example, in California, you may choose an age of majority between twenty-one and twenty-five.

Can I set up one UTMA custodial account for the benefit of all of my children?

No. Each child must have his or her own UTMA custodial account. If you have more than one child, you will need to divide your assets between your children in order to place those assets in UTMA custodial accounts for each child.

> *An UTMA custodial account is not a good tool for transferring shared assets, like your family home.* If you want certain assets to be held jointly for the benefit of all of your children, then you will need to use a trust rather than an UTMA custodial account.

My child may inherit more than $250,000. Should I place my child's inheritance in an UTMA custodial account?

The UTMA custodial accounts work best for modest inheritances. If your child stands to inherit less than $250,000, the custodian will probably spend down most of this amount before your child reaches the age of majority under your state's UTMA law. From orthodontics and summer camp expenses to the cost of a college education, there probably won't be much left for your child to fritter away once your child reaches the age of majority under UTMA.

For larger inheritances, however, a customized trust is a better option. With a trust, you can set limits on when and how your child can access the assets. For example, you could provide that your child will obtain access to half of the assets upon college graduation, and the remainder of the assets at age thirty-five. (See pages 275 through 278 below to learn more about trusts.)

Do all states offer UTMA custodianships?

Every state but South Carolina and Vermont offer UTMA custodianships. If you live in a state that has not adopted UTMA, then your best option is to establish a trust to hold your child's inherited assets. (See pages 275 through 278 below for more information.)

For more information on UTMA custodial accounts, including an up-to-date chart of UTMA ages of majority by state, go to the American Funds website, at americanfunds.com/advisor/products/ugma-utma.html.

Trusts

What is a trust?
A trust is a property management structure in which assets are held for the benefit of one or more individuals (the beneficiaries).

Why should I consider using a trust for my child's inheritance?
A trust allows you to make all the rules regarding how you would like your child's assets to be managed, invested, and spent on your child's behalf. For example, you can decide when and how your child will obtain access to the assets in the trust.

One of the major advantages of using a trust rather than an UTMA custodial account is that you don't necessarily have to divide your assets among your children when you die. Rather, you can place your assets in a family pot trust for the benefit of all of your children.

Aren't trusts just for rich families?
This is a common misconception. The word "trust" often makes people think of yachts and Ferraris! The reality is that a trust is just a management structure that you can easily establish in your will or during your lifetime. A trust can be a useful tool for all types of families, from the super-rich to the middle class.

Who would be responsible for managing the assets in my child's trust?
You choose a trustee to manage the assets in your child's trust. You

should appoint the person you selected as your child's financial guardian (see pages 267 through 270 above) to serve as the trustee of your child's trust.

What rights and responsibilities does a trustee have?

Your child's trustee would have the discretion to spend, invest, and manage your child's assets as he or she sees fit, subject to any restrictions you establish. For example, you could provide that your trustee may only invest your child's assets in diversified mutual funds. You could also limit your trustee's ability to sell your family home until your youngest child has graduated from college.

> *Consider including a provision allowing the trustee to use a limited amount of the assets for the benefit of your child's guardian and the guardian's family.* Raising another person's child can be logistically challenging and stressful. One way to ease the burden is by providing a limited amount of financial support for your child's guardian and his or her family. For example, you might allow the trustee to use some of the assets in your child's trust to pay for a renovation to your child's guardian's home, so that the arrival of your child does not cramp the rest of the guardian's family. Or, you might permit the trustee to pay for your guardian's family to take a couple of vacations each year (with your child in tow, of course).

When would my child have access to the assets in a trust?

That's entirely up to you. You can decide when and how your child will obtain access to and control over the assets in your trust.

Are there any disadvantages to establishing a trust rather than an UTMA custodial account?

A trust is definitely more complicated to set up than an UTMA custodial account. You will almost always need a lawyer to establish a trust for you. Leaving assets to your child in an UTMA custodial account is a more straightforward "do-it-yourself" option.

There are also potential tax disadvantages with using a trust rather than an UTMA custodial account. Trust assets are taxed at a special rate that specifically applies to trusts, while the assets in an UTMA custodial account are taxed at individual tax rates. This often results in a lower tax rate for assets in an UTMA custodial account as compared with assets held in trust.

Finally, there are simplified tax reporting requirements for UTMA custodial accounts as compared with trusts. You can learn more about the tax rules governing trusts in the instructions for Form 1041, the U.S. Income Tax Return for Estates and Trusts, available at irs.gov.

Can I set up one trust for the benefit of all of my children?

Yes. You can establish a family *pot trust* to hold your assets for the benefit of all of your children. With a pot trust, you won't have to divide your assets between your children upon your death. Rather, you can have all the assets placed into one combined trust. The trustee of a pot trust would then be able to spend the assets on your children's behalf as necessary. Depending on your children's needs, your trustee might end up spending more on one child and less on another. For example, if one child has unusually high medical expenses, the trustee might use more of the assets in the trust for that child and less for your other children.

> *Family pot trusts work especially well for shared assets, such as the family home.* Otherwise, you would either have to give your family home to just one of your children or sell your home and divide the proceeds among your children.

My child has a significant disability. Can I set up a trust to hold my child's assets for the rest of her life?

Yes. You can establish a special needs trust for the benefit of your child. One of the major advantages of using a special needs trust is that the assets in the trust will not impact your child's eligibility for government benefits, such as Medicaid and Supplemental Security Income.

You can learn more about the unique considerations involved with a child who needs lifelong financial support in Special Needs Trusts: Protect Your Child's Financial Future by Stephen Elias and Kevin Urbatsch (Nolo, 2013).

What is the difference between a "living trust" and a "testamentary trust"?

A *living trust* is a trust that you create during your lifetime. Unless you establish an irrevocable living trust, you can amend the terms of a living trust, or revoke the trust entirely, while you are still alive.

A *testamentary trust* is an irrevocable trust that you establish in your will. After you die, the terms of the trust cannot be changed. Assets that are placed in a testamentary trust cannot be released from the trust except in accordance with the terms specified in your will.

Will I need a lawyer to set up a trust?

As a general rule, it is best to retain an experienced trusts and estates attorney to establish a trust for you.

Property Guardianship

What is a property guardianship?

A property guardianship is a very basic property management structure in which a financial guardian manages any assets that belong to your child that are not in another management structure, such as an UTMA custodial account or a trust. A property guardian will be responsible for spending and investing the assets on your child's behalf until your child reaches the age of majority in your state (eighteen in most states).

Who would be responsible for managing the assets in my child's property guardianship?

You choose a property guardian to manage the assets in your child's property guardianship. You should appoint the person you selected as your child's financial guardian (see pages 267 through 270 above) to serve as the property guardian of your child's property guardianship.

What rights and responsibilities does a property guardian have?
A property guardian typically has much less discretion than the custodian of an UTMA custodial account or the trustee of a trust. Property guardians are generally subject to court supervision, and must adhere to strict rules regarding how and when they can spend assets for the child's benefit. Complying with these requirements often involves lots of administrative expenses, court time, and overall hassle for the property guardian.

When would my child have access to the assets in a property guardianship?
Your child would obtain complete access to and control over the assets in a property guardianship as soon as he or she reaches the age of majority in your state (eighteen in most states).

> *The age of majority for a property guardianship is different than the age of majority for UTMA custodial accounts.* In most states, the age of majority for purposes of a property guardianship is eighteen, while the age of majority for UTMA purposes is twenty-one. What this means is that your child will almost certainly gain access to his or her assets sooner with a property guardianship as compared with an UTMA custodial account.

Should I consider leaving all of my assets to my child in a property guardianship?
A property guardianship is rarely a good choice for the management of your child's inheritance because of the court supervision and administrative hassles involved for the property guardian and also because your child will likely gain access to the assets in the account by age eighteen. If you would like to establish a simple management structure for your child's assets, an UTMA custodial account is a far better choice.

Name a property guardian in your will, just in case. It's a smart idea to specifically appoint the person you have selected to serve as your child's financial guardian as your child's property guardian in your will, just to handle any of your child's assets that are not placed in a custodial account or a trust for your child while your child is a minor. For example, if your child earns a significant amount of money after your death (perhaps by becoming a child model), or if your child inherits assets from a relative, then your child's property guardian will be responsible for managing those funds until your child reaches the age of majority in your state.

Creating a Will

After you have tackled the really difficult questions of who should serve as your child's guardian and how you would like your child's assets to be managed after your death, you'll be ready to put it all in writing and make it legal. Here we'll answer some of the basic questions you may have on creating a will.

Does my will control the distribution of all of my assets in the event of my death?

No. Many different types of assets pass by contract, rather than by will. In other words, the terms of a will have no impact on the distribution of certain types of assets. These assets include:

- *Joint banking and brokerage accounts.* The assets in a joint banking or brokerage account will pass to your joint owner in the event of your death. If you have a joint account with your spouse, and your spouse is still alive when you die, your spouse will automatically acquire sole and complete ownership of all of the funds in that account.
- *Real estate you own in joint tenancy.* Property held in joint tenancy will pass to your co-owner in the event of your death. If you

and your spouse own a home together, and both names are on the deed to the property, then your spouse will automatically obtain sole and complete ownership of your home.

- *Retirement accounts, such as 401(k) plans or IRAs.* The funds in your retirement accounts will be distributed to the person you named as the beneficiary of those accounts. If you have a 401(k) plan, your spouse will be the beneficiary of that account unless your spouse signed a written waiver that is on file with your plan administrator at the time of your death.
- *Life insurance proceeds.* The proceeds of your life insurance policy will be paid to the person you named as the beneficiary of the policy.
- *Funds in a payable-on-death account.* If you have a bank or brokerage account with a pay-on-death designation, then the funds in that account will be distributed in accordance with your pay-on-death designation when you die.
- *Real estate with a transfer-on-death designation.* If you have real estate with a transfer-on-death designation, then that property will be distributed in accordance with your transfer-on-death designation when you die.
- *Assets held in a living trust.* If you established a trust during your lifetime, those assets will remain in trust for the benefit of your designated beneficiaries after your death.

Check your beneficiary designations and account ownerships carefully! Make sure that you complete and submit all necessary beneficiary designation forms. Don't forget to name a contingent beneficiary as well. If you name your child as the primary or contingent beneficiary of any asset, make sure that you name a financial guardian for your child's assets and establish a property management structure in your will.

What types of assets pass by will?

Your will controls the distribution of all bank and brokerage accounts, real estate, tangible property (like jewelry and antiques), and intangible property (like creative works and patents) that you own in your name only, with no beneficiary designation. For example, if you have a brokerage account that is not held jointly with someone else, then the funds in that account will be distributed in accordance with the terms of your will.

Property you own as a "tenant in common" with someone else will be distributed according to the terms of your will. Unlike a joint tenant, a tenant in common does not have survivorship rights. For example, let's suppose that you and your brother own a home together as tenants in common. If you were to die, your half of that home would not automatically pass to your brother. Rather, you could name a beneficiary for your half of that home in your will.

Will my spouse and I each need our own wills?
Yes. In many cases, spouses prepare mirror image wills that set forth the same basic terms.

Make sure you and your spouse name the same legal guardian and financial guardian for your child in your wills. If there is a conflict between your will and your spouse's will, then it will be up to a court to make these all-important determinations.

Are there any special legal requirements for creating a valid will?
Yes. To create a legally valid will, you must comply with a few basic requirements:

- The document should clearly state that it is your last will and testament.
- Your will should be typewritten, not handwritten. Only some states accept handwritten wills. A typewritten will is the best option.
- You must sign and date your will in the presence of two witnesses. Those witnesses should then sign and date the will themselves.

An informal note or letter does not qualify as a legal will. Definitely don't scribble your last wishes on a napkin and hope that someone will find it in the event of your death!

Will I need to name an executor in my will?

Yes. An *executor* is someone who will handle all of the many administrative and financial tasks involved in wrapping up your affairs and making sure that your final wishes are honored. Your executor will obtain court approval for your will through the probate process, pay your debts and any administrative expenses, and help to handle the distribution of your assets.

Serving as executor can be a time-consuming and onerous job. Fortunately, your executor can hire expert help as needed and use the assets in the estate to pay for those services.

A useful resource for executors is The Executor's Guide: Settling a Loved One's Estate or Trust by Mary Randolph (Nolo, 2014).

Who should I name as the executor of my will?

If you are married you may want to name your spouse as the executor of your will, unless you think that your spouse would be overwhelmed by the responsibility. You should also name an alternate executor in the event that your spouse dies before you or is unable to handle the job.

You don't need to name a financial expert or a lawyer as the executor of your will. Instead, just name someone competent and caring who would be willing to handle the responsibility. It's a good idea to ask the person for permission before naming him or her as the executor of your will.

Do I need to hire a lawyer to prepare my will?

If your family structure and your financial situation are both very simple, then you may be able to draft a will entirely on your own using commercially available books or software.

When in doubt, hire a lawyer. If you want to create a trust in your will, for example, or if yours is a blended family, then the best course of action is to retain an experienced trusts and estates attorney to prepare your will.

A useful "do-it-yourself" resource is Quicken Will-Maker Plus, available at nolo.com. While there are a variety of other will preparation tools available online, Nolo has a well-established reputation for accurate and user-friendly self-help legal materials.

How much will it cost for a lawyer to prepare my will?
It depends on the level of complexity involved. Some lawyers charge a flat fee to prepare basic estate planning documents, while others charge by the hour. Don't be afraid to ask for a "ballpark" estimate of the number of hours that your lawyer is likely to spend. Your lawyer should be able to give you a reasonable estimate after getting a sense of your estate planning needs.

How can I find a qualified trusts and estates attorney to prepare my will?
Word of mouth is often the best way. Ask friends and family members whose opinion you trust for the names of estate planning attorneys they have used. You can also reach out to your local bar association's lawyer referral service. To find contact information, you can use the American Bar Association's Lawyer Referral Directory, available at http://apps.americanbar.org/legalservices/lris/directory/home.html.

Once I have signed my will, do I have to file my will with the court?
No. You don't have to file your will with a court or any other government institution. You just have to keep your will in a safe place and make sure that at least one or two family members or close friends know where to find your will in the event of your death.

Don't keep your will in a safe-deposit box. It can be incredibly difficult to access a bank safe-deposit box after the owner's death. A better choice is to keep your will in a desk drawer somewhere in your home, ideally in a fireproof box.

Consider keeping your original will on file with your trusts and estates attorney. This way, you won't have to worry about losing or damaging your original will. You should still keep a copy of your will, as well as contact information for your trusts and estates attorney, in an easy-to-find place in your home.

Other than preparing a will, is there anything else I should do to protect my family in the event of my death?
Yes. First, you should make sure your family is protected with adequate life insurance. (See Chapter 5 for more information on purchasing life insurance.)

Second, you should check the ownership status and beneficiary designations of any assets that do not pass by will. These assets include:

- joint banking and brokerage accounts;
- real estate you own in joint tenancy;
- retirement accounts, such as 401(k) plans or IRAs;
- life insurance proceeds;
- funds in a payable-on-death account;
- real estate with a transfer-on-death designation; and
- assets in a living trust.

Make sure that you complete and submit all necessary beneficiary designation forms. Don't forget to name a contingent beneficiary as well, just in case.

Finally, you should consider putting together a sealed information packet to help your family members sort out your affairs in the event of your death. This information packet should include:

- A copy of your life insurance policy and the name and phone number of your insurance broker.
- A list of all of your bank and brokerage accounts, including

account numbers and passwords.

- A list of all of your retirement accounts, including account numbers and passwords.
- A list of all real property you own in whole or in part.
- A list of any other property you own, and where that property can be found. If you have a safe-deposit box, for example, make sure you include instructions for accessing the contents of the safe-deposit box in the event of your death.
- A list of all of your debts, loans, and credit card accounts, including account numbers and passwords.
- Details on all the vehicles you own or have leased.
- Instructions on where to find important personal documents such as your marriage certificate, your children's birth certificates, your children's Social Security cards, and your children's passports. You may even want to include copies of each of these important documents in your information packet.
- Instructions on where to find important financial and property-related documents, such as the deed to any property you own. You may want to include copies of these important documents in your information packet.
- A list of personal details for each of your children, including the names and numbers of health care providers, important health-related information (like a list of allergies), the names and numbers of your children's schools, and any other child-related details that might be helpful.
- Any other instructions or useful pieces of information that others in your family might not know. For example, you may wish to include a copy of your homeowners' insurance policy and your automobile insurance policy, as well as a list of the various companies that service your home on a regular basis.

You can give this information packet to a trusted relative or friend with instructions that it should only be opened in the event of your death. You should also keep a copy of the information packet in the same place you keep your will.

Keep your information packet up to date. Though it might seem tedious, creating an information packet could save your family countless hours of confusion in the event of your death. Look over the information packet at least once a year and make any necessary changes or updates.

If you need help getting your information packet together, a useful resource is Get It Together: Organize Your Records So Your Family Won't Have To by Melanie Cullen and Shae Irving (Nolo, 2014).

Changing Your Will

A will is not a document that is set in stone for all eternity. As your life changes and your family grows, you may need to update your will to include new beneficiaries, name a different guardian, or adjust your estate plan.

Can I change my will at any time and for any reason?

Yes. You can change your will as often as you would like. Just remember that you will need to sign and date your new or revised will in the presence of two witnesses. Both witnesses must also sign your revised will.

Under what circumstances should I consider changing or updating my will?

You should revisit your will every time your life changes in some significant way. For example, you will need to update your will if:

- you have another child,
- you marry or divorce, or
- one of your named beneficiaries passes away.

You will also need to revise your will if you wish to name a different guardian, or if you change your mind about how you would like your assets to be distributed in the event of your death.

> *Failing to update your will when you marry or have another child could impact your estate plan.* If you don't specifically mention one of your children in your will, then that child may have an automatic right to inherit a portion of your assets when you die. Similarly, your new spouse may be entitled to a portion of your estate unless your spouse specifically disclaims his or her share in a prenuptial or postnuptial agreement.

Should I revise my will if I move to a new state?
In most cases, a will you create in one state remains valid even if you move to a different state. However, it would be wise to consult with a trusts and estates attorney in your new state, or at least check your new state's laws, to make sure that no changes are required.

> *Be particularly careful if you are married and you move from a community property state to a common law state or vice versa.* Moving from a community property state to a common law state, or vice versa, could impact your spouse's entitlement to a share of your assets in the event of your death. (If your will leaves all of your assets to your spouse, then you don't need to worry about this.)

Will I need a lawyer to change my will?
If you used a lawyer to draft your original will, then it is best to consult that same attorney (or an attorney in your new home state, if you have since moved) to revise your will. But if you drafted your will yourself, you may able to draft a new or revised will entirely on your own.

Should I destroy my original will if I change my will?
Yes. It's a good idea to tear up your original will when you sign a new or revised will. Make sure that your new or revised will explicitly states that it supersedes all prior wills.

Estate Taxes

Very few parents have to worry about the possibility of paying federal estate taxes. Under federal law, your family will only owe estate taxes if the value of your estate exceeds a certain very large amount ($5.43 million in 2015). If you leave all of your assets to your spouse, your spouse will not owe any estate taxes, regardless of the size of your estate, because property transfers between spouses are completely tax free.

Depending on the state in which you live, however, your family may owe state estate taxes. These taxes apply to much smaller estates than the federal estate tax. New Jersey, for example, imposes an estate tax on estates worth $675,000 or more. In addition to estate taxes, some states also impose an inheritance tax on individuals who inherit property in the state.

What is an estate tax?

An estate tax is a tax that your estate must pay to the government after your death.

Will my family owe federal estate taxes in the event of my death?
Not unless you are a millionaire! Thanks to the federal estate tax exemption, your family will not have to pay estate taxes unless you leave well over $5 million in assets when you die. (The federal estate tax exemption in 2015 was $5.43 million.) For estates that exceed the exemption amount, however, federal estate taxes are steep. The highest federal estate tax rate is 40 percent.

Any assets you leave to your spouse are federal estate tax exempt, regardless of the amount. Let's pretend you won the lottery and you left $10 million to your spouse. Your spouse would not owe a single dollar in federal estate taxes on that amount because transfers between spouses are always federal estate tax exempt.

Will my family have to pay estate taxes on my life insurance proceeds?

It depends on whom you name as the beneficiary of your life insurance policy and the size of your estate.

If your spouse is the beneficiary of your life insurance policy, then no estate taxes will be owed regardless of the size of your estate because transfers between spouses are exempt from estate taxes.

If you name someone other than your spouse as the beneficiary of your life insurance policy, then your family may owe estate taxes on your life insurance proceeds if the total amount of your estate, including the proceeds of your insurance policy, exceeds the estate tax exemption. (In 2015, the estate tax exemption was $5.43 million.)

> *Life insurance proceeds will not count as part of your estate if you transfer ownership of your life insurance policy more than three years before your death.* You can exclude life insurance proceeds from your taxable estate by naming someone else as the owner of your life insurance policy or by transferring your policy to a life insurance trust more than three years before you die. If you are concerned that your life insurance proceeds may subject your family to federal estate taxes, you may want to talk to an experienced trusts and estates attorney about transferring ownership of your life insurance policy.

Can I avoid federal estate taxes by giving away all of my property during my lifetime?

The federal estate tax system is designed to prevent people from avoiding estate taxes by giving away their assets during their lifetime. If you give away substantial amounts of money during your lifetime, the amount of those gifts will count against your lifetime estate tax exemption. For example, let's suppose that you have three children and you give each child $1 million during your lifetime. You would then only be entitled to an estate tax exemption of $2.43 million if you died in 2015.

You can give away a certain amount of money each year without reducing your estate tax exemption. The federal government lets you have an annual gift exclusion ($14,000 per person in 2015). If you give away this amount or less to any of your friends or family members, your gifts will not reduce your estate tax exemption. The exclusion applies per gift recipient, not per gift giver. For example, if you have two children you could have given each child $14,000 in 2015, for a total of $28,000, without worrying about the estate tax exemption. Many parents take advantage of the gift tax exclusion to reduce the size of their estates slowly over the course of many years.

If your assets are sizable enough that you have to worry about federal estate taxes, consult with an experienced trusts and estates attorney. A good lawyer can implement strategies for minimizing your estate taxes and preserving your assets.

Will my family owe state estate taxes in the event of my death?

It depends on where you live. The following states impose taxes on the estates of state residents: Connecticut, Delaware, the District of Columbia, Hawaii, Illinois, Maine, Maryland, Massachusetts, Minnesota, New Jersey, New York, Oregon, Rhode Island, Vermont, and Washington. Tennessee also imposes a state estate tax, but it will not apply to deaths after January 1, 2016.

State estate tax exemptions are much lower in many states than the federal estate tax exemption. In 2015, New Jersey taxed estates that exceeded $675,000, while Rhode Island taxed estates that exceeded $921,655. On a positive note, state estate tax rates are much lower than the federal estate tax rate.

What is an inheritance tax?

An inheritance tax is a tax that someone who inherits property must pay to the government.

Which states impose state inheritance taxes?
The following states impose inheritance taxes: Iowa, Kentucky, Maryland, Nebraska, New Jersey, and Pennsylvania.

> *Inheriting spouses do not have to pay the inheritance tax in any state.* Very low inheritance tax rates apply to children who inherit property from their parents. In some states with inheritance taxes, children who inherit property from their parents do not owe any inheritance taxes whatsoever.

For More Information

Estate planning is complicated! Fortunately, there are plenty of resources available to help you make your decisions and implement your plan. Here are a few books to get you started:

- *The American Bar Association's Guide to Wills and Estates* (Random House Reference, 2013).
- *Plan Your Estate* by Denis Clifford (Nolo, 2014).
- *Estate Planning Basics* by Denis Clifford (Nolo, 2013).
- *The Complete Idiot's Guide to Wills and Estates* by Dr. Stephen Maple (Alpha, 2009).
- *Estate Planning for Blended Families: Providing for Your Spouse & Children in a Second Marriage* by Richard E. Barnes (Nolo, 2009).
- *Get It Together: Organize Your Records So Your Family Won't Have To* by Melanie Cullen and Shae Irving (Nolo, 2014).

Appendix A

State Minimum Wages, Overtime Rules, and Workers' Compensation Requirements

STATE	MINIMUM WAGE	OVERTIME RULES	WORKERS' COMPENSATION
Alabama	$7.25	Time and a half due after forty hours worked per week. Overtime pay is not required for live-in nannies.	Not required.
Alaska	$7.75	Time and a half due after forty hours worked per week. Overtime pay is not required for live-in nannies.	Not required.
Arizona	$8.05	Time and a half due after forty hours worked per week. Overtime pay is not required for live-in nannies.	Required only if you have three or more employees.
Arkansas	$7.50	Time and a half due after forty hours worked per week. Overtime pay is not required for live-in nannies.	Not required.
California	$9.00 San Francisco: $11.05 San Jose: $10.30 San Diego: $9.75	*Live-out nannies*: Time and a half due after nine hours worked per day or forty hours worked per week. *Live-in nannies*: Time and a half due after nine hours worked per day or forty-five hours worked per week.	Required.
Colorado	$8.23	Time and a half due after forty hours worked per week. Overtime pay is not required for live-in nannies.	Required if your nanny works forty or more hours per week or five or more days per week.

STATE	MINIMUM WAGE	OVERTIME RULES	WORKERS' COMPENSATION
Connecticut	$9.15	Time and a half due after forty hours worked per week. Overtime pay is not required for live-in nannies.	Required if your nanny works more than twenty-six hours per week.
Delaware	$7.75	Time and a half due after forty hours worked per week. Overtime pay is not required for live-in nannies.	Required if your nanny earns $750 or more in a three-month period.
District of Columbia	$9.50	Time and a half due after forty hours worked per week. Overtime pay is not required for live-in nannies.	Required if your nanny works 240 hours or more per quarter.
Florida	$8.05	Time and a half due after forty hours worked per week. Overtime pay is not required for live-in nannies.	Not required.
Georgia	$7.25	Time and a half due after forty hours worked per week. Overtime pay is not required for live-in nannies.	Not required.
Hawaii	$7.75	Time and a half due after forty hours worked per week. *Live-in nannies*: Time and a half due after forty-four hours worked per week. *For all nannies*: Time and a half due for all hours worked on the seventh consecutive day of work each week.	Required for nannies who earn $225 or more per quarter.
Idaho	$7.25	Time and a half due after forty hours worked per week. Overtime pay is not required for live-in nannies.	Not required.

STATE	MINIMUM WAGE	OVERTIME RULES	WORKERS' COMPENSATION
Illinois	$8.25	Time and a half due after forty hours worked per week. Overtime pay is not required for live-in nannies.	Required if your nanny works forty hours or more per week. Also required if you have two part-time nannies who together work forty hours or more per week.
Indiana	$7.25	Time and a half due after forty hours worked per week. Overtime pay is not required for live-in nannies.	Not required.
Iowa	$7.25	Time and a half due after forty hours worked per week. Overtime pay is not required for live-in nannies.	Required if your nanny earns $1,500 or more per year.
Kansas	$7.25	Time and a half due after forty hours worked per week. Overtime pay is not required for live-in nannies.	Required for nannies who earn $20,000 or more per year.
Kentucky	$7.25	Time and a half due after forty hours worked per week. Overtime pay is not required for live-in nannies.	Required only if you have two or more employees who each work more than forty hours per week.
Louisiana	$7.25	Time and a half due after forty hours worked per week. Overtime pay is not required for live-in nannies.	Not required.
Maine	$7.50	Time and a half due after forty hours worked per week. *Live-in nannies*: Time and a half due after forty hours worked per week.	Not required.
Maryland	$8.00	Time and a half due after forty hours worked per week. *Live-in nannies*: Time and a half due after forty hours worked per week.	Required if your nanny earns $1,000 or more per year.

STATE	MINIMUM WAGE	OVERTIME RULES	WORKERS' COMPENSATION
Massachu-setts	$9.00	Time and a half due after forty hours worked per week. *Live-in nannies*: Time and a half due after forty hours worked per week.	Required if your nanny works sixteen hours or more per week.
Michigan	$8.15	Time and a half due after forty hours worked per week. Overtime pay is not required for live-in nannies.	Required if your nanny works thirty-five hours or more per week or if you have three or more employees.
Minnesota	$7.25	Time and a half due after forty hours worked per week. *Live-in nannies*: Time and a half due after forty-eight hours worked per week.	Required if your nanny earns $1,000 or more in a calen-dar quarter.
Mississippi	$7.25	Time and a half due after forty hours worked per week. Overtime pay is not required for live-in nannies.	Only required if you have five or more employees.
Missouri	$7.65	Time and a half due after forty hours worked per week. Overtime pay is not required for live-in nannies.	Not required.
Montana	$8.05	Time and a half due after forty hours worked per week. Overtime pay is not required for live-in nannies.	Not required.
Nebraska	$8.00	Time and a half due after forty hours worked per week. Overtime pay is not required for live-in nannies.	Required unless the employee is a domestic servant.
Nevada	$8.25	Time and a half due after forty hours worked per week. Overtime pay is not required for live-in nannies.	Not required.

STATE	MINIMUM WAGE	OVERTIME RULES	WORKERS' COMPENSATION
New Hampshire	$7.25	Time and a half due after forty hours worked per week. Overtime pay is not required for live-in nannies.	Required.
New Jersey	$8.38	Time and a half due after forty hours worked per week. Overtime pay is not required for live-in nannies.	Required.
New Mexico	$7.50 Albuquerque: $8.60 Santa Fe: $10.51	Time and a half due after forty hours worked per week. Overtime pay is not required for live-in nannies.	Not required.
New York	$8.75	Time and a half due after forty hours worked per week. *Live-in nannies*: Time and a half due after forty-four hours worked per week. *For all nannies*: Time and a half due for all hours worked on the seventh consecutive day of work each week.	Required if your nanny (1) works forty hours or more per week, (2) is a live-in nanny, or (3) is professionally certified.
North Carolina	$7.25	Time and a half due after forty hours worked per week. Overtime pay is not required for live-in nannies.	Only required if you have three or more employees.
North Dakota	$7.25	Time and a half due after forty hours worked per week. Overtime pay is not required for live-in nannies.	Not required.

STATE	MINIMUM WAGE	OVERTIME RULES	WORKERS' COMPENSATION
Ohio	$7.25	Time and a half due after forty hours worked per week. Overtime pay is not required for live-in nannies.	Required.
Oklahoma	$7.25	Time and a half due after forty hours worked per week. Overtime pay is not required for live-in nannies.	Required for nannies who earn $10,000 or more per year.
Oregon	$9.25	Time and a half due after forty hours worked per week. Overtime pay is not required for live-in nannies.	Not required.
Pennsylvania	$7.25	Time and a half due after forty hours worked per week. Overtime pay is not required for live-in nannies.	Not required.
Rhode Island	$7.75	Time and a half due after forty hours worked per week. Overtime pay is not required for live-in nannies.	Not required.
South Carolina	$7.25	Time and a half due after forty hours worked per week. Overtime pay is not required for live-in nannies.	Required if you have four or more employees.
South Dakota	$8.50	Time and a half due after forty hours worked per week. Overtime pay is not required for live-in nannies.	Required if your nanny works more than twenty hours in any calendar week.
Tennessee	$7.25	Time and a half due after forty hours worked per week. Overtime pay is not required for live-in nannies.	Not required.

STATE	MINIMUM WAGE	OVERTIME RULES	WORKERS' COMPENSATION
Texas	$7.25	Time and a half due after forty hours worked per week. Overtime pay is not required for live-in nannies.	Not required.
Utah	$7.25	Time and a half due after forty hours worked per week. Overtime pay is not required for live-in nannies.	Required if your nanny works more than forty hours per week.
Vermont	$9.15	Time and a half due after forty hours worked per week. Overtime pay is not required for live-in nannies.	Not required.
Virginia	$7.25	Time and a half due after forty hours worked per week. Overtime pay is not required for live-in nannies.	Not required.
Washington	$9.47	Time and a half due after forty hours worked per week. Overtime pay is not required for live-in nannies.	Required if you have two or more employees who each work forty hours or more per week.
West Virginia	$8.00	Time and a half due after forty hours worked per week. Overtime pay is not required for live-in nannies.	Not required.
Wisconsin	$7.25	Time and a half due after forty hours worked per week. Overtime pay is not required for live-in nannies.	Not required.
Wyoming	$7.25	Time and a half due after forty hours worked per week. Overtime pay is not required for live-in nannies.	Not required.

Appendix B

State Tax Benefits for 529 Plan Contributions

Alabama	Annual state tax deduction for contributions to an Alabama 529 plan of up to $5,000 per person and up to $10,000 for married couples.
Alaska	N/A (no state income tax).
Arizona	Annual state tax deduction for contributions to *any* 529 plan of up to $2,000 per person and up to $4,000 for married couples.
Arkansas	Annual state tax deduction for contributions to an Arkansas 529 plan of up to $5,000 per person and up to $10,000 for married couples.
California	N/A
Colorado	Unlimited annual state tax deduction for contributions to a Colorado 529 plan.
Connecticut	Annual state tax deduction for contributions to a Connecticut 529 plan of up to $5,000 per person and up to $10,000 for married couples.
Delaware	N/A
District of Columbia	Annual state tax deduction for contributions to a District of Columbia 529 plan of up to $4,000 per person and up to $8,000 for married couples.
Florida	N/A (no state income tax).
Georgia	Annual state tax deduction for contributions to a Georgia 529 plan of up to $2,000 per beneficiary.
Hawaii	N/A
Idaho	Annual state tax deduction for contributions to an Idaho 529 plan of up to $4,000 per person and up to $8,000 for married couples.
Illinois	Annual state tax deduction for contributions to an Illinois 529 plan of up to $10,000 per person and up to $20,000 for married couples.
Indiana	Annual state tax credit for contributions to an Indiana 529 plan of up to $1,000 per person or married couple.
Iowa	Annual state tax deduction for contributions to an Iowa 529 plan of up to $3,163 per beneficiary. Married couples can deduct up to $6,196 per beneficiary per year.
Kansas	Annual state tax deduction for contributions to any 529 plan of up to $3,000 per beneficiary. Married couples can deduct up to $6,000 per beneficiary per year.

Kentucky	N/A
Louisiana	Annual state tax deduction for contributions to a Louisiana 529 plan of up to $2,400 per beneficiary. Married couples can deduct up to $4,800 per beneficiary per year.
Maine	Annual state tax deduction for contributions to *any* 529 plan of up to $250 per beneficiary.
Maryland	Annual state tax deduction for contributions to a Maryland 529 plan of up to $2,500 per beneficiary.
Massachusetts	N/A
Michigan	Annual state tax deduction for contributions to a Michigan 529 plan of up to $5,000 per person and up to $10,000 for married couples.
Minnesota	N/A
Mississippi	Annual state tax deduction for contributions to a Mississippi 529 plan of up to $10,000 per person and up to $20,000 for married couples.
Missouri	Annual state tax deduction for contributions to *any* 529 plan of up to $8,000 per person and up to $16,000 for married couples.
Montana	Annual state tax deduction for contributions to *any* 529 plan of up to $3,000 per person and up to $6,000 for married couples.
Nebraska	Annual state tax deduction for contributions to a Nebraska 529 plan of up to $10,000 per tax return (or up to $5,000 if married filing separately).
New Hampshire	N/A (no state income tax except on dividend and interest income).
New Jersey	N/A
New Mexico	Unlimited annual state tax deduction for contributions a New Mexico 529 plan.
New York	Annual state tax deduction for contributions to a New York 529 plan of up to $5,000 per person and up to $10,000 for married couples.
Nevada	N/A (no state income tax).
North Carolina	N/A
North Dakota	Annual state tax deduction for contributions to a North Dakota 529 plan of up to $5,000 per person and up to $10,000 for married couples.
Ohio	Annual state tax deduction for contributions to an Ohio 529 plan of up to $2,000 per beneficiary.
Oklahoma	Annual state tax deduction for contributions to an Oklahoma 529 plan of up to $10,000 per person and up to $20,000 for married couples.
Oregon	Annual state tax deduction for contributions to an Oregon 529 plan of up to $2,170 per person and up to $4,345 for married couples.

Pennsylvania	Annual state tax deduction for contributions to *any* 529 plan of up to $14,000 per beneficiary. Married couples can deduct up to $28,000 per beneficiary.
Rhode Island	Annual state tax deduction for contributions to a Rhode Island 529 plan of up to $500 per person and up to $1,000 for married couples.
South Carolina	Unlimited annual state tax deduction for contributions to a South Carolina 529 plan.
South Dakota	N/A (no state income tax).
Tennessee	N/A (no state income tax except on dividend and interest income).
Texas	N/A (no state income tax).
Utah	Annual state tax credit for contributions to a Utah 529 plan of up to $93 per beneficiary. Married couples can take a credit of up to $185 per beneficiary per year.
Vermont	Annual state tax credit for contributions to a Vermont 529 plan of up to $250 per beneficiary. Married couples can take a credit of up to $500 per beneficiary per year.
Virginia	Annual state tax deduction for contributions to a Virginia 529 plan of up to $4,000 per beneficiary. Unlimited state tax deduction for contributions to a Virginia 529 plan for taxpayers age seventy and over.
Washington	N/A (no state income tax).
West Virginia	Unlimited annual state tax deduction for contributions to a West Virginia 529 plan.
Wisconsin	Annual state tax deduction for contributions to a Wisconsin 529 plan of up to $3,000 per beneficiary.
Wyoming	No state-sponsored 529 plan. Also, no state income tax.

Appendix C

UTMA/UGMA Age of Majority by State

Alabama	21
Alaska	Custodians may designate an age of majority from eighteen to twenty-five. The default age of majority is twenty-one.
Arizona	21
Arkansas	Custodians may designate an age of majority from eighteen to twenty-one. The default age of majority is twenty-one.
California	Custodians may designate an age of majority from eighteen to twenty-one. The default age of majority is eighteen.
Colorado	21
Connecticut	21
Delaware	21
District of Columbia	Custodians may designate an age of majority of either eighteen or twenty-one. The default age of majority is eighteen.
Florida	21
Georgia	21
Hawaii	21
Idaho	21
Illinois	21
Indiana	21
Iowa	21
Kansas	21
Kentucky	18
Louisiana	18
Maine	Custodians may designate an age of majority from eighteen to twenty-one. The default age of majority is eighteen.
Maryland	21
Massachusetts	21
Michigan	Custodians may designate an age of majority from eighteen to twenty-one. The default age of majority is eighteen.

Minnesota	21
Mississippi	21
Missouri	21
Montana	21
Nebraska	21
Nevada	Custodians may designate an age of majority from eighteen to twenty-one. The default age of majority is eighteen.
New Hampshire	21
New Jersey	21
New Mexico	21
New York	Custodians may designate an age of majority of either eighteen or twenty-one. The default age of majority is twenty-one.
North Carolina	Custodians may designate an age of majority from eighteen to twenty-one. The default age of majority is twenty-one.
North Dakota	21
Ohio	Transferors may designate an age of majority between eighteen and twenty-one. The default age of majority is twenty-one.
Oklahoma	Custodians may designate an age of majority from eighteen to twenty-one. The default age of majority is eighteen.
Oregon	Transferors may designate an age of majority between twenty-one and twenty-five. The default age of majority is twenty-one.
Pennsylvania	21
Rhode Island	21
South Carolina	21
South Dakota	18
Tennessee	Transferors or custodians may designate an age of majority between twenty-one and twenty-five. The default age of majority is twenty-one.
Texas	21
Utah	21
Vermont	18
Virginia	Custodians may designate an age of majority of either eighteen or twenty-one. The default age of majority is eighteen.
Washington	21
West Virginia	21

Wisconsin	21
Wyoming	21

Appendix D

UTMA Age of Majority by State

Alabama	21
Alaska	Custodians may designate an age of majority from eighteen to twenty-five. The default age of majority is twenty-one.
Arizona	21
Arkansas	Custodians may designate an age of majority from eighteen to twenty-one. The default age of majority is twenty-one.
California	You may designate an age of majority from eighteen to twenty-five in your will, trust, or insurance policy. Custodians may designate an age of majority from eighteen to twenty-one. The default age of majority is eighteen.
Colorado	21
Connecticut	21
Delaware	21
District of Columbia	Custodians may designate an age of majority of either eighteen or twenty-one. The default age of majority is eighteen.
Florida	21
Georgia	21
Hawaii	21
Idaho	21
Illinois	21
Indiana	21
Iowa	21
Kansas	21
Kentucky	18
Louisiana	18
Maine	Custodians may designate an age of majority from eighteen to twenty-one. The default age of majority is eighteen.

Maryland	21
Massachusetts	21
Michigan	Custodians may designate an age of majority from eighteen to twenty-one. The default age of majority is eighteen.
Minnesota	21
Mississippi	21
Missouri	21
Montana	21
Nebraska	21
Nevada	You may designate an age of majority from eighteen to twenty-five in your will, trust, or insurance policy. Custodians may designate an age of majority from eighteen to twenty-one. The default age of majority is eighteen.
New Hampshire	21
New Jersey	21
New Mexico	21
New York	Custodians may designate an age of majority of either eighteen or twenty-one. The default age of majority is twenty-one.
North Carolina	Custodians may designate an age of majority from eighteen to twenty-one. The default age of majority is twenty-one.
North Dakota	21
Ohio	You may designate an age of majority from eighteen to twenty-one. The default age of majority is twenty-one.
Oklahoma	Custodians may designate an age of majority from eighteen to twenty-one. The default age of majority is eighteen.
Oregon	You may designate an age of majority from twenty-one to twenty-five. The default age of majority is twenty-one.
Pennsylvania	You may designate an age of majority from eighteen to twenty-five in your will, trust, or insurance policy. The default age of majority is twenty-one.
Rhode Island	21
South Dakota	18

Tennessee	You or the custodian may designate an age of majority from twenty-one to twenty-five. The default age of majority is twenty-one.
Texas	21
Utah	21
Virginia	Custodians may designate an age of majority of either eighteen or twenty-one. The default age of majority is eighteen.
Washington	21
West Virginia	21
Wisconsin	21
Wyoming	21

INDEX